THE CANADIAN CLASS STRUCTURE

McGraw-Hill Ryerson Series in Canadian Sociology

General Editor — Lorne Tepperman
Department of Sociology
University of Toronto

IDEOLOGICAL PERSPECTIVES ON CANADA, Second Edition
M. Patricia Marchak

SOCIAL MOBILITY IN CANADA
Lorne Tepperman

UNDERSTANDING DATA
B. H. Erickson and T. A. Nosanchuk

THE NEW URBAN POOR
S. D. Clark

SOCIOLOGICAL THEORIES OF EDUCATION
Raymond Murphy with the collaboration of Ann Denis

DEMOGRAPHIC BASES OF CANADIAN SOCIETY, Second Edition
(General Editor: S. D. Clark)
Warren Kalback and Wayne McVey

THE SURVIVAL OF ETHNIC GROUPS
Jeffrey G. Reitz

WOMEN, FAMILY AND THE ECONOMY
Sue Wilson

THE URBAN KALEIDOSCOPE: Canadian Perspectives
Leslie W. Kennedy

RELIGION: Classic Sociological Approaches
Roger O'Toole

THE DISREPUTABLE PLEASURES, Second Edition
John Hagan

THE CANADIAN CLASS STRUCTURE, Third Edition
Dennis Forcese

Forthcoming

THE SOCIOLOGY OF MASS COMMUNICATIONS IN CANADA
Arthur Siegel

WOMEN, THE FAMILY AND THE ECONOMY, Second Edition
Sue Wilson

DEVIANCE: Tolerable Differences
Robert Stebbins

SOCIOLOGY OF AGING
Maureen Baker

THE CANADIAN CLASS STRUCTURE

THIRD EDITION

DENNIS FORCESE

Carleton University

McGraw-Hill Ryerson Limited

Toronto Montreal New York Auckland Bogotá Cairo Guatemala
Hamburg Lisbon London Madrid Mexico
New Delhi Panama Paris San Juan São Paulo Singapore
Sydney Tokyo

THE CANADIAN CLASS STRUCTURE, Third Edition

ISBN: 0-07-548805-1

2 3 4 5 6 7 8 9 0   W   5 4 3 2 1 0 9 8 7 6

Printed and bound in Canada

Care has been taken to trace ownership of copyright material contained in this
text. The publishers will gladly take any information that will enable them to
rectify any reference or credit in subsequent editions.

Canadian Cataloguing in Publication Data

Forcese, Dennis, date.
  The Canadian class structure

(McGraw-Hill Ryerson series in Canadian sociology)
Bibliography: p.
Includes index.
ISBN 0-07-548805-1

1. Social classes — Canada. I. Title. II. Series.

HN110.Z9S625 1986   305.5'0971   C85-099822-0

Contents

Preface to the First Edition

This book is an overview of what is known about social stratification in Canada. The extensive list of references is indicative of my attempt to integrate the pertinent information. The result is a rather selective introduction to the many aspects of institutionalized inequality in Canada.

I have not attempted to write a work of theory in the ambitious sense, but simply a presentation and interpretation of my perceptions of the facts of the Canadian social class structure. Certainly this is not a work that attempts to affiliate itself with or regurgitate any particular ''classic'' theory. I think it eclectic, rather than a contrived effort at making a Karl Marx, a Max Weber, or even a Ludwig Gumplowicz fit the Canadian circumstance. I have been accused by some colleagues, perhaps not in jest, of advocating sociological parricide. There is truth in the charge, not that I wish to deny the insight and guidance of the ''classics,'' but that I weary of repeated classical exegesis. So, though I deal in first concepts, assumptions, and findings, and though alternatives and their origins are summarized in the text, this is definitely not a book of great names revisited.

It may well be the case that this is but an elaborate rationalization for my own mal-integrated approach to the study of social stratification; that is, of course, for the reader to judge. I am satisfied that it has not been an excuse to avoid the articulation of personal values or goals regarding social stratification. There are theoretically derived premises explicitly presented in the book: the non-inevitability of social class stratification; the existence of class conflict in Canada; and the desirability of political action to the goal of a genuinely egalitarian society.

I should point out that my emphasis differs from the pure power and stratification school of analysis, best represented by John Porter's *The Vertical Mosaic.*. I am of the view that Porter's work remains the single outstanding contribution to the sociological study of Canadian society, and for that reason alone I would feel foolish in spending any more time than I do in summarizing some of his already well-known findings and interpretations. Instead, I have chosen to emphasize non-elites in Canadian society. Conceding the economic basis of power, I am interested in the relations of Canadians to the fact of concentrated wealth and power, and of the relations of non-elite Canadians with one another. Particularly, the nature of class awareness and resentment and possible bases of class action and social change have preoccupied me, as much or more than an exploration of the rigidities of institutionalized inequality. I do not expect that social change will emanate from the elite or ruling class; rather, if we are to have change, we must expect it from the hitherto ''smug'' middle-class majority, and from *organized* industrial and rural workers. This said, I confess that I am not yet certain whether it stands as an expression of pessimism or of optimism.

DPF
Ottawa

Preface to the Second Edition

The Canadian Class Structure has apparently been widely read and used in undergraduate instruction. I gather, therefore, that many of my colleagues found it a useful instructional tool. Some reviewers have been good enough to suggest that it has met the purpose for which it was intended: to introduce the undergraduate to the controversy and complexity of social stratification analysis, and to do so without any silly pretense of value neutrality.

Others, though, have objected to the "ideological" tenor of the book. For example, one scoffed at what is characterized as my conviction that a society without stratification is possible. I argue no such thing, of course, as my discussion of minimal stratification should make clear. To the contrary, I insist that some manifestations of inequality are inevitable. The principal theoretical thesis of the book remains the view that stratification may be ameliorated, not eliminated. Moreover, I insist that stratification need not take the form of class differentiation, as defined by inherited economic disparities. The principal empirically illustrated view is that in Canada class stratification seems to be becoming increasingly rigid and stable.

In working through my interpretation of stratification in Canada I explicitly employ two conceptions of social class. For heuristic reasons there is resort to the imperfect operationalization of social class permitted by occupational data, so well suited to a description of middle class characteristics. There is also resort to a dichotomized representation of class, with the distinction vested in extremes of prestige, power, and more basically, propertied wealth. In each case I suggest that collective consciousness or awareness is the basis of action.

The changes in this edition of the book are basically these:
1) An updating where possible of pertinent statistical and research data.
2) Some more explicit attention to women in the Canadian class structure.
3) A clarification of my opinion regarding the probability and the desirability of effective class politics and the realization of change in stratified Canadian society.

The last perhaps deserves additional comment. If I were to criticize *The Canadian Class Structure*, above all else it would be on grounds of equivocation with respect to the question of revolutionary action.

I have not escaped ambivalence in this revised statement, but I have attempted to explain its bases. Fundamentally I take the view that there must be an effective class conflict and class action that escapes the lethargy of evolutionary welfarism and the excess of violent revolution. I do not, however, suggest that this is a probable feature of future Canada; rather, as a logical conclusion from the information assembled in the book, the entrenchment of welfare stratification is more likely. To put it somewhat differently, the ambivalence that persists regarding the malleability of Canadian society is a reflection of a disparity in ideological aspiration on the one hand, and more pessimistic empirically based conclusion on the other. Consequently, where the book begins with an argument asserting that a classless society is achievable, it concludes in the view that such a society is not probable.

In this edition I persist in my attempt to avoid encumbering the book with the concepts, or rhetoric, or disputes of any one school of social science theory. Although clearly interpretive and opinionated, I have sought to ignore conceptual and theoretical quibble in order to convey an image of the nature and the consequences of stratification in Canada.

In attempting to achieve that measure of detachment the book perhaps lacks the conviction or affiliation that some might wish. Surely, however, no one can mistake my work as detached social science, even if such were possible.

In conclusion, I suggest that the informed reader is not intended to love or endorse the book wholeheartedly. There are too many instances of selection, opinion, and interpretation for that to occur. I would, however, be pleased to have readers reacting to the book and its themes, using the information for alternative interpretation and for instruction. And perhaps along the way I will convince some people of some things.

D.F.
November 1978

Preface to the Third Edition

We are, media pundits assure us, in a neo-conservative period. Political leaders attack social service expenditures, and members of the new generation occupying Canada's universities are intent, not upon political or social reform, but upon qualifying for that scarce and crucial commodity, a job. The theoretically feasible prospect of an egalitarian society seems more utopian than ever.

In preparing this new edition of *The Canadian Class Structure*, I find no grounds for amending the basic argument—the basic pessimism—of previous editions. Rather, I am satisfied to provide more current data, and to renew my conclusion that class stratification in Canada is rigid and unyielding. Middle-class women may be doing better than a decade or so ago, as measured by greater labour force participation and income. But working-class women still labour in dead-end menial jobs, and families headed by single women are the front-line of Canadian poverty. Middle-class persons, men and women, still do well, perhaps even better than in the recent past, with two-income families more common in the 1980's. But working-class persons still struggle in the economic margins, sometimes employed, and very often not.

Class inequality is very much with us in the 1980's, and Canadians seem further from, rather than nearer, an egalitarian society.

D.F.

THE CANADIAN
CLASS STRUCTURE

CHAPTER 1

Stratification in Perspective

The Ubiquity of Inequality

Mankind has never wanted for utopian conceptions of society. Recorded history offers repeated visions of some better form of social existence wherein human beings live in perfect and fulfilling harmony. Such utopias have always had to come to grips with inequality. Some thinkers have done so with an image of the best and most fulfilling form of inequality, such as Plato's emphasis upon a society of communal property, yet governed by an enlightened ruling class. Similarly, Auguste Comte envisaged a socialist society guided by social engineers or sociologist priests. Others, such as in the early Christian tradition, have resisted notions of necessary distinctions among men, and have insisted upon a fundamental equality. Thomas More, who gave us the word "utopia," writing in 1516 argued for a communal ownership, ideally guided by Christian love and brotherhood.

The 18th-century liberal ideology of the new American republic also projected a utopian image. It promised an equality of opportunity founded on a society of free and independent property holders. This equality was constitutionally guaranteed and celebrated. Yet, though the object of this liberal sentiment was a goal less difficult than full equality of condition, in the sense of only guaranteeing equal opportunity to compete for unequal rewards, the United States from the outset failed to realize its utopian inspiration. The opportunity for wealth, like wealth itself, has proved to be inheritable, such that each generation of Americans begins its quest for the "American dream" from enormously variable starting points.

Another utopian image that continues to intrigue idealists and social critics is that of Karl Marx. The Marxist dream was of a classless society whose members realized their potential as human beings and no longer suffered the inequities and humiliations of inferior status and benefits. For Marx, industrial society such as that of 19th-century England was bourgeois class society, a system in which the *bourgeoisie* or owners of property ruled and exploited the *proletariat* or wage slaves. Eventually, Marx reasoned, the vast proletariat would develop a *class consciousness*, recognize the common misery of their lives, and act as an effective political force to violently overthrow the bourgeoisie. Private property, the basis of wealth and power, would be abolished. Each person would work for himself,

1

producing according to his skills and inclination and receiving according to his needs. Human society would have evolved to its highest form, and humankind would be fulfilled. (Marx, 1947; 1955; Anderson, 1974.)

The power of such an image is obvious—as obvious as the other-worldly appeal of Christianity. Yet, despite dedicated converts, despite nations formally committed to Marxist goals, somehow the goal of perfect equality has proved elusive, and Marxist nations find themselves coping with inequalities that seem to be becoming increasingly rigid. (Bottomore, 1965: 47–60; Parkin, 1972: 137–159; Djilas, 1957.)

Some sociological theorists believe the failure inevitable, for they believe that hierarchical differentiation or inequality in society is intrinsic to human behaviour. For example, Kingsley Davis and Wilbert Moore wrote of the *functional necessity* of some form of differentiation or stratification. (Davis and Moore, 1942.) In order to survive, they argued, societies must see to the performance of certain functionally necessary tasks. And since tasks are not all equally attractive, a society must contain practices that ensure that persons are assigned specific roles and motivated to perform them. An unequal system of rewards realizes such *role allocation*, argued Davis and Moore, and motivates the performance of the requisite behaviour associated with such roles. In their view, the forms of stratification might differ widely, and the variation in rewards might be extreme or slight, but some variation must necessarily come to pass if a society is to persist as a viable unit.

The functionalist view makes much of the difficulties of role allocation and of motivation, assuming that the performance of socially relevant tasks is dependent upon pay-off for the performers. Gouldner (1970) suggests that functionalism is a variation on the theme of 19th-century utilitarianism, in that it takes culturally relative definitions of the utility or value of specific roles and tasks to be indicative of some functional necessity. In contrast to functionalist emphasis upon system maintenance, Marx made light of the problems of social organization and what historically has been human maximization of reward. On the one hand, functionalists suggest that rewards, and, by implication, material rewards, must be unequally allocated or human society is impossible. On the other hand, Marxists suggest that society will develop to a stage wherein human beings can divest themselves of any inclination to distribute wealth differentially.

Sociologists other than the functionalists have argued the inevitability of inequality. For example, Gaetano Mosca (1939) was of the view that there would always be a ruling class, because society, with its complexity, requires that there be political organization. Thus, there must be inequalities in power. And since people are self-seeking, the powerful will acquire privilege or wealth. (Mosca, 1939; Lenski, 1966.) Similarly, in 1911, Robert Michels (1958) published his study of the German Social Democratic Party and concluded that there obtains an ''iron law of oligarchy.'' Because specialized tasks must be undertaken, requiring expertise and the human expenditure of time and effort, inevitably a minority within any human organization will come to monopolize decision-making or power. The masses will tend to opt out of regular participation and decision-making, from lack of interest or information and because of the sheer cost in time and effort. Those already making decisions will consolidate their positions of power and advantage. (Michels, 1958.)

Taking a similar tone, John Porter (1965) suggests that the highly complex and specialized nature of modern society has necessitated complex and specialized government and corporate organization. Those making decisions in these government and economic organizations have enormous power. Unlike the American sociologist C. Wright Mills (1959), who deemed such persons ''the power elite,'' Porter did not believe that these decision-makers act in full consensus; they are in competition and conflict, as well as in collusion. But they do rule society. (Porter, 1965: 22–28.) Moreover, they maintain their power and privilege even when they or their descendants lack merit.

Porter suggested that power is a means to the exploitation of property and resources and is therefore crucial. In a somewhat similar fashion, Dahrendorf (1959) offered what he believed to be a necessary modification of Marxism, and stressed that in modern societies there is a basic struggle for political power as the basis of differential control of property and wealth. Writing early in the 20th century, Weber (1946; 1947; 1958) also stressed non-economic considerations. Weber noted that persons distinguished among themselves by prestige as well as by power and economic possession. Lenski agrees, and speaks of prestige, power, and privilege. (Lenski, 1966.) Thus, many sociologists today take the view that there are three principal dimensions of stratification: the honorific (prestige), the political (power), and the economic (wealth). The Weberian three-fold distinction suggests that stratification is complex, rather than merely a matter of economic differentiation, especially in the modern nation state. The complexity suggests that full equality may fail to materialize even when there is equal distribution of wealth.

Modern Marxism offers analyses that are remarkably similar to Weber's. Property and wealth remain fundamental, but political power located in the state is viewed as crucial. (Panitch, 1977.) The state can and does intervene economically, acting as owner, employer, regulator, redistributor, and perpetuator of economic resources. In its extreme manifestation, intervention and control by the ''socialist states'' of Eastern Europe act to fully determine privilege and the structure of inequality. (Lane, 1971.)

Human history contains examples of societies that approximated the Marxist ideal, insofar as they briefly avoided disparities in material reward or wealth. Yet there is no convincing example of a viable human society in which there has not been *some* differentiation in prestige and in power. That is, even where a society has had few persisting differences in the material possessions of its members, these societies have been characterized by distinct and recognized differences in the prestige or honour assigned to people and in the power or ability of people to control the behaviour of others. These minimal differences in prestige and power have derived from individual characteristics or skills and from social positions of responsibility. The differences may be awarded individuals in recognition of or reward for their behaviour and use of skills to the perceived advantage of the collectivity. But honour and power also have been inherited across generations, with the result that individuals come to enjoy benefits irrespective of their own achievements or contributions to society. Even in simple societies, such inheritance is not altogether avoided. We can illustrate inequality of prestige and power, in the absence of inequality of wealth, by considering very simple human societies.

Hunting and Gathering Societies

In simple hunting and gathering societies, we have an example of the most rudimentary level of human social organization. People at this level of social existence are literally dependent for their existence upon foodstuffs they collect from the natural environment: the plants women gather and dig up and the animals men bring home from the hunt. There is no cultivation of plants or herding of animals. Nor, with the exception of some peoples who occupy lush and abundant environments, are there permanent settlements. The small bands of people, 10 to 30 in number, are nomadic; they must move with the seasons to secure their subsistence. And there is typically no accumulation of wealth; the absence of an economic surplus is a distinguishing feature. (Lenski, 1966; 95–116.) A conspicuous exception, the Kwakiutl of what is now British Columbia, were able to accumulate considerable wealth; yet rank was distinguished, not by accumulation *per se*, but by reciprocal exchanges of property, or, in the extreme, by "rivalry potlatches," offering resources for consumption or destruction. Thus the *potlatch* was a means of establishing and validating relations of social status. (Druker, 1965; 55–66.)

The usual hunting and gathering society is aptly described as communal. As was the case with Inuit bands before contact with Europeans, it is unquestioningly accepted that there be full co-operation and sharing. Without necessarily recognizing the consequences, this communal ownership and consumption, administered through the organization of the extended family, guarantees the maintenance and security of the collectivity. No matter which hunter is responsible for the kill, for example, the meat will be distributed through the band, along kinship lines, until everyone has a share.

There is a limited technology, in a hunting and gathering society, such as pointed digging sticks, spears, bows and arrows; there is no control over the production of foodstuffs, except what is vested in knowledge of plants and animals and skill in obtaining their yield. Thus, essentially, hunting and gathering peoples remain subject to the fluctuations of climate, much more than agriculturalists, for their yield is modest and is not preserved or stored. The life of a hunting and gathering band is thereby harsh and precarious, co-operation is essential, and deviance intolerable. There are no legal paraphernalia, however, such as we are familiar with to ensure minimal conformity. Laws are not formally articulated, nor are persons designated as responsible for ensuring obedience to such laws. The very isolation of such peoples, lacking exposure to alternate societies and ways of life, ensures a basic uniformity of behaviour, for there has been uniformity of socialization. That is, unlike the case of large complex societies such as our own, the members of a hunting and gathering band will face few options in life. There is a simple division of labour by gender and age, and people all learn the expected behaviours. Within the limits of socialization, where deviance does occur in the small band, the norms and sanctions of kin are effective controls. Ultimately, there are fearful sanctions of ostracism and banishment for persistent or serious offences. Given a harsh environment and the need for co-operation, banishment may become a virtual death sentence. In societies such as the Inuit, execution is the ultimate penalty, and is the responsibility of kin and the immediate band.

Because of the rudimentary level of existence, there is little social differentiation in such societies. There are certainly no social classes, in the sense of individuals within a society being differentiated by wealth. But there is some differentiation; more important, there is some hierarchical or vertical differentiation, specifically by power and prestige, and this hierarchical differentiation to some extent persists across generations, for it is inherited. It thereby constitutes what we take to be a minimal social stratification.

At the most elementary level, we find differences in ascribed social position related to birth and biological maturation and, in turn, normatively defined in relation to the elementary division of labour. Thus, for example, women gather foodstuffs and men hunt. In addition, not only do roles differ, varying values are assigned to them and the people who fulfill them; it is at this point that hierarchical differentiation occurs. Women, for example, characteristically enjoy less prestige and power than do men; children less than adults. Moreover, in addition to such inequality by ascription, some individuals demonstrate valued skills or attributes relatively lacking in others. Such persons are respected and assume greater prestige, and their suggestions and initiatives are valued. They have greater influence than other members of the band; they become leaders. Sometimes this leadership is formalized; sometimes, as among some Inuit, there is little formalization — no conception, for example, of chieftainship. (Weyer, 1932; 21-0-214.) Insofar as these skilled individuals elicit deference and others comply with their directions, leadership status is distinguished from that of rank and file members of the band. For example, the skilled hunter is extremely important to the survival of the band, and his skills are recognized and his advice, at least in hunting, is respected. There will usually not be laws or norms requiring compliance with such advice and punishments for failure to comply; but insofar as an individual has valuable skills, the probability of compliance is great, because it is in the interest of the collectivity. Thus, individuals come to be distinguished on the basis of their contributions to the group, or, as Lenski put it, we find "functional inequality." (Lenski, 1966: 105.) Skills other than those related to hunting may be recognized, such as the mystical and practical skills of a *shaaman* or medicine man to whom people will turn for advice and assistance. (Lenski, 1966: 100–101.) If the skills of hunter and spiritual/medical leader coincide in a single individual, that individual may become very powerful indeed, for he is granted the voluntary compliance of other members of the band.

In stressing differentiation by skills, we suggest a fluid system of inequality, relating to individual qualities and achievement. But such skills are not entirely a function of the luck of the biological draw. In some part they can be accounted for by socialization, and are thereby socially inherited. The sons of the hunter, or of the *shaaman*, are more likely to learn their father's skills than are other members of the band. That is, the parent will impart information to his sons, while the other members of the band will tend to expect that the child of a skilful person will have inherited these skills, thereby generating a self-fulfilling prophecy. Thus, although a biologically determined capacity is necessary, it is important to realize that the opportunity to shape such a capacity is also important, and it is more likely to be shaped in a manner consistent with existing differentiation.

Because skilled individuals have the opportunity to pass skills on to whomever they choose, whether their own children or others, and because other members of the band are inclined to expect certain behaviour from persons associated with those of recognized skill, the son of a great hunter and leader is given greater opportunity to establish high status than would be given other members of the band. This is just a short step, then, from establishing hereditary leadership, which in some instances does become formally institutionalized. The son of the leader or headman is given the benefit of the doubt, and would more likely have to discredit himself to lose status rather than prove himself to secure leadership status.

The point of this description is that some hierarchical differentiation exists in the simplest form of human social organization. This differentiation constitutes minimal stratification when it is inherited across generations. It is not stratification of a complex sort, for role differentiation and population size are slight, in keeping with the slight technology that can support only a small population. Nor, for the same reasons and in the absence of differential wealth, do we find ranked collectivities or aggregates that we could view as classes. But some individuals are distinguished from others in prestige and in power — women from men, children from adults, the elderly from the vigorous adults, and the skilled from the unskilled. In this most egalitarian of known human societies, perfect equality or the complete absence of stratification in its broadest sense is not realized. Inequality is not due to some innate and sinister drive to power or will to dominate or greed, but is the product of a collectivity organized for survival.

Minimal Stratification

If one contrasts such simple hunting and gathering societies with modern industrialized Canada, we can perhaps be less incredulous when we encounter contemporary stratification. Hunting and gathering peoples are small in number, and accumulate virtually no possessions. They have a minimal division of labour and only kinship organization. Yet differentiation by prestige and power does occur. Little wonder that it occurs, therefore, in more complex societies, with large populations, a considerable technology and variations in skill, a vast range of durable material possessions, and an access to mass communication that renders visible many alternate ways of life. Questions of livelihood and social order become problematic, and the distribution of benefits and the regulation of deviance major social tasks.

Existing knowledge of all forms of society or levels of social organization suggests that *some hierarchical social differentiation or stratification has always existed* (Lenski, 1966). Given the minimal subtle variations in influence and prestige that characterize human relations, some hierarchical differentiation and even a fragile inheritance is probably inevitable. We stress that this is a far different statement than it would be to say that unequal wealth or class society is inevitable. And it is certainly not an endorsement of any given degree or kind of differentiation or inequality. Indeed, to be perfectly clear, we are of the view that differentiation in a complex society could theoretically approximate that of a hunting and gathering society, in that we find no empirical or theoretical basis suggesting the necessity, as opposed to the effectiveness and near ubiquity, of inheritable economic differences. Minimal stratification by prestige and by influence or power is inherent in human social interaction and organization. The more complex the social organization, the greater the incidence of differential economic rewards in addition to differential prestige and power. Because commodities, money, and other forms of material property are visible, quantifiable, and ostensibly scarce, disparate material rewards and their inheritance increase with social complexity. Differences in economic rewards are practical or expedient. But it is not necessary that economic rewards be differentially, as opposed to equally, assigned to persons, especially to the extent of massive disparities. Nor is it necessary that material rewards be passed on to heirs.

Thus, without resorting to the language of functionalist theory, or the assumption of necessary economic differentiation, or the endorsement of large disparities and the institutionalization of such disparities over time and across generations, we do assert that some minimal degree of social stratification is inevitable. But what is highly variable is the nature and the extremity of stratification systems. Stratification as we find it in Canada is not inevitable. Nor, to make a very personal statement of value, is it to be condoned. Rather, it can be explained, understood, and changed. But whatever the changes and however desirable they may be, some stratification will persist. *What is crucial, because of its enormous impact upon human lives, and because theoretically it is remediable and not inevitable, is economic stratification or class stratification.*

Minimally Stratified Society: The Hutterites

Recent history has witnessed numerous attempts to realize the goal of the economically egalitarian society; and they have typically collapsed far short of the ideal. A dramatic exception that illustrates our thesis of minimally inevitable stratification in the absence of class is that of the Hutterite communal colonies, scattered throughout the provinces of Manitoba, Saskatchewan, and Alberta.

The Hutterites are an Anabaptist religious sect, motivated by a conception of Christian community and equality. Founded by Joseph Hutter, they fled from Germany to Russia during the European counter-Reformation of the 17th century. Czarist retribution for Hutterite resistance to conscription prompted the Hutterite migration to North America. Colonies were founded in North Dakota and Minnesota, but greater numbers settled in the prairie provinces in Canada. (Peters, 1965; Bennett, 1967; Bennett, 1969.)

There they have literally prospered and multiplied. And they have done so without compromising with the secular society surrounding them. They are unlike the adherents of the other Anabaptist sects, the Mennonites and the Amish, who have, with few exceptions, abandoned any communal organization and whose members have largely been assimilated into the larger North American society. They maintain a rural existence segregated from the stimuli of modern urban Canada.

The Hutterites live in colonies of a maximum size of about one hundred. When a colony exceeds that number, a new colony is established, because, until recently, land for expansion in the Canadian West has been readily available. There are continual challenges to continued expansion of the Hutterite colonies, however, for, as perceived by other farmers, and to some extent in fact, their communal organization, pooling of resources, and modest consumption permit them the capital to expand where the individual farmer (as opposed to corporate agriculturalists) may not. In addition, the Hutterites are largely self-sufficient, and, as their opponents stress, they spend little money in surrounding communities. Their major expenditures are on new machinery, and these are not purchases usually made from local merchants. In Alberta, where the majority of the Hutterite population — more than 40,000 — live, the *Communal Properties Act* limited Hutterite expansion. (Russell, 1974.) In 1973, the Lougheed government repealed the Act, but public pressure for limits upon Hutterite expansion persist. At the present time, municipal zoning laws hamper their growth.

The Hutterites are extremely efficient agriculturalists. They employ the most modern techniques and machinery, and, because of their collective organization, they can afford to. But the agricultural output is for the collectivity, not individuals. The Hutterites emphasize "all things common." People dress alike, in basic black, with modest colour variations in items of clothing such as a man's shirt or a woman's kerchief. Women are readily recognized by their Mother Hubbard dresses and kerchiefed heads; the men by their black suits or work-clothing, and beards if married. Each family has private quarters, but the adults eat together in a communal dining hall, segregated by sex. The hall also doubles as a place of worship, for there are no churches. The children eat together, separate from the adults, under the care and supervision of the Hutterite teacher and his wife.

Individuals have virtually no possessions. Insistence on uniform clothing and the prohibition against accumulating wealth or acquiring items of adornment are meant to minimize differences, much as was intended by uniformity of dress in Mao's China. A young unmarried girl might have a few items of clothing and keepsakes in her hope chest, but little else.

The Hutterite form of organization is sustained by segregation of the colony members from outside contact, especially during childhood, and by religious ideology. A characteristic of failed communal settlements otherwise similar to the Hutterites is that they lack a shared ideological allegiance learned in the absence of alternative conceptions of social life. The Hutterite children are rigorously socialized to one life style. There are no books, radios, magazines, or television sets — except sometimes in the quarters of the elected leader of the colony, the preacher.

But though they are able to maintain this egalitarian structure, it cannot be said that there is no differentiation. There are, for example, the minimal differences derived from ascribed characteristics — i.e., gender and age. Certain roles are defined as suitable for women, and others for men. A woman is excluded from much of the labour involved in cultivation or ranching, but is responsible for cleaning, cooking, and mending. A woman could never be a preacher. Similarly, age demands respect, and only with maturity can one marry.

Moreover, beyond an elementary division of labour by age or gender, a related differentiation is the extent to which various male roles demand enhanced skills or are assigned prestige. Thus, of crucial importance to the colony are the positions of German teacher and of preacher. In addition, there are church elders, a colony boss, and farm boss. (Ryan, 1977: 84–91.) These persons are respected, and they make decisions and can command compliance. Thus, although material items are held in common, there is differentiation along the dimensions of prestige and power. Thereby, in a rudimentary sense, there is hierarchical differentiation. This constitutes a system of stratification to the extent that it is inheritable across generations. It seems to be true that, as in hunting and gathering societies, there is an inheritance of skills by virtue of socialization. Children do acquire the skills and the reputation of their parents to some extent, thereby aiding later election to influential positions. But this inheritance lacks formalization and legitimation; on the contrary, it is defined as ideologically undesirable. In a precise sense, stratification exists, but it is remarkably slight, especially in contrast to a society such as our own.

Even the Hutterites fall short of the perfectly egalitarian society. But it is an economically egalitarian society. As in hunting and gathering societies, material wealth is shared equally, although people are differentiated by prestige and power, which in human relations never seem to be equally distributed. However, unlike hunting and gathering societies, the Hutterites have realized their economic equality or classlessness while existing well above a subsistence level. It is a prosperous society, but the distribution of wealth is uniform among its members. There would be enormous institutional obstacles, but we stress that, theoretically, any society could function similarly in the absence of gross material differentiation—even Canadian society.

Forms of Complex Stratification

We have been using as our definition of stratification the notion that there must be persisting or inherited hierarchical differentiation in possessions, prestige, or power. Usually, the three dimensions are coincident. Within this broad definition, it is possible to distinguish different forms of stratification, such as "class stratification", in Canada.

The institutionalized inequalities found in societies are not identical in organization. Their extent, in wealth, for example, varies from society to society, as do disparities in prestige and power. In some societies the extremes of wealth and poverty extend over a broad range; in others the range is relatively narrow. In some societies, such as in pre-industrial or agrarian societies, we find a marked polarization between a very rich minority of the population and the mass of the population, largely a rural peasantry. Wealth, power, and prestige are concentrated, and there is no significant middle stratum. This is in contrast to industrialized societies, where, although one can still point to extremes of wealth and poverty, the majority of the population have historically constituted a middle stratum, enjoying a standard of life far superior to that of the impoverished masses of agrarian societies.

Whatever the precise composition of the inequality, it is important to realize that it is a structured thing, very resistant to change. In sociological terms, it is *institutionalized*; that is, persisting through inherited organization and learning or socialization.

Variations in stratification systems are exemplified not only by the extent and distribution of wealth, but by the degree to which the stratification is rigid or closed, as opposed to open or "permeable." (Svalastoga, 1965: 40.) Some are more rigid than others. Some permit greater opportunity for an individual to increase his wealth or power and prestige — i.e., greater opportunity for upward *social mobility*. Conversely, such open societies would also feature greater likelihood of downward social mobility. Such societies would depend to a greater extent upon individual achievements rather than upon inheritance; an individual would achieve a rank or social status (*achieved status*) as opposed to inheriting it or having it ascribed to him (*ascribed status*).

All societies offer some opportunity for mobility, but no society excludes rank by ascription or inheritance. Mobility opportunities are greater in industrialized societies than in non-industrialized societies. In that relative sense, industrial societies are open rather than closed societies.

Open societies, such as Canada's, have generally been class societies, in that mobility has been measured against the criterion of wealth. The boundaries between these classes are indistinct and not formalized, but they represent obvious variations in prestige, power, and, above all, income or wealth. But because these strata are not formally sanctioned in law or custom, people may not have a clear conception or consciousness of belonging to a class, in the sense of an awareness of a commonality of situation and interests. Such an awareness is far less problematic in rigid stratification systems.

Estate

In traditional societies, distinctions were more apparent. A person owned property and possessed wealth or he did not. A person had formal rank, usually hereditary, or he did not. Societies characterized by formal demarcation of strata are significantly different from class societies, precisely because the differentiation is legitimated, that is, viewed as right and proper, sanctioned by tradition and often by law. Some of the clearer examples are to be found in mediaeval Europe. For example, feudal England was a society in which there existed three distinguishable sectors: the aristocracy, the clergy, and the common people. These *estates* were legally recognized. Such legal differentiation distinguishes an estate from a class society. Each estate was itself stratified, but, by law, the aristocracy comprised the privileged minority of society, the hereditary landowners. Within the aristocracy, one's place in the hierarchy depended principally on the extent of one's lands, and, not unrelated, allegiance to the monarch. The pre-eminent aristocrat, the king or queen, is at the pinnacle of the feudal estate stratification system. The commoners made up the peasant mass of society, and also included a smaller number of craftsmen and tradesmen resident in the towns. The rural peasantry were bound to local lords and confined to the land they worked.

These distinctions were hereditary. Mobility, or achieved status, while not unknown, was not the norm. The church was a principal means of mobility, since, given its vows of celibacy, its clergy were dependent upon recruitment. By entering the church, a common man could improve his status, for the church transcended both the aristocracy and the peasantry. Although the more prominent churchmen were normally members of the aristocracy, and themselves important landowners, people could achieve high rank in the church despite being born to a very modest status. (Mayer and Buckley, 1969: 33–38.) A famous example from English history is that of Thomas Becket, a merchant's son who became Archbishop of Canterbury with a power that threatened the king's.

Another historical example of estate society may be taken from Canadian history, in the case of New France. The hereditary nobility, or seigneurs, were the large landholders, and their serfs or habitants were under legal obligation to perform specified services. The clergy of the Roman Catholic Church shared in the political administration of this New France. With the British conquest, the legal nature of this feudal system was broken, although its outline lived on in land distribution and community organization. The Catholic Church, controlling educational opportunities and land as well as religious ideology, persisted in its dominating influence well into the 20th century. From the outset, the frontier as well as the church provided opportunities for social mobility. But as the frontier gradually closed after the British conquest of New France, Quebec society settled into the stable pattern of small rural land holdings which persists to the present in rural Quebec.

Caste

More enduring than estate societies are caste societies. The best example is that of traditional India; despite changes since Indian independence, even today Indian caste distinctions survive. A *caste* is a religiously-sanctioned stratum into which an individual is bound for life. Each caste is associated with an occupational role, certain norms of behaviour, and specified privileges. For example, in traditional Indian society, the superior caste in the Hindu community was the priesthood (Brahmans). Next in standing were the warriors (Kshatryias). The third caste consisted of merchants, craftsmen, and peasants (Vaisyas). A fourth caste consisted of those performing manual labour and acting as servants for the three superior castes (Sudras). Indians came to distinguish several thousands of castes, many of them peculiar to local areas and associated with some specific and hereditary occupation. In 1901, the Indian census reported 2,378 such castes. (Barber, 1957: 80.) In turn, each such caste was divided into sub-castes. (Mayer and Buckley, 1969: 30–33; Barber, 1958: 80–81.) Each was viewed as inviolate, with the expectation that an individual must conform to his caste requirements or suffer the penalty, after death, of reincarnation in an inferior caste. The most inferior status is that of *outcastes*, known as the "untouchables" or the "unclean," contact with whom by caste members required subsequent acts of purification. Barber (1957: 81) reports that in 1931 one-fifth of the Indian population, or 50 million people, were outcastes.

The caste system has proved remarkably persistent, having survived wave after wave of immigrating peoples and conquests, most recently British control of the Indian subcontinent. With Independence, the Indian government declared caste distinctions illegal, and today there are opportunities for mobility, often in government, and deliberate attempts to extend education to all castes, including the outcastes. But the traditional behaviour persists, with new castes and caste functions growing up to meet the government's attempts to introduce modernity to India. Today it is estimated that approximately 25 percent of modern India's population are untouchables — approximately 165 million people. Most live in poverty, and are frequently the targets of violence. (Kashmeri, 1985: 4.) Particularly at the local village level, India, overwhelmingly rural, still finds itself characterized by caste distinctions (often reinforced by ethnic and religious distinctions), and persistence of what is perhaps history's most complex and elaborate system of institutionalized inequality.

Class

The preceding descriptions of estate and caste societies are grossly oversimplified. Within estates or castes there are considerable differences, with the result that each itself comprises a hierarchy of many strata. But they are fundamentally distinguished from class societies in that they are clearly and visibly stratified, as sanctioned or legitimated in custom, law, and religion. In class societies, such clear-cut strata and formal legitimation are absent, and to some degree repudiated as morally offensive. In a sense, the stratification is more subtle and less rigid in a class society, in that upward mobility or movement from stratum to stratum is accepted and, in fact, encouraged. Relatively, class societies are open societies, and estate and caste societies are closed. But although, in this relative sense, class societies are open, advantages are inherited. The class positions of individuals are usually transmitted across generations, with privileges of prestige, power, wealth, and the resources that these command, shared and passed on informally and legally through the family. The family into which one is born is the medium governing access to advantage and class standing in modern societies. Inherited benefits include not only wealth but access to such key institutions as universities and prestigious employers.

Classes are aggregates of persons distinguished by inherited access to wealth or income. Power and prestige or life style are dimensions correlated with such wealth. In large part, inherited wealth or property and occupation are crucial to a person's class and the class membership of a dependent. Classes are not formally demarcated, and the boundaries are fluid. But they do represent distinctive shared or common positions of relative privilege, and that privilege is inherited, whether directly as wealth or indirectly as opportunity to acquire wealth. Especially to the degree that such aggregated individuals are conscious of their common positions, they constitute social classes. Such awareness characterizes the Canadian circumstance, despite the egalitarian ethic that deters acknowledgement of the existence of social class in Canada.

Measuring Social Class

Unlike the legal and religious definitions of estate and caste societies taught to succeeding generations, the strata or classes that make up the stratification systems of modern societies are difficult to identify precisely. This is particularly true of modern industrialized societies, as contrasted to developing societies, for their role differentiation or division of labour is all the more elaborate. There are no formal or legal labels that distinguish a working class from a middle class or an upper class in modern Canada. Rather, there are many imperfect indicators of class membership that Canadians more or less explicitly respond to and that the researcher can use, albeit somewhat arbitrarily.

The number of strata the social scientist distinguishes is also arbitrary, as are the cutting points distinguishing one stratum from another. They are a matter of judgement and definition, as if, for example, one were to state that the boundary between the working class and the middle class is an income level of $15,000. But classes are not merely arbitrary sociological inventions. Not just some social scientists, but most Canadians, even while at the same time denying the reality of classes, will vaguely distinguish strata, such as working or lower, middle, and upper class. And we almost all have some understanding of the kind of people to whom these labels refer, although we usually do not go about precisely designating class characteristics and boundaries.

Some researchers, such as W. Lloyd Warner, made fine distinctions. In his community studies, Warner at times spoke of strata within each of the lower, middle, upper-middle, and upper classes. He found that people were able to make such distinctions within their own broad stratum, as when lower-class individuals distinguished the "shiftless" from the good worker. The upper class (I) consists of persons of wealth, and wealth that extends over several generations; these are established families, the "silk stockings." The upper-middle class (II) consists of achievers, persons who are doing well financially, but may have been upwardly mobile; who very often are in professional occupations; and who frequently are the visible "community leaders." The lower-middle class (III) are "working people," but doing relatively well financially, typically within white collar (clerical) occupations. The upper-lower class (IV) are "poor but honest" workers, persons working in factories, and often immigrants. The lower-lower class (V) approximate those whom Marx termed the "lumpenproletariat," in that they are perceived as the "people who scrape the bottom," persons on welfare. (Warner, 1949: 66–67.) Whatever the distinctions, it is the case that no so-called class is homogeneous in its characteristics, or free of some additional hierarchical gradation.

Class distinctions are perceived on the bases of many indicators, the most fundamental of which is money — that is, inherited and earned wealth. The various indicators that have been applied by particular researchers for identifying class composition can be used with varying degrees of precision. The grosser the distinctions we wish to make, the easier time we have of it. For example, we could dichotomize and distinguish only the extremes of wealth and poverty. The distinction between two classes could be in terms of possessions, such as money and negotiable securities, land, or housing. We would still have to decide arbitrarily what accumulation of possessions distinguished the superior or the inferior stratum, and where the cut-off points would be, but we could make the distinctions and be rather straightforward about it. But in each group we would be lumping together persons who in many ways are distinguishable. A theoretically more meaningful dichotomization would be to distinguish those who own productive property from those who lack such property and work for wages or salaries, or even are unemployed. That this would obscure considerable differences within each stratum is all too apparent, and, for most sociologists, such a dichotomization would be of little utility. But it does summarize a fundamental difference between capitalists or those who control the means of production, and employees or the unemployed, those who are dependent upon owners or the state for their livelihood.

If finer distinctions are required, the task of measurement is complicated. Not only do we have the matter of arbitrary cutting points, but also the limited visibility of indicators. In feudal societies, symbols of wealth such as clothing or housing were highly distinctive by stratum, and very visible. But in modern Canada, short of extremes, people dress approximately alike or drive automobiles approximately alike, even wear clothing and drive automobiles for which they have inadequate income. Quite obviously there remain distinctions in the quality and cost of clothing, automobiles, or housing, as well as other consumer items, and in the ease with which different persons can acquire them. The difficulty is in systematically identifying and distinguishing them, or in determining those few which would serve to be indicative of the others. In modern Canada, one such indicator, for example, might be housing, given the extent to which the single dwelling unit has become a scarce commodity. The notion that certain key items are indicative of one's class membership has resulted in research procedures designed to measure social class by references to possessions.

F. Stuart Chapin developed four indexes of class, one of which he came to favour as most effective: the "living-room scale." (Chapin, 1928; 1933; Guttman, 1942.) Chapin found that evaluation of living room items was an effective representation of all possessions and of social status, in that the living room was the centre of family interaction and display. He evaluated the material and the "cultural" status of the items and their condition — matters such as presence, quantity, and nature of books and magazines, for example. To take an improvised example from Chapin's notion, one would expect different magazines in an upper-middle class home as opposed to a working-class home, such as *Saturday Night* as opposed to *Reader's Digest*, or shelves of Book-of-the-Month selections as opposed to either the utter absence of books, or paperback titles such as Harlequin romances. Or to consider furniture, the upper-middle class home is not likely to have a television set in the living room whereas a working-class home would. This is not a matter of invidious comparison, but a recognition that different kinds of possessions and their uses do correlate highly with incomes, suggesting effective methods of measurement.

In his community studies, Warner developed two principal methods of identifying classes; he called them Evaluated Participation (E.P.) and the Index of Status Characteristics (I.S.C.). He found the results from each to be highly correlated. (Warner, 1949.) They were first used in his famous Yankee City studies (1941). The E.P. depends on the ratings or perceptions of a representative sample of members of the community. It is an attempt to specify the nature of the over-all "social-class configuration" of a community, as well as to specify the participation or life style of individuals within the configuration; the research depends upon the consensus or "matched agreement" of the respondents. (Warner, 1949: 47–71.) The I.S.C. uses four visible socio-economic items: occupation, source of income, house type, and dwelling area (Warner, 1949: 41) as indicators of class membership. The occupational dimensions distinguished amongst independent businessmen, (and according to size of business), and professionals, clerks, skilled, semi-skilled, and unskilled workers. The income dimension distinguished amongst inherited and earned wealth, profits, salaries, wages, and welfare. Houses were distinguished by size and condition, and their location or neighbourhood by reputation, facilities, and condition. (Warner, 1949: 122–154.) These were all scaled.

Such measurement approaches are particularly useful if we are dealing with a relatively small community. But if we wish to identify not simply social class membership in Cornwall, Ontario, or Kamloops, British Columbia, but social class in Canada, we would face the prospect of evaluating the possessions of millions of individuals, or, equally unrealistic, of requiring a panel of informants knowledgeable about the class characteristics of the entire society. We could, of course, resort to some representative sample, and survey some proportion of the total population, but this would be a relatively inefficient research procedure, compared to available alternatives.

A means of coping with measurement, other than by sampling or participant observation, is to analyze existing statistics collected by agencies such as Statistics Canada. Included among such available data, for example, is a breakdown of population by factors such as occupation, education, income, or even housing. Taken very literally, and recognizing room for error, two factors, education and/or income, have generally been used to provide crude but useful indicators of stratification. Such information is especially useful if we are comparing Canada to other nations. Income distribution, or educational distribution, would allow gross comparison of stratification systems, for example in terms of opportunities for mobility open to the population at varying levels of educational achievement. We could also arbitrarily identify strata.

A related device that has been used in many nations, and seems to produce approximately the same results in all industrialized nations, Canada included, is some form of *occupational ranking scale*. This technique was pioneered in the United States, with the NORC (National Opinion Research Centre) scale (1947), which ranked occupations and suggested cutting-points or categories of ranked occupations by prestige. These rankings, when aggregated, produced an occupational ranking scale that has proved quite reliable and stable over time. And it has correlated highly with similar scales in other industrialized societies, including Canada. (Svalastoga, 1965: 23–31; Pineo and Porter, 1967.)

In Canada, Bernard Blishen has worked with census data for 1951, 1961, and 1971, and has devised successive scales that correlate highly with those of other societies. (Blishen, 1958; 1967; Blishen and McRoberts, 1976.) Instead of prestige scores derived from a sample of Canadians, Blishen integrates public data regarding the educational requirements and the incomes associated with identifiable occupations in Canada as reported by Statistics Canada. The occupations are thereby rank-ordered, and cutting-points are specified that serve to distinguish six strata of occupations in the latest version of the Blishen socio-economic index. (Blishen and McRoberts, 1976.) The cutting-points that were accepted as approximating class-like strata are artifacts of the measurement scale, and recognized to be heuristic or the invention of the researcher. For example, of the six classes that may be distinguished, three indicate gradations within the middle class, and three within the lower or working class. Note that the scale, in that it is dependent upon occupational designations within the labour force, does not really incorporate upper class designations related to propertied wealth or state power.

Table 1-1: Examples of Blishen Rankings, 1971 Census Data

	Socio Economic Index		Overall Rank
Class 1 (Index 70 +)	Administrators, Teaching and Related Fields	75.2846	1
	Physicians and Surgeons	74.2246	6
	Chemical Engineers	70.8910	18
Class 2 (Index 60.00–69.99)	Petroleum Engineers	69.7069	21
	Writers and Editors	62.8184	64
	Sociologists, Anthropologists and Related Social Scientists	60.5728	83
Class 3 (Index 50.00–59.99)	Officials and Administrators unique to Government.	58.8662	94
	Inspectors and Regulatory Officers, non-Government	54.2791	131
	Bookkeepers and Accounting Clerks	50.7098	160
Class 4 (Index 40.00–49.99)	Photographers and Cameramen	49.5214	175
	Musicians	43.3157	240
	Tellers and Cashiers	40.4164	274
Class 5 (Index 30.00–39.99)	Bookbinders and Related Occupations	38.8055	291
	Paper Product Fabricating and Assembly Occupations	35.2914	329
	Plasterers and Related Occupations	30.4749	387
Class 6 (Index Below 30)	Hotel Clerks	30.0380	393
	Bartenders	26.4920	449
	Farmers	23.0227	480

Source: Blishen and McRoberts and *Canadian Sociology and Anthropology*, 1976: 73–79.

Measurement devices like this serve to identify real differences in Canadian society. They do not identify real classes, in the sense of integrated and conscious groups. But they do approximate such identification and permit a magnitude of analysis — national rather than local — that would not otherwise be feasible. Blau and Duncan, Svalastoga, and most sociologists argue that in modern industrial society the three fundamental dimensions of stratification — prestige, power, and privilege — are all reflected in occupation. This suggests that occupations are the best indicators with which to work. (Blau and Duncan, 1967: 6–7; Svalastoga, 1965: 29.) It should be realized that this is by no means a unanimous view. Some sociologists have been very critical of an occupational emphasis in stratification studies, suggesting that it leads to an emphasis upon status groups and not the fundamental existence of economically-based classes. Usually such critics insist that the basic distinction must be between owners of the means of production and non-owners. Others would refine this fundamental distinction by noting an upper class of wealth and power vested in property and in government position; an old middle class of small property-holders; a new middle class of professionals; and a working class of skilled and unskilled workers. (Parkin, 1971: 18–23; Anderson, 1973: 16; 122–23.) Each of the many alternative conceptualizations is arguable, and fussing over theoretical conceptualization has all too often deterred class analysis.

Much of the data we shall use for Canada is dependent upon occupation as the indicator of stratification. It may not be the best indicator, but it is widely available, and it allows the researcher to distinguish a very real non-propertied middle class. At times we shall distinguish specific occupations or sub-sets of occupations, following Canadian census distinctions. On other occasions, however, we will aggregate occupations, in the view that the fundamental distinctions are between the upper class of large property owners, controlling the means of production, and non-owners. Among non-owners of productive property we may distinguish an upper stratum of managers and professionals and a lower stratum of sales and clerical occupations. These "white collar" strata, along with small businessmen, approximate the middle class. The lower or working class may be viewed as consisting of skilled and unskilled manual workers, employed or unemployed. Farmers, whose occupational category is ambiguous so far as stratification is concerned, we take to run the breadth of the industrial class spectrum, essentially sharing an affinity with the middle class and the lower class, depending upon the size and productivity of their holdings. Along with small businessmen, they control property, but on a modest scale; the Marxist concept of *petite bourgeoisie* seems reasonably appropriate for them, excepting the extremes of the small marginal or tenant farmer and the large "agri-business" owner.

Class Consciousness

Social classes distinguished by indicators such as prestige rankings, occupational rankings, or even property are not classes in the sense in which the concept was intended by Karl Marx. Marx emphasized that economically distinguishable strata must develop a group awareness or *class consciousness* that would realize itself in political action. It is undoubtedly the case that in Canada today there are working class, middle class, and upper class persons who believe themselves to be so, and who act in their personal and class interests, seeking to preserve or alter the existing distribution of wealth to their advantage. But entire classes do not act as interest groups or political actors. Nor do all members of such classes recognize their membership in them, a failure that Marx called *false consciousness*. Individuals often act contrary to their apparent class interests, as when a worker, perhaps even a labour union member, supports conservative policies, winning the label of ''working class Tory.'' (McKenzie and Silver, 1966.)

The conception of class consciousness is premised upon the importance and probability of class action to realize class interests. Consciousness means not only some awareness of situations shared in common, but also organized action to realize class-related objectives. We shall be considering the extent to which Canadian social classes have demonstrated a class consciousness, in the sense of recognizing and acting as a commonality.

Minimal Inequality plus Maximal Opportunity

Thus far we have emphasized the pervasive existence of some form of hierarchical differentiation. However, as remarked earlier, there is nothing in our analysis that suggests as necessary, or in any way condones, the extremes of wealth and power existing today in Canada and every other nation in the world, including socialist and communist nations. If one worries over filling positions and motivating behaviour, as did Davis and Moore (1945), one could utilize a system of honorific rewards in place of a system of material rewards, although there would be difficulties, inefficiencies, and delays extending over generations in implementing such a system. Eliminating gross economic disparities would still involve some hierarchical differentiation by prestige and power. Conceivably, given equal material rewards, there still might be competition for more attractive activities or roles, those which are perceived to be more intrinsically satisfying. But even such differentiation could be moderated, by rotating roles, as was done to a degree in the People's Republic of China.

If we must reconcile ourselves to some degree of vertical differentiation, we need not be reconciled to systems that deprive members of society of the means to existence, or existence of a quality comparable to that of more wealthy, prestigious, or powerful members of society. The differences in wealth which in Canada today are translated into differences in life style, as represented by quantity and quality of foodstuffs, medical service, and various consumer and service benefits, need not persist. That is, quite simply, differentiation could be quite minimal, devoid of material differences, and characterized by minimal disparities in power and prestige. The inter-generational inheritance of disparities could be explicitly pro-scribed and deterred. To prevent all social inheritance would undoubtedly be impossible. But through gradual socialization and enforcement, such inheritance could be minimized. Society would approximate the perfectly egalitarian society, thereby. We emphasize that this levelling up need not concede or endorse elaborate welfarism. Rather, as a statement of a theo-retical and morally desirable condition, as opposed to a probable or politi-cally practical condition, it is to suggest the possibility of a radically different form of social organization, consisting of shared resources and variable role performance implemented through socialization and honorific reward.

Ostensibly, nations dedicated to organizing themselves in keeping with Marxist principles were seeking a situation such as I have described, through elimination of material or economic differentiation (although no society has achieved this or persisted in doing so). They never, however, sought to moderate differences in power and prestige, at least for the leaders who needed authority in order to successfully consolidate a revolution and enforce communist definitions of society. An imperfect and limited attempt to minimize all forms of differentiation in a national society was made in Maoist China, where disparities obviously persisted. Yet communal own-ership and production, uniformity of clothing, and the interchange of intellectual and manual tasks were intended to approximate a broadly-based egalitarianism that now seems on the wane.

The point is that there is no evidence suggesting that stratification must take any specific form, or that gross differences among people must persist, especially in material possessions. Thus, whatever its political unlikeli-hood, we may conceive of a Canadian society of virtually equal economic distribution. The extent of differentiation, therefore, may be minimized in theory, if not historical precedent.

Nor need there be inter-generational institutionalization of any differ-ences. That is, such differences among persons as do occur need not be perpetuated across generations, as they now are in all nations, including communist nations.

Societies such as Canada are characterized not only by marked and rather extreme stratification, but also by *inequality of opportunity*. Not only do some people have more things than others, they also have greater opportunity to acquire additional material items, not because of biological advantage or superiority, but because of social legacy. As opposed to other societies, such as traditional agrarian societies generally, in Canada, as in the industrialized nations of Europe and in the United States, we empha-size *achievement* over *ascription*. Quite literally, people are to receive what they earn. But quite obviously we have not eliminated people's ability to receive material advantage directly through inheritance, nor their inherit-ing greater opportunity.

Putting it conversely, there is considerable inheritance of disadvantage in Canada. There are social obstacles to success. Rather than equality of opportunity, the children of persons of higher status are more likely themselves to realize high status than are the children of low-status parents. Even access to work, to regular employment, is not equally distributed in Canada. Unemployment, with its dependency and deprivation, is tolerated as a normal circumstance. Opportunities for social mobility do exist in Canada; but a middle-class child, particularly a male, has a greater probability of mobility to a higher income or occupation than does a working-class child. This is so even if other things are equal, which they are not, because of the influence of region in Canada, and depending on one's ethnic group membership or origin.

Variation in opportunity will be considered throughout this book. For example, we will consider unequal access to education. The point we wish to establish here is that we must be aware, not only of the existence of inequality of wealth, power, and prestige, but also of inequality of opportunity to influence and alter the benefits and the status that one has from birth. Working-class children are unlikely ever to achieve middle-class, let alone upper-class, status. Or, to take the not unimportant converse, children of high-status individuals are unlikely to be downwardly mobile, to occupy a social rank subordinate to that of their parents. Effort and ability are not utterly irrelevant, but family status immediately translates into differential access to society's means to achievement, including adequate education and economic resources.

The very concept of social stratification includes the notion of rigidity or persistence; the system of differentiation in possession and advantage passes on from generation to generation through the family. But there is a theoretical alternative, one that is supposed to exist in practice in Canada and other western societies. Inequality of reward could co-exist with full and equal competition, so that the most worthy were the most rewarded. There would be inequality of condition, but equality of opportunity, as opposed to the inequality of condition and opportunity that characterizes stratified societies. (Gilbert and McRoberts, 1975.)

In such a society, the inter-generational transmission of class membership and its advantages would be eliminated. Certain people might receive greater rewards than others, but these would not be passed on to heirs. It must be stressed, however, that to dedicate oneself to equality of opportunity is different from dedicating oneself to equality of condition. Full equality of opportunity would still permit a system of considerably unequal rewards; it would be a *meritocracy* of reward dependent upon performance, with the competition renewed in each generation. It is a view, therefore, which concedes hierarchical differentiation, but rejects the necessary inheritance of that differentiation. Equality of condition goes a stage further, including equal competition for benefits, but insisting that differential benefits may be minimal, and will exclude unequal material reward. (Gilbert and McRoberts, 1975.)

Both possibilities, it should be noted, are premised upon the view that the bulk of differentiation in modern societies cannot be attributed to genetic or biological differences, as some argue, but to social conditions. Undoubtedly some biological variations do affect human performance and differentiation, and these would persist. Accordingly, some inheritance or generational continuity in social status will probably also persist in any social future, insofar as these relate to biologically vested skills or personal attributes. That is, unless, to continue our utopian speculation, they were altered by some program of fully controlled breeding in order to homogenize biological inheritance. The obvious irony of this last suggestion is that, in its very nature, it is a challenge to idealist conceptions of human freedom and dignity. But with some such biological inheritance taken for granted, we emphasize that inequality of condition and of opportunity are socially based, and thereby subject to social alteration. It is from this awareness that we may go on to consider some of the specifics of social stratification in Canada.

Conclusion

Social stratification consists of inherited and hierarchical distinctions among people in society. Persons who share an approximately common social position, as distinguished principally by wealth, but also by power and prestige, are thought of in our society as belonging to a social class. Such classes are not legally and clearly demarcated, but there are several approximate means of identifying them, especially by concentrating upon occupation and property.

Class societies offer greater opportunities for mobility than do closed societies, such as the caste or estate stratification systems of agrarian societies. But such greater opportunities fall far short of equal competition for benefits. Rather, unequal benefits are accumulated and passed on through the family to succeeding generations in the form of wealth or learned skills. The relative class composition is maintained thereby.

The inequalities that characterize a stratification system are not immutable. Even if some hierarchical differentiation is inevitable, the extent of disparity, especially economic disparity, may be extensively moderated. Certainly the institutionalized inequality that characterizes Canadian society as we will describe it in the following chapters is remediable.

The transformation of the Canadian class structure may not be a politically attractive, realistic, or probable outcome. Some evidence that we shall consider suggests that the stratification system is becoming more extreme and rigid, rather than less so. Yet a society incorporating equality of opportunity, or additionally the more difficult equality of condition, is conceivable, and arguably possible. Whether it is desirable is a matter of individual moral judgement.

CHAPTER 2

The Structure of Inequality

The Myth of Classlessness

In Canada, as in the United States, we have tended to subscribe to the myth of a classless or a middle-class society. (Porter, 1965: 3.) This does not mean that Americans or Canadians have no perception of class. In fact, upper-class and working-class North Americans do have a clear sense of class identification related to inherited wealth, education, job skills, income, choice and conditions of work, and prestige. (ISR, 1982.) What classlessness has meant is peculiar to the middle class. Middle-class Canadians tell researchers that they perceive themselves as living in a homogeneous middle-class society. We are taught to think in such a fashion by our parents, peers, the media, and the school. Additionally, we are taught that we succeed or fail by our own efforts. For middle-class persons, this is a notion readily accepted. The school system is such that middle-class students are more apt to succeed academically and go on to satisfactory occupations and incomes and then continue to associate with other healthy, product-consuming, middle-class people. The myth of a middle-class society of equal opportunity is thereby perpetuated. As one author sums it up, "Canadians see their society as 'classless' because the vast majority of persons with whom they interact are, just as they themselves are, members of the middle class. It is precisely because we perceive our structure in this way, that we ignore both the extremes, that is, the poor and the rich. The larger the middle class, the less visible the extremes." (Hofley, 1971: 104.)

The middle class insulate themselves from extremes of wealth and poverty. Middle-class working experiences and residential communities are remarkably homogeneous, with the result that middle-class Canadians only associate with people like themselves. Paupers and millionaires are merely the stuff of television drama, and thereby unreal. The peculiar life styles of power and wealth, or helplessness and impoverishment, do not intrude upon the daily lives of most Canadians. As we travel from home to work and back, to shopping centres or movie theatres, we do so in our private capsules along routes that never penetrate the slums or the exclusive communities of a city. And as we Canadians, for the most part, do live in cities, we never really see, let alone experience, rural poverty.

Thus it is important to be aware that, although sociologists are capable of distinguishing strata in Canada, conveniently designated as classes, and although these classes do represent, as we shall discuss, very real and significant differences in style of life, class is to some extent a subjective matter as well as an objective economic condition. In the absence of a full awareness of the experience and the consequences of class distinctions in Canada, class-related inequalities are tolerated and persist, to the terrible disadvantage of many Canadians.

Nationalism and Class Awareness

A factor contributing to a moderation of class awareness is national pride and ideology. It is a well-worn feature of human collectivities that internal cleavages are obscured and a form of solidarity is achieved by indulging in opposition to some other group. This extends from the trivial to the sinister, from national flags and national hockey teams to national armies and foreign conflicts. We generally are socialized to accept an unquestioning allegiance to a nation and its decision makers, although, in the Canadian experience, this socialization has had a regional as well as a national viability.

In these early years of Canada's second century, nationalism has moved well beyond such slogans and sentiments of the 19th century as "no truck or trade with the Yankees." The nationalist urge has a considerable significance and validity, although it may serve to deter genuine structural changes in Canada. Concern over Canadian ownership, control, and utilization of industry and natural resources or the composition of Canadian universities are matters fundamental to the nation; yet perhaps this concern keeps us from dealing with the question of what kind of nation we are, and at what cost.

National celebrations are double-edged events. So far as we are seeking to build an admirable society, we can derive satisfaction from the achievements of Canadians and revel in a sense of pride and solidarity. A major international exposition such as Expo 67 in Montreal, or an Olympic success like the one enjoyed by Canadian athletes in the summer of 1984, is a "good news" event. Yet, while winning a Canada Cup or some similar achievement may be of value to a nation, there is an additional, latent cost. Specifically, attention is diverted from fundamental human issues within Canadian society, issues of inequality and human well-being. Nationalism, in effect, is the luxury and indulgence of the privileged, and the opiate of the deprived. It is a moot point whether Canadians would be better off without such successes and their celebration, but, in all probability, Canadians would be more attentive to social problems and prospects for social change — albeit not necessarily change for the better.

The Marxist analyst would unhesitatingly suggest, with reason, that the Canadian "ruling class" in some measure deliberately manipulates agencies of socialization, such as the schools and the mass media, in order to consolidate its position of class advantage. Thus the federal state licenses, scrutinizes, and subsidizes the broadcast media, and similarly shapes publishing, with the support of nationalists deploring "American" influence. The national "publicly owned" television and radio network is explicitly intended to create and serve a national solidarity.

For example, indicative of this effort to generate a positive Canadian concept of identity was the Canadian Broadcasting Corporation's 1973 production of Pierre Berton's *The National Dream*. Such television efforts at making Canadian history "interesting," like Berton's several books, are fashioned after the heroic genre, a nation of grand vistas, men, and deeds. A hallmark of such programs is that they romanticize and emphasize anything that may be seen to contribute to a sense of Canadian nationhood. Such myth-making reduces serious political deficiences and conflicts to the basic denominator of nation building. An illustration from *The National Dream* is the celebrated notion that the Canadian Pacific Railway earned its keep from the outset, for it "saved the nation" by transporting troops to the West to put down Louis Riel and his rebels. The point to be taken is the assumption of the interests of Upper Canada as legitimate, as against the distinctive interests of another region of British North America. The actions of the Indian and Métis populations are said to be invalid in that they contradicted the ideological and economic interests of British-Ontario mercantilists in the precariously established new nation. A contrary view is that expansion into the Northwest, in competition with the Americans, was Canada's "first war," and a colonial war, not a mere police action against disloyal subjects; yet such an interpretation is not in keeping with national "pop" mythology.

In a time when we proudly display Canadian flags on the bumpers of automobiles produced by European, Japanese, or American subsidiaries, we celebrate a fragile national pride. We direct our attention from internal problems and inadequacies, and indulge in chauvinistic self-deception. Nationalism evokes an image of an undifferentiated collectivity. A nation is represented as an organism to be pridefully distinguished from others, rather than as contending classes within a politically-defined territory.

There is a genuine dilemma, for to aspire to change Canadian society requires that Canadians control their own society. To that extent, concerns such as those relating to the control and content of the media of socialization, and control of the Canadian economy, are legitimate. So, too, a sense of social pride and purpose, of national mission, is a means for organizing a distinctive and perhaps morally satisfactory society, an egalitarian society. But, ironically, such nationalism may also retard realization of a satisfactory society.

Nationalism, including economic nationalism, is likely to involve a "liberation" of national wealth to the advantage of Canadians already disproportionately privileged, and would allow and perpetuate impoverishment and dependency on welfare, under the mantle of national pride and class-lessness. It permits the persistence of the myth of classlessness.

Micro-stratification

Class distinctions exist in Canada. Despite assertions of classlessness, equality, and national unity and pride, people's lives are governed by social differences. There is some tendency to think of stratification exclusively in terms of large strata of classes characterizing a society. We are led to do so by Marxist theory, and generally by a total societal orientation, as in this volume, in which we are attempting to describe Canadian society. Such social classes will occupy us through much of our discussion, but we must also note the import of more local stratification, obtruding upon the day-to-day living of Canadians.

From early community studies, we know that people make fine distinctions among themselves. For example, as we previously noted, persons whom we might characterize as working-class may distinguish those who are unemployed as "shiftless" and those who labour to make ends meet, "poor but honest." (Warner and Lunt, 1941 and 1942; Lynd and Lynd, 1929 and 1937.) In a Toronto working-class neighbourhood it was found that the respectably employed were distinguished from those who "go wrong," who were viewed as "welfare bums." (Lorimer and Phillips, 1971: 110–111.) Similarly, middle-class persons distinguish clerical workers from the self-employed and professionals, while upper-class persons are aware of the "*nouveau riche*" and "old money." (Warner and Lunt, 1941 and 1942; Lynd and Lynd, 1937.)

Not only does this illustrate that there are finer distinctions than those we conventionally associate with class, it notes that perception of distinctions varies with one's social position. The working-class person who distinguishes among members of his community in considerable detail is at the same time unaware of the distinctions among the middle and upper classes: they all live well and have money. The converse is also true. The upper-class individual will tend to lump together those of "inferior" social status. (Warner and Lunt, 1941 and 1942.)

Social distinctions noted only on a national level may obscure the salient features of the experiences of Canadians. For example, a region of Quebec may be characterized by low income levels and educational achievement on the part of its inhabitants, and we may thereby locate it broadly in a system of social stratification: it tells us something about the life styles and the opportunities for mobility of persons living in such a location. At the same time, however, it overlooks the finer perceptions of the inhabitants themselves. These perceptions influence people's behaviour and patterns of interaction, affecting, for example, whom they converse with, entertain, date, marry, and so on.

The day-to-day meanings and distinctions in social status were described by Everett Hughes. In a Quebec parish, he found, as researchers have found consistently, that the businessmen and professionals of the town were the leaders. But, in addition, status differences were indicated in ways other than by occupation. For example, owning or renting a pew in church was a sign of "stable position," and generally the professionals, business-men, and local farmers did so, whereas labourers and the employees of town businesses did not. (Hughes, 1943: 95.) Similarly, attending high mass was indicative of higher and more stable social status. (Hughes, 1943: 97.)

In a study conducted in the inter-lake region of Manitoba, people engaged in the fishing industry were found to have a well-demarcated sense of local stratification. (Siemens and Forcese, 1963; Forcese, 1964.) Not only were the fishermen able to designate leaders with a high degree of consensus: what the uncharitable person might call the pecking order became apparent. Generally, fishermen acknowledged as superior those among their fellows who were better educated and earned more money. These persons tended to be of Icelandic ethnic descent, and, over all, the Icelanders enjoyed higher status than fishermen of other ethnic origins. At the bottom of the local hierarchy were the native peoples. These "class" perceptions in turn influenced interaction more broadly, in terms of contacts among family members, exchange of social visits, and mutual aid.

Another illustration of what we call micro-stratification may be taken from a study of "Jasper," as John Bennett called a region of southwestern Saskatchewan that he studied. (Bennett, 1969.) Bennett declined to argue that the 7,360 people of this area had a well-defined class structure; yet criteria of hierarchical differentiation were apparent. In the area lived ranchers, farmers, Hutterites, and native peoples. The ranchers as a group had the greatest prestige. At the opposite extreme were the native peoples, who were outcaste-like "non-people." (Bennett, 1969: 66; 74.) Even among the ranchers, distinctions were apparent, as between the "town ranchers," "hill ranchers," "bench ranchers," and "sandhill and shortgrass ranch-ers." (Bennett, 1969: 66–68.) As a group, the ranchers were of British-Canadian and American origins; although their holdings varied in size and productivity, they maintained close kin ties. Similarly, the farmers were distinguished according to their holdings; "prairie farms" were the rural middle-class prosperous farms, often British-Canadian owned. On the other hand, the "marginal dry-land farmers" were more often of Ukrainian origin, with some Scandinavian and German representation. (Bennett, 1969: 66–74.) Generally, persons with large holdings constituted an élite-like group in the region; the ranchers dominated town politics, along with local merchants and professionals, and the farmers dominated "agrarian politics," extending to provincial and federal levels. (Bennett, 1969: 183.) In addition to these distinctions, prestige was differentially assigned according to people's perceived worth, reminiscent of the prestige awarded the skilled hunter in hunting and gathering societies. Those who were seen to be efficient operators, and frugal, sober, co-operative, friendly, and the like, were held in high regard. Bennett thus speaks of ''social credit,'' in the sense that such persons had credit or earned prestige. (Bennett, 1969: 184; 219.)

Such local or micro-distinctions are very salient to people's everyday behaviour, and are usually more meaningful than the broader class differences in society as a whole, which are less visible to individuals. But, in addition, local distinctions do reflect larger societal patterns; the example of single-industry towns in Canada is illustrative.

Community Stratification: Single Industry Towns

A characteristic Canadian community is the small town existing around a single industry, such as a mine, paper mill, or railroad. Such towns differ from those scattered about the country which grew up as local service centres or early foci of settlement. These ''old'' communities are home to high proportions of impoverished Canadians, particularly in the Atlantic region. But active, single-enterprise towns are not impoverished; they enjoy a precarious prosperity. They depend upon a primary or extractive industry or some major development, most likely hydroelectric. Unlike communities with value-added manufacturing industries, single-enterprise towns exist as long as there is a profitable volume of natural resources to exploit. As long as the mine or the forest holds up, or the company does not need to retool for continued resource exploitation, there may be a ''good living'' for the people employed as workers in these towns, and for those few merchants and professionals who serve them. For example, a surveyor working on the James Bay Hydroelectric Development construction site was provided with a four-bedroom house, furnished, for $110 per month. He did not pay for electricity or fuel, nor did he pay school or property taxes. The James Bay Energy Corporation also provided him with full health care, recreational facilities, and air fare to the south twice a year for the whole family. By one account, in 1978 the average weekly pay among all employees ranged from ''$800 for a labourer to $1,100 for a skilled tradesman''. (*The Gazette*, Oct. 21, 1978).

There are hundreds of single-enterprise communities in Canada, many of them in the North beyond the agricultural zone. (Siemens, 1973.) For immigrants or for migrants from other parts of Canada, especially from rural Quebec and more recently from the Maritimes, such towns have represented opportunity. For example, in the 1960's, Manitoba operated a recruiting program designed to bring labour to Manitoba mining towns like Thompson, offering wages far higher than those normally available in rural or urban areas. For Indian, Métis or Inuit, the new northern towns often transformed their existence. Life styles were imported for which native peoples were ill-prepared and which damaged the indigenous cultures. At the same time, often because of the sheer prejudice of the employers and supervisors, the native peoples have rarely been allowed full and effective participation in the labour market. (Riffel, 1975.)

Historically, the single-enterprise town has been the creation of a principal employer. Such company towns depended utterly upon the company, and the company ran things. In the town, the employees depended on the company not only for wages, but also for shelter, services, and transportation to and from its isolated location. The workers were recruited and imported by the company, and not linked by any prior organization or union. Or, as was the case at James Bay, provincial legislation curtailed union activity. Looking specifically at northern Ontario and Quebec, Clark remarks that much of the labour force was drawn from rural Quebec, and argues that such migrants helped keep industry union-free. Not only was the company in control, but, in addition, the Roman Catholic Church lined up in opposition to unionization. (Clark, 1971: 72.)

Because the towns are the creation of the employer and the planner, Lucas describes them as communities without tradition, and "towns of technology." (Lucas, 1971: 20.) Their residents have tended to be young, married, of rural background, having no more than high-school level education, and from ethnically diverse backgrounds. (Jackson and Poushinsky, 1971: 32–40.) They are thus approximately working-class to lower-middle class in origins. They also tend to be very mobile geographically. In one study, a sample of the residents of Fort McMurray, Alberta (pop. approx. 6,000), more than half of the respondents (125 people) had moved five or more times, from town to town, "good job" to job. (Matthiasson, 1971.) Generally, such towns have provided economic opportunities for young, poorly-educated Canadians, offering them relatively high-paying jobs, where in the south they might lack a job altogether.

These towns seem today to be characterized by good services or facilities, although complaints are characteristic, and participation in community organization slight. (Wichern, 1972: v.) The high degree of geographical mobility, the physical isolation of the towns, and their newness all act to inhibit any sense of community and community action. For example, the town of Churchill Falls was created in Labrador in 1960 for the development of Churchill Falls' hydroelectric potential. The town was characterized by modern facilities, such as good schools and housing, and very high wages. But it was also characterized by overt conflict, and no sense of community. As Robert Plaskin remarked of Churchill Falls, "It is one thing to adapt to company-town life but quite another when the community is the essence of that idea: a place where the company is not only the main employer, but also the only employer; a place where the company owns the house you live in, the streets you drive on, the restaurant you eat in, the store that sells you food, the theatre you watch films in, and everything else for miles around, including the cars, the airports, the school, the hospital." (Plaskin, 1978: 11.)

Until recently, these towns had been formally fully under the control of company administrators or provincial government administration. Not until the 1960s was there a clear pattern of local self-government, usually at the demand of the residents, rather than at the initiative of the company or government administrators. (Wichern, 1972: iv-v.) Lucas suggests stages of town development; the "mature community" has seceded from company government to local civic government. (Lucas, 1971: 91.) When we do find communities of long-standing self-government, the leadership of the community is vested in relatively few individuals.

When Michels (1962) offered his "iron law of oligarchy," he had been dealing with political party organization; but, quite consistently, sociologists have found similarly that a minority of individuals or an élite conduct effective decision-making in towns and cities. Their leaders are characteristically the proprietors of businesses and professional persons.

A town familiar to anyone who has travelled the CNR mainline through Saskatchewan is Biggar: "New York is big but this is Biggar." In 1960, Richard Laskin found that Biggar's adult population of about 1,600 generated 5,100 memberships in 136 voluntary associations. These associations required 666 officers, but only about 96 persons made up the effective leadership. Laskin identified a total of 411 leaders, one-third of whom were married to one another, reducing the leadership to less than one-quarter of the families in the town. When Laskin then grades the leaders in terms of importance of the organizations and of the offices held, he distinguishes 18 "top" leaders and 78 "secondary" leaders — a total of 96. Skilled workers were well-represented, constituting 44 percent of the "top" leadership and 36 percent of the secondary leaders. But the largest proportion of leaders was from among the proprietors, managers, and professionals, representing 50 percent of the "top" and 46 percent of the "secondary" leaders. (Laskin, 1961: 29–31.)

Thus, the small town provides a stratification system in microcosm. The small-town businessman, lawyer, or doctor, ultimately subordinate to or dependent upon the corporate owners and managers, probably does not rank very highly in terms of status in Canadian society as a whole, especially relative to the national élite, which we shall describe. But within their communities they are of top rank, because of their influence with other townspeople.

The ethnic stratification of these towns is also a reflection of the larger society. The company officers, and the professionals, have tended to be Anglo-Canadians, and the workers French Canadian, or European immigrants. In Railtown, where the railway provided the sole industry, Lucas noted persons of British background in top-level positions, including those mechanically skilled among the workers. The rank-and-file labourers were French Canadian, Polish, Ukrainian, Italian, and native Indian. (Lucas, 1971: 30.)

Relating to their place in the over-all picture of stratification in Canada, the remarkable feature of these towns is their dependency and precariousness. If a Marxist had wished to create a prototype of capitalist-worker relations, he could have done little better than to devise such communities. They offer a situation wherein there is a virtual class polarization in the sense that there is no substantial middle class of clerical and service employees, or even many small merchants or professionals — although the small latter group is, as we have noted, of influence. In recent history, the standard of services provided the labour forces of these communities seems to have been respectable, and the workers have earned incomes perhaps not otherwise possible. But they do so at the discretion of the company. Even when the company does not formally govern the town, it still owns it, often literally, as in the ownership of the houses and other buildings. If the company closes down, the town closes down, and the workers are obliged to move on.

However, in the ''mature'' community, moving on is not so easy. Aging with the town, the work force becomes less mobile, in part because their skills may be obsolescent, but also because, as Lucas notes, they have an investment in their homes. (Lucas, 1971: 91.) Letting the town die leaves the workers without employment, and without a home or the money invested in a home.

Thus, when Canadian International Paper decided to close down their mill in Temiscaming, Quebec, after 50 years of operation, the community of 2,400 built around the industry seemed effectively to be closed down. In this instance, because they were not mobile, the workers fought to keep the mill alive. As the National Film Board titled its film on the affair, it was ''The Town that Wouldn't Die.'' With direct government investment and the support of a new corporate investor, plus the workers themselves purchasing shares in the mill, it has thus far continued operation. The town residents fought for their lives — including the local merchants who were particularly active in leading the opposition to the mill's closing, consistent with the findings elsewhere stressing the leadership role of the small-town middle class or petite bourgeoisie. In most instances, however, the workers and their unions helplessly accept their fate, as in the paper mill closings of 1984 in eastern Quebec, in towns such as Pt. Gatineau. Slowly the town withers, with the more vigorous residents moving on, and others just hanging on, tied to a now-devalued home. An Ontario example, Burchell Lake, is an abandoned town, the casualty of closure of a copper mine. Similar towns are estimated in excess of 400 across Canada, where some of the residents cling on in the face of a departed resource venture. (*Maclean's*, January 21, 1985: 46–47.)

These towns are the temporary creatures of interests external to them. Companies centred in urban areas, often outside Canada, control them, so that they are in a sense artificial communities of persons of subordinate class status, irrespective of whether or not the residents are conscious of their subordination, or find it immediately salient. They are typically communities of people who, in the large society, are of lower or working-class status.

City and Farm

Another aspect of the Canadian pattern of privilege is the existence of dominant urban centres. In particular, for Canada as a whole, Toronto and Montreal have been pre-eminent. Within regions, other urban centres have had considerable influence, like Winnipeg in the prairies, especially early in the century. Vancouver on the west coast, and increasingly Edmonton in Alberta and through the Canadian northwest, have also acted as major centres of wealth and influence.

About one-half of the Canadian population lives in cities of 100,000 or more. Cities generally, and especially major centres, are the loci of finance, production, transportation and communications, community services, education, and cultural activities. Starkly indicative of economic influence is the degree to which raw material is transformed into usable products in cities. Thus, Kerr observed of the 1960's, "Montreal and Toronto accounted for about 37 per cent of all 'value added' in manufacturing in Canada. These two cities had more employees in manufacturing than the four western provinces combined, and over twice those of the Atlantic provinces." (Kerr, 1968: 227.) If one extends the concept of city boundaries to include a 50-mile radius of Toronto and Montreal, Kerr found concentrated there over two-thirds of the manufacturing activity in Canada. (Kerr, 1968: 227.) Similarly, "cultural" production, as in television, filmmaking, and publishing, clusters in Toronto. It is because of this concentration of financial, industrial, and cultural decision-making, with its resulting prosperous lifestyles, that Montreal and Toronto must be viewed as affecting the lives of every Canadian. This is increasingly so with improved communication and transportation efficiency.

Moving out from these two major metropolitan areas, we find other cities whose influence is characterized by specialized economic dominance. Thus, in the West, Vancouver is characterized by forest products industries, utilities, and pipeline industries; Calgary and Edmonton by oil and gas industries; and Winnipeg — at one time expected to develop a status comparable to that of Toronto and Montreal — grain distributing and general merchandising, retail and wholesale industries. (Kerr, 1968: 242.)

That these activities are reflected in the pattern of distribution of wealth was illustrated in income tax figures in the 1960s, with the greatest proportion of the total income tax paid in Canada coming from Toronto and Montreal. The 1960s pattern of metropolitan dominance has not changed greatly. Some shift of corporate power from Montreal to Toronto occurred after the election of the Parti Québecois, and the resource industry centres of Calgary and Edmonton experienced a flurry of growth in the 1970s.

Within the broad framework of relative affluence, there is a clear and enduring distribution of persons by social class throughout the metropolitan area. Investigation consistently points to a marked degree of ethnic and economic stratification. As in the United States, the inner Canadian city tends to be the loci of lower-status persons engaged in unskilled or semi-skilled occupations. Immigrant populations locate in the older, inner areas of the city, succeeding to homes that have housed earlier waves of immigrants. In such areas, for example, are to be found the immigrant populations of Italian, Portuguese, or Asian descent in the city of Toronto, the destination of the overwhelming majority of immigrants to Canada.

One may also find old British-Canadian neighbourhoods that have persisted in their ethnic identity and are working-class in composition. Historically, Cabbagetown in Toronto has been such a case. Lorimer and Phillips described a Toronto example, the neighbourhood of Minster Lane, east of the Ontario-Parliament district. In 1961, the average family income in Minster Lane was $4,025, as compared to the over-all metropolitan Toronto average family income of $5,831. (Lorimer and Phillips, 1971: 8.) The residents were long-time home-owners in the neighbourhood, about half of them owning their houses. But they were relatively poor, working class, and of British origin. The men who were employed, half of them earning less than $3,000, worked at such jobs as truck driving, warehousing labour, baking, and carpentering. Those who did work were the "respected" members of the community. (Lorimer and Phillips, 1971: 7–8; 35.)

In contrast to the downtown areas of Canadian cities, the suburbs are made up of middle-class professionals, often from Anglo-Canadian backgrounds. Thus the upper-middle class suburb of Crestwood Heights, with its doctors, lawyers, and managers, is oriented to occupational success. (Seeley, Sims, and Loosely, 1956.) Clark found that the majority of people moving into Toronto suburbs after World War II were Canadian-born, of British origins, and Protestant, and viewed themselves as "middle-class." (Clark, 1966: 98–99.) Clark notes also that from about 1961 there was some decline in WASP (White-Anglo-Saxon-Protestant) dominance, with some Jews and successful non-Anglo immigrant families moving into suburban communities. (Clark, 1966: 99.) Undoubtedly the non-WASPs were in quest of what might have been viewed as a better standard of life with respect to quality of housing, even at the cost of giving up the community and ethnic ties that would have characterized their inner-city lives. Yet additionally, as Clark concludes, they were people aspiring to an improvement in social status by seeking association with middle-class people already established in the suburbs. (Clark, 1966: 103–104.)

Even with such ethnic infiltration, the suburbs have tended to remain "pure." That is, certain suburbs are perceived to be, and are, largely upper-middle class and Anglo-Canadian, and often explicitly defined as exclusive. Rockliffe Village in Ottawa, Wellington Crescent in Winnipeg, or Westmount in Montreal have been stark examples of élite residential communities within urban centres. Similarly, Clark concluded that Toronto suburbs such as Etobicoke, Don Mills, Scarborough, and particularly "exclusive" suburbs such as Thorncrest Village, remained Anglo-Canadian bastions. (Clark, 1966: 100 and 212.)

The extent to which similar stratification by suburbs is true of other Canadian cities is less well documented, but in all probability much the same. It is not remarkable to suggest that in Canadian cities, as in the United States, there has been a middle-class exodus to the suburbs. Where the cities are characterized by growth through immigration, the old downtown area becomes the setting of the "new" non-Anglo ethnic groups, such as has been true of the "North End" of Winnipeg. The middle-class suburbs are characterized by, and perceived to have, specific ethnic identities, usually Anglo-Canadian, such as the suburb of St. James in Winnipeg, or at times Jewish, as with Tuxedo in Winnipeg.

A newer and conflicting urban tendency is for the more affluent middle class to attempt to rehabilitate the city core, by upgrading and renovating housing. The working-class employed and unemployed are thereby displaced, and the poor housing that once accommodated them is withdrawn from the market, creating enormous urban housing problems. Despite the chic move back to city centre, and the existence of some highrise suburban working-class ghettos, the persisting urban pattern is that of the more affluent moving to the suburban fringe. In the vicinity of metro Toronto, areas such as York Region, Oshawa, and Peel County are growing rapidly. One estimate puts growth at 35 percent since 1976, while metro Toronto's population has declined .75 percent in that period. (*The Toronto Star*, November 25, 1984.) The inhabitants are the relatively affluent, middle-class employed.

There is reason to state that residential segregation in Canada is as much by ethnic background as it is by socio-economic status, recognizing that in Canada the two factors are so intimately related. It has even been suggested that ethnic background is more important than socio-economic status (social class) in Canadian patterns of residential segregation. (Darroch and Marston, 1971.) Yet, over time, as successive waves of immigrants are assimilated in the sense of achieving some economic success in Canadian society, we may expect to find some continued breakdown in the segregation of suburbs, much as Clark described it for Toronto, as some immigrant families move into predominantly Anglo-Canadian suburbs. This limited movement to the suburbs may be observed in Ottawa, for example, with some Italian-Canadian families moving from city-centre to the newer suburbs. But the present urban subcommunities or suburbs characteristically have been and remain the centres of Anglo-Canadian upper-and middle-class Canadians. And the prosperity enjoyed by these Canadians has not been characteristic of all regions.

As Canada has become an urban society, its remaining rural population has become an invisible minority. Rural poverty is extreme, a form of subsistence economy. Even the rural middle class, that is, the farmers, have experienced a long-term deterioriation in economic benefits. In constant 1981 dollars, farmers earned less in 1984 than in 1974. At the same time, the value of farms has deteriorated. (*The Toronto Star*, June 5, 1985.)

Most farms are heavily in debt. For example, in contrast to the common public image of land-rich farmers, only about 7 percent of farm owners in the west—a "small élite"—own land and equipment. It has been observed that by urban standards the majority of prairie farmers are not well off, and make much less in cash income than would workers in urban construc-

Figure 2-1 Realized Net Farm Income in Billions of Dollars

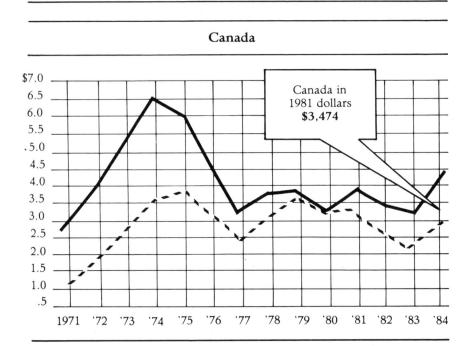

Source: *The Toronto Star*, June 5, 1985. Reproduced by permission of the Minister of Supply and Services Canada.

tion industries. ''In 1970, a period of agricultural depression, the average farm income across the prairie was $2,500 — less than a farm family would make on welfare.'' (Robertson, 1973; 11.)

Regional Inequality

Canada is generally conceded to be among a minority of the nations of the world, in that it is considered a developed or industrialized nation. Some analysts would dispute this by pointing up the high proportion of national income generated by extractive as opposed to manufacturing industries, or the high degree of foreign ownership. But it is nonetheless the case that, by most indicators of development, such as average per capita income, per capita energy consumption, or standard of living, Canada belongs to an élite group.

Such indicators suggest an affluent society. Yet it is a misleading suggestion, for the considerable affluence that does exist obscures the disparate concentrations of affluence and poverty in Canada. Poverty among the aboriginal populations of the North and the western provinces is not visible in such a simple figure. Nor is the welfare existence of populations in rural areas of the Maritimes, or in the slums or subsidized housing projects of our large metropolitan centres. Relative to size, the greatest proportion of impoverished Canadians is to be found in rural locations and small villages of between 1,000 to 10,000 residents. As a proportion of regional populations, the greatest incidence of poverty occurs in the Atlantic provinces, followed by Quebec, the Prairies, British Columbia, and, decidedly last of all, in Ontario. (Podoluk, 1968: 187–201.) Conversely, looking at the distribution of high-status occupations, Blishen pointed out that, of the 1961 male labour force, the greatest proportional representations of high-status occupations in the regions were in Ontario, the west, and Quebec, with the least in the Maritimes. This correlates with the regional income levels displayed in Table 2-1. As we shall emphasize repeatedly in subsequent discussion, Canadian society is distinguished by regional stratification — that is, a hierarchy of privilege that clusters by region.

There are collectivities or strata based on social status that extend across the regions of Canada, so that one may still speak of nation-wide classes. But the regional economic character obtrudes, as does the local stratification we have previously noted.

Any given occupation will be differentially evaluated and rewarded in different regions. For example, a medical doctor will have approximately the same social status in St. John, or Brandon, or Montreal, if we take the occupation and its educational and income correlates as a measure. But it is only an approximation. The income of a surgeon in a large urban centre will be greater than that of the general practitioner in Trout Lake. Similarly, within a small town, the doctor may assume an almost god-like importance and prestige, whereas, in an urban centre, a doctor is one of many doctors and other high-status professionals. Moreover, among his peers, themselves largely urban doctors, success and ability are equated with a specialized practice in an urban community, and thereby will be associated with greater prestige. Or, to take an example from the other extreme, the labourer working for the city of Toronto will earn more than the labourer working for the city of Saskatoon; the work is the same, but the remuneration varies. Occupational scales such as we previously described aggregate by occupation and obscure their regional and local variations.

More important than variations in occupational worth, opportunities for social mobility vary from region to region. Such opportunities are far more numerous in large urban areas than in the smaller cities of Canada or the rural areas. Indeed, opportunities for employment are greater. This has long been understood by Canadians who leave rural and small-town homes in order to make it in the big city, especially the big central-Canadian cities. Little wonder, then, that we take for granted the phenomenon of ''going down the road.''

This is all somewhat obvious. Each of us has a notion of where we are apt to get a job or earn more money. But, however obvious it is, there is an important point to be made. Although most Canadians, if asked, would say that they were ''middle class,'' and although we can estimate a class structure in Canada by occupation, there are nonetheless important differences in lifestyle and mobility opportunity from region to region. In that sense, there are several regional stratification systems: one for the Maritimes, another for Quebec, another for urban Ontario, still others for the Ontario hinterland, for the Prairie provinces of Manitoba and Saskatchewan, for Alberta, or for British Columbia.

Regional disparity exists, not because the federal government recognizes it, but because it has evolved with Canadian development. In a sense, the Canadian West and North have served as the colonies of the industrialized East, as westerners have argued. Historically high tariff and rail freight rates have profited eastern Canadian manufacturing industries and permitted the extraction resources of the West to be processed in central Canada, then resold at high cost in processed form. Although today the western provinces are experiencing relative prosperity, vested in resource industries, the perception of ''colonial'' status persists. The insistence by non-industrialized provinces, such as Alberta, that they and not the federal government should control their natural resources, is an aspect of this regional stratification.

Generally, if we consider 1974 federal government development grants as an indicator of regional status, three kinds of regions may be distinguished: high-incentive regions, moderate-incentive regions, and low-incentive regions. They approximate the incidence of economic deprivation.

These designations of the Department of Regional and Economic Expansion (DREE) targeted those areas of Canada intended for the development of industries and employment, working to the DREE mandate of "regional equality of opportunity."

The Maritimes constituted the high-incentive area, indicating the greatest economic deprivation. The moderate-incentive areas encompassed the rural regions of Quebec, Ontario, Manitoba, Saskatchewan, and, to a lesser degree, Alberta and British Columbia. The low-incentive region included only the rural, small-town areas along the lower St. Lawrence from Drummondville, Quebec, to Renfrew, Ontario. Additionally, some special areas, towns or small cities in the Maritimes, Quebec, and the prairie provinces — all major underdeveloped regions — were singled out.

The obvious point is that, of the populated regions, only the west coast, southern Ontario, much of Alberta, and some of Saskatchewan were excluded, apparently as comprising prosperous Canada.

We can see the pattern more clearly if we examine regional variations in the proportion of Canadians employed in industrially-related activities, such as manufacturing, wholesaling, and finance. Overwhelmingly, southern Ontario and southern Quebec (the urbanized areas) outstrip all other regions of Canada. In extractive or primary industries, excepting in isolated single-industry towns, workers earn characteristically lower incomes. Such employment is distributed across the rest of the country, the hinterland of a small area of central Canada. If we consider the income data, we find that, since 1971, income gains are marked in the West; income decline is marked in Quebec. A hierarchy of relative advantage in Canada has persisted over modern Canadian history. Data on average family incomes in 1981, by province, indicate that Alberta income now exceeds the traditional leader, Ontario, at 28,500 versus 27,300. British Columbia (26,800), Saskatchewan (24,000), Quebec (23,600), and Manitoba (23,300) follow. Put differently, by 1981, Ontario incomes were still the highest, 107 percent of the Canadian average, but British Columbia and most recently the Prairies had achieved second and third standing respectively, at 105 percent and 102 percent of the national average. (See Figure 2-2.) Quebec had declined through the 1960s and 1970s to 92 percent of the national level, while the Atlantic provinces, with slight improvement in the 1970s, remained at the lowest levels. (Canada, March 1984, 23.) In Figure 2-3, the data indicate after-income-tax income as a factor slightly moderating the regional income differences. Whether before or after tax income, the Atlantic remains markedly lower than other regions, and Ontario still more advantaged than the aggregate of the Western provinces, even with the effect of Alberta. The same image is evident in Gross National Product per capita by region. (See Figure 2-3.)

Another perspective on regional disparity and its stability over time may be gained from a perusal of levels of unemployment. The Atlantic region manifests the highest rate of unemployment, and the Prairies the lowest.

Figure 2-2 Average Income in Different Regions

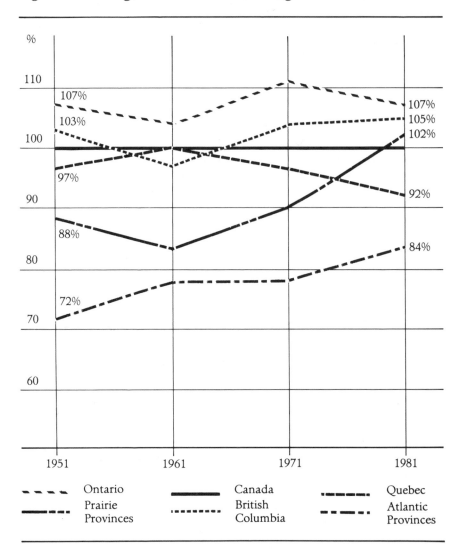

Source: Canada, March 1984:23. Reproduced by permission of the Minister of Supply and Services Canada.

Ontario and the Prairies have consistently been below the Canadian national unemployment average. (See Figure 2-4.) Of the provinces, the greatest unemployment is in Newfoundland, estimated in March 1978 to be 16.5 percent of the labour force. At the same date, New Brunswick was 13.3

Figure 2-3 Average Provincial Income and Income Tax Paid, 1981

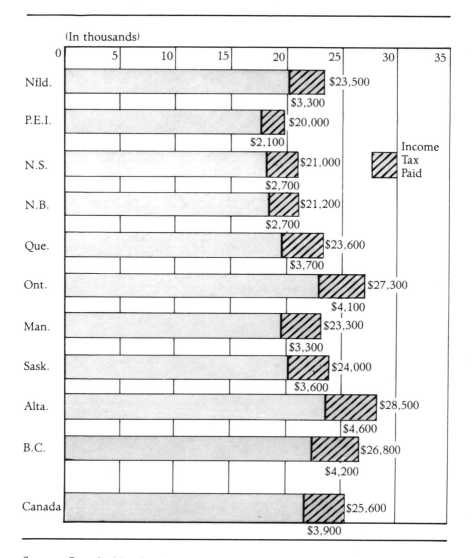

(In thousands)

Province	Income	Income Tax Paid
Nfld.	$23,500	$3,300
P.E.I.	$20,000	$2,100
N.S.	$21,000	$2,700
N.B.	$21,200	$2,700
Que.	$23,600	$3,700
Ont.	$27,300	$4,100
Man.	$23,300	$3,300
Sask.	$24,000	$3,600
Alta.	$28,500	$4,600
B.C.	$26,800	$4,200
Canada	$25,600	$3,900

Source: Canada, March, 1984:24. Reproduced by permission of the Minister of Supply and Services Canada.

percent and Quebec was 11.5 percent. (Bank of Montreal, 1978: 2.) Next is British Columbia. But, unlike the Atlantic region, Quebec, or the Prairies, there is a considerable migration to British Columbia, thereby magnifying the unemployment figure, and, to some degree, shifting unemployment

Figure 2-4 Regional Unemployment

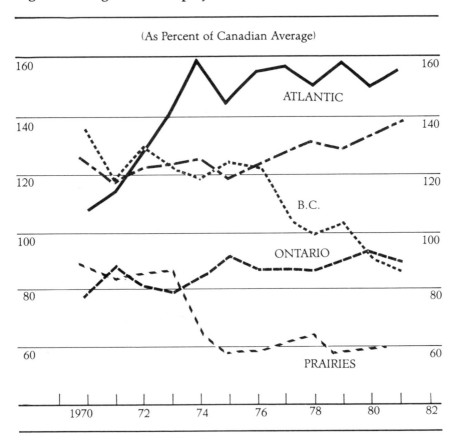

(As Percent of Canadian Average)

Source: Bank of Montreal *Business Review*, December, 1981.

from other regions, such as the Prairies. Thus, in some part, the Prairie region's favourable rate of unemployment reflects out-migration, while Ontario's favourable rate (derived in part from in-migration) reflects its industrialized prosperity. Also reflected in the favourable Prairie rate is the prosperity of Alberta, with the lowest unemployment rate of the provinces, at 4.5 percent in the late 1970's. (Bank of Montreal, 1978: 2.) Generally it has been in those regions such as Quebec and the Atlantic provinces where the work force is engaged in primary rather than in industrial activities that out-migration has been highest in recent Canadian history, while Ontario, British Columbia, and Alberta have been acquiring population from other regions of Canada and from other nations. (See Figure 2-4, Figure 2-5, and Table 2-2.)

Figure 2-5 Net Migration, 1970–80

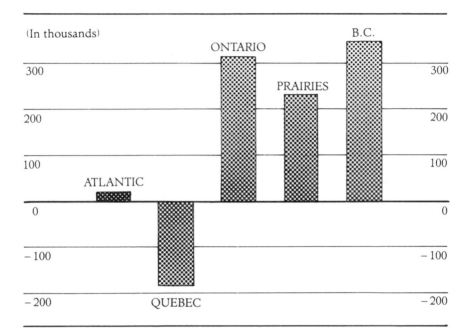

Source: Bank of Montreal *Business Review*, December, 1981.

Table 2-1: Average Family Incomes 1981 by Province

Province	Pre-tax Income	Income Tax Paid	Income Tax as a Percentage	After-tax Income
Newfoundland	23,500	3,300	14.04	20,200
Prince Edward Island	20,000	2,100	10.50	19,900
Nova Scotia	21,000	2,700	12.86	18,300
New Brunswick	21,200	2,700	12.74	18,500
Atlantic	21,425	2,700	12.60	19,225
Quebec	23,600	3,700	15.68	19,900
Ontario	27,300	4,100	15.02	23,200
Manitoba	23,300	3,300	14.16	20,000
Saskatchewan	24,000	3,600	15.00	20,400
Alberta	28,500	4,600	16.14	23,900
British Columbia	26,800	4,200	15.67	22,600
West	25,650	3,925	15.30	21,725
Canada	25,600	3,900	15.23	21,700

Source: Adapted from Figure 1, Canada 1984.

Table 2-2: Percentage Distribution of Interprovincial Migration by Province of Origin and Destination. Average for 1971–72 through 1982–83

Province	Origin	Destination
Newfoundland	3.3	2.7
Prince Edward Island	1.0	1.0
Nova Scotia	5.6	5.7
New Brunswick	4.5	4.6
Quebec	13.9	7.6
Ontario	25.8	23.4
Manitoba	7.8	6.3
Saskatchewan	6.9	6.2
Alberta	15.8	22.5
British Columbia	13.6	18.3
Yukon and Northwest Territories	1.8	1.7
Total	100	100

Source: Statistics Canada on data from *International and Interprovincial Migration in Canada*, Catalogue No. 91-208, Annual, and Catalogue No. 91-210, Annual.

Ethnic Stratification

Charter Groups

In addition to regional and urban-rural differentiation related to stratification, we have been alluding to the fact that one's position in Canadian society is influenced by ethnic background. In 1965, the most important book in Canadian sociology appeared, John Porter's *The Vertical Mosaic* (1965). The title succinctly summarized the principal thesis of the work, that there is a clear and persistent relationship in Canada between social class and ethnic group or origin.

This was perhaps not a startling or surprising statement, for the honest observer of Canadian society would have long since noted this relationship. John Porter himself had published several papers on the theme over the previous twenty years. But, although not new, the thoroughness of the analysis was new. And like many things people think they know, ethnic stratification in Canada not only had to be stated, but proven.

Porter wrote of the two "charter groups" who historically have comprised the nation — persons of Anglo-Saxon or British ethnic origins, and those of French origins. Each was party to the founding of the

Canadian federal state; each constituted a nation, in a sense (1965). Yet the one group was a conqueror, the other a conquered people. The Canadian state was founded in a tradition of conquest and the related definition of superiority and inferiority. As Rioux has argued, with the conquest, the old French aristocracy and the clergy united with the English to form a new ruling group or "aristocratic compact." (Rioux, 1971: 18–20.) The influence of this alliance persists to the present, despite massive post-war changes — witness the slight French-Canadian representation in industry, except as workers.

The participation of the two "charter groups" in Canadian society has never been equal. They occupied, as aggregates, different strata along the stratification hierarchy. To put it simply, those of British origin have tended in disproportionate numbers to occupy high social-class positions, of high income, prestige, and power, while French Canadians have tended disproportionately to occupy lower-class social positions. Across the nation, persons of British origin have earned approximately 10 percent more than the national average. This has been true of all the provinces separately, except for Newfoundland (where the labour force is virtually of British origin, at 94 percent), and Quebec, where in the 1960s those of British origin enjoyed a startling level of income superiority, 40 percent above the provincial average. Consistently, in all provinces, French Canadians earn less than the provincial income averages. (Canada, 1969: 17.)

The significant exceptions to the pattern of British-Canadian dominance and French-Canadian subordination have been in politics, the bureaucracy excepted, and in the control of the media. French Canadians have had access to high-status political positions, including of course, that of the Prime Minister of Canada. Moreover, they have occupied positions of formal political power within the province of Quebec. In addition, ownership of the major Francophone newspapers has been French-Canadian. The French in Quebec also dominate farming, and have size-able representation in the retail trade and the construction industry. But in all other sectors of the economy they are in a minority ownership position within the province, and, of course, in the nation as a whole. (Hall, 1973.)

Generally it has been the case that control of commercial or economic interests has rested with those of British origins. Thus, for example, the large chartered banks have been controlled by Canadians of British origin, as have Canadian industries. To illustrate this feature of our society, consider Canada's two largest metropolitan centres, Montreal and Toronto. In Montreal, when we move beyond political leadership, which is French Canadian, and examine the economic "élite," we find disproportional Anglo-Saxon representation. Where British participation in the Montreal labour force, including many professionals, has been declining, Anglo-Saxon dominance persists at the top, in major commercial organizations. (Rennie, 1953.) This commercial/managerial domination continues to show up in incomes. Research by François Vaillancourt, reported to the

Economic Council of Canada in 1979, confirmed the persistence of Anglophone income advantage, with indication of only slight moderation in the past decade (cited in *The Gazette*, Montreal, May 11, 1979).

Similarly, in Toronto, the Scots and the English have dominated high-status positions, and, additionally, Kelner argues that the Irish now also have "entrance group status," since at least 1931. (Kelner, 1969.) Richmond had reported a few non-British corporate leaders in Toronto (Richmond, 1968: 70) and signs of multi-ethnic professions; similarly, Kelner (1969: 32) had reported greater access by non-Anglo-Saxons. But she concluded that the "core" élite was still "pure," while the lower or "strategic élites" where non-Anglo-Saxon ethnic groups were gaining access were not accepted by the "core-élite," did not significantly interact with the "core-élite," and were less influential. (Kelner, 1969: 23.)

Mosaic

Still looking at Toronto, and in contrast with its élite component, we find large numbers of Italian and Portuguese immigrants or descendants. After the British, persons of Italian descent make up the largest ethnic group in Toronto, with more than 250,000 people, the majority of whom are first generation. (Jansen, 1971: 207.) They tend to be employed as labourers, and generally are encouraged to come to Canada for unskilled and semi-skilled jobs. (Jansen, 1971: 212–213.) This is quite unlike the basis for recruiting in the United Kingdom and western Europe, favoured locations for professional recruitment and high-status entry to Canada.

Ethnic stratification, as it relates, at least, to the "charter groups," may be "diminishing." (Boyd *et al.*, 1985: 335–393.) Yet there are obvious differences in entrance status among immigrants, ones that favour English-speaking immigrants from England and the United States. Moreover, a major analysis suggesting moderating ethnic stratification nonetheless finds persisting English-Canadian advantage over French Canadians. And the researchers find that persons of Jewish and British groups have higher occupational status than others—whether attributable to ethnicity *per se* or to family origin. (Boyd *et al.*, 1985: 335–393.)

National figures show that the labour force is clearly stratified by Canada's several ethnic groups. For example, examining occupational categories in Canada by ethnic background in 1971 reveals that high-status occupations such as the medical and administrative or managerial are occupied by persons from Great Britain, or those who are Jewish, in greater proportion than other ethnic groups. The exception is the high proportion of Asiatics in medicine. (Canada, 1974: 279–280.) Consistent with occupational status (and with educational attainment) Jewish-Canadian males tend to achieve high incomes. A survey of native-born wage earners recently confirmed that Jewish male Canadians, who by and large are urban residents, earned more than one-third as much as other Canadian wage earners. (*The Globe and Mail*, May 3, 1985.) Thus, relatively, other ethnic groups are distributed in greater proportion in lower status and income occupations, from labour to white collar. Service occupations and labour sectors such as farming, forestry, logging, and mining are heavily represented by the French, Italian, Polish, and native Indian populations.

The income return associated with different occupations is well-known to most Canadians. Some occupations, such as medicine and law, are consistently well-rewarded, although not experiencing recently the growth in income that is associated with many other occupations. (See Table 2-3.) And these occupations are differentially accessible by ethnic and class background.

Table 2-3 : 1980 Average Employment Income for Full-Year/Full-Time Workers in Selected Occupations Showing Percentage Change in Average Employment Income in Real Terms 1970–1980, Canada

	Number with 1980 Employment Income	Average Employment Income 1980	Percentage Change in Real Terms 1970–1980
Elementary/Kindergarten Teachers	117,865	21,223	38.0
Nurses	71,810	18,098	33.3
Real Estate Salesmen	34,775	23,162	27.5
Mail Carriers	19,290	18,576	25.0
Policemen and Detectives (Government)	45,465	25,183	24.2
Truck Drivers	139,625	18,507	23.8
Secretaries and Stenographers	208,215	12,886	16.1
Machinists and Machine tool setting-up occupations	30,875	18,838	15.7
Motor Vehicle Mechanics and Repairmen	89,705	16,515	13.3
Chefs and Cooks	50,650	11,336	10.5
Social Workers	19,055	19,832	10.4
General Office Clerks	74,130	13,342	10.1
Systems Analysts and Computer Programmers	43,145	22,945	6.9
Physicians and Surgeons	22,065	56,539	– 1.5
Lawyers and Notaries	24,795	39,039	– 16.0
All Occupations	6,212,125	18,902	18.6

Source: Canada, April 1984: 22. Reproduced by permission of the Minister of Supply and Services Canada.

Also suggestive are 1981 data on labour force participation of selected ethnic populations. These data do not distinguish among occupations, but do indicate, especially for males, degree of access to the labour force. Native peoples, both men and women, have the lowest participation rates. (See Table 2-4.) There is research evidence suggesting that "visible" minorities — that is, non-white Canadians, with the exception of Japanese and Chinese — have greater difficulty than others in securing employment. Recent work done for the Ontario Human Rights Commission, for example, compared white and non-white business school graduates. It was found that although they were more active in seeking jobs, non-whites received fewer job offers. (*The Sunday Star*, June 5, 1983.)

Given the varying positions of ethnic groups in the economic order in Canada, as indicated by occupation and income representation, it is an obvious corollary that persons of different ethnic backgrounds have different life styles. That is, all Canadians, depending on ethnic origins, do not live the same way in terms of consumption of basic commodities, luxury items, or shelter. It is apparent, for example, to put it crudely, that if the stratification system is such in Canada as to favour certain groups, these groups include the persons who will dress better, eat better, and have better shelter. And the different ethnic groups will tend to be segregated by community, even within our cities. For example, we have already noted evidence that ethnic background is an important basis for residential segregation, particularly as it is related to income.

The English and the French charter groups, the one privileged and the other economically underdeveloped, have constituted the major and most

Table 2-4: Participation Rates for Selected Ethnic Origins by Sex, Canada, 1981

Ethnic Origin	Male	Female
Multiple Origins	81.0	61.2
Single Origin	78.0	51.2
British	77.8	51.5
French	76.3	47.9
German	82.2	53.1
Italian	82.0	55.2
Ukrainian	77.9	53.7
Dutch	83.6	52.1
Scandinavian	78.6	51.7
Chinese	79.0	61.0
Other Asiatic	83.4	60.8
Native Peoples	60.7	36.7

Source: Canada, April 1984:16. Reproduced by permission of the Minister of Supply and Services Canada.

visible components of the "vertical mosaic." As Canada attracted immigrants from other nations, other ethnic groups found niches in the Canadian stratification hierarchy. As successive waves of immigrant peoples reached Canada, they tended to be associated with distinguishable regions of Canada. Thus, added to the Scots of the Maritimes, the English of Ontario, and the French of Quebec, came German settlements in the Maritimes and Ontario, and middle-European populations such as the Ukrainians on the Prairies. And always at the bottom of the class order, the "non-people," the native peoples and Métis.

The structure of privilege, weighted in favour of the English-speaking person of United Kingdom origin — the WASP, or white Anglo-Saxon Protestant — relegated the late-coming immigrant peoples to inferior occupations, and to the new, less-populated, frontier territories. Not only did such people, as individuals, face obstacles to mobility, from blatant prejudice to sheer unequal resources, they settled regions of the country that were often of marginal productivity, slipping out of the agricultural belt. Those who settled the arable land of the Prairies experienced wildly fluctuating prices for their crops. When mineral resources were added to grain as staple western products, these populations still filled the role of primary producers, processing continuing to be confined to central Canada.

This in general has been the basis of western-Canadian, ethnic-related perception of subordinate status and subsequent protest, as we shall consider them in Chapters 4 and 5.

Current Immigration

Ethnic stratification is not just a matter of historical experience. We can distinguish a pattern of immigration in which certain ethnic groups enter the nation to fill low-status positions, others to occupy high-status positions. For example, British and American immigrants are more likely to be highly-educated persons, with professional training, than are people from other nations. They are privileged and favoured immigrants, for "they are like us," and easily assimilated. Opportunities for emigration from such nations are good because Canadian immigration officers are posted full-time in English-speaking countries, and are readily accessible to possible immigrants, unlike the situation in, for example, Africa or Latin America. Not only are immigrants from the United Kingdom and the United States advantaged relative to other immigrants, in Quebec and in the Maritime provinces, they are more likely to fill high-status positions than are Canadian-born applicants. Rarely do immigrants from the United Kingdom enter the Canadian working-class. (Richmond, 1969.) On the other hand, Italian immigrants to Canada consistently assume unskilled tasks, and rarely do their members include professionals. Generally, professional credentials from nations other than the United States, England,

Table 2-5: Distribution of Immigrant Population Destined for the Labour Force by Occupation, Canada, 1980 and 1981

Rank in 1980	Occupational Group	1980		1981	
		Number	Percentage	Number	Percentage
1	Fabricating, assembling and repairing	10,383	16.3	6,296	11.1
2	Clerical	7,207	11.3	7,044	12.4
3	Natural sciences, engineering and mathematics	5,032	7.9	6,932	12.2
4	Service	4,648	7.3	4,250	7.5
5	Managerial, administrative	3,065	4.8	3,601	6.3
6	Construction	2,918	4.6	2,194	3.9
7	Machining	2,867	4.5	2,529	4.4
8	Medicine and health	2,681	4.2	2,903	5.1
9	Sales	2,476	3.9	2,151	3.8
10	Farming, horticulture, and animal husbandry	2,462	3.9	2,931	5.1
11	Teaching	1,895	3.0	1,677	2.9
12	Processing	1,544	2.4	1,170	2.1
13	Transport equipment operating	1,195	1.9	691	1.2
14	Artistic, literary, performing arts	1,111	1.7	1,131	2.0
15	Social sciences	498	.8	555	1.0
16	Material handling	447	.7	361	.6
17	Other crafts and equipment operating	441	.7	313	.5
18	Religion	425	.7	469	.8
19	Fishing, hunting, trapping	227	.4	135	.2
20	Entrepreneurs	266	.4	293	.5
21	Sport and recreation	119	.2	111	.2
22	Mining and quarrying, including gas and oil	75	—	67	.1
23	Forestry and logging	41	—	19	—
	Not stated and other	11,722	18.4	9,146	16.1
	Total	63,745	100.0	56,969	100.0

Source: Canada, October 1984: 98. Reproduced by permission of the Minister of Supply and Services Canada.

or, to some degree, western Europe are not freely recognized by Canadian authorities, whether in government or in professional associations, thereby reinforcing this immigration pattern.

This point, that different ethnic groups enter the nation at different status levels, was illustrated by Bernard Blishen, who considered the extent to which various immigrant groups were under- or over-represented in higher status positions in Canada. The higher-status positions are classes one to three of Blishen's occupational ranking scale. In the summary reproduced in Table 2-6 for the provinces of Ontario and Quebec in 1970, all groups above the line in each of the three classes are over-represented; all those below the line, under-represented. The groups appear in order or degree of representation.

Note that the Italians are consistently the least equally represented for each of the three upper classes in each of the two provinces. Persons of American or British birth are the most over-represented for each class in each province. In Quebec, Canadians, which means French Canadians, are under-represented in each of the three higher classes.

The pattern of ethnic privilege is also clear on a region-by-region basis. In each region, and especially in the Maritimes and Quebec, persons of British or American background not only were better represented than immigrants of other ethnic origins, but they were also better represented in the top three classes than were native-born Canadians. (Blishen, 1970: 124.) Besides, in each region, the percentage of British and American immigrants in the upper strata had increased since 1946. Conversely, in each region, the ethnic group with the lowest representation in the upper strata was the Italian, while in both the Maritimes and Quebec, Europeans generally were better represented in the upper strata than were the Canadian-born. (Blishen, 1970: 124.)

The traditional pattern of immigrant recruitment has reduced both the opportunities for high-status positions for Canadian-born persons, and the pressures to train them for such positions. Throughout Canadian history, as Porter demonstrated, professionals have tended to be imported (Porter, 1965: 54–56), usually from England and more recently from the United States. These persons are easily assimilated, for in language and custom they are similar to the dominant Anglophone charter group, and they have skills required in an industrialized nation.

Canada has therefore been able to tolerate a situation, in contrast to the United States, where fewer native-born persons were being trained for skilled positions, as a result of immigration recruitment. As we shall see in Chapter 3, Canada's proportion of population educated at universities did not begin to expand until the 1960's, and there are still indications that we tend to import the highly skilled rather than train our own.

Once an immigrant has arrived, ethnic background affects a further degree of career success. Anthony Richmond found that the children of

Table 2-6: Rank Distinction of Canadian and Foreign Born (1946–1961) in Quebec and Ontario by Degree of Over- and Under-representation in Classes 1–3

	Class 1		Class 2		Class 3	
	Quebec	Ontario	Quebec	Ontario	Quebec	Ontario
1	U.K.	U.S.	U.S.	U.S.	U.S.	U.S.
2	U.S.	Asian	U.K.	U.K.	U.K.	U.K.
3	Scand.	U.K.	Scand.	Canadian	Scand.	Canadian
4	Asian	Canadian	Asian	Scand.	Hungarian	Scand.
5	Hungarian	Hungarian	Oth. Europe	Asian	Asian	Asian
6	USSR	Scand.	Hungarian	German	German	German
7	Polish	USSR	German	Oth. Europe	Polish	Hungarian
8	Oth. Europe	Polish	USSR	USSR	Oth. Europe	USSR
9	German	Oth. Europe	Polish	Hungarian	USSR	Oth. Europe
10	Canadian	German	Canadian	Polish	Canadian	Polish
11	Italian	Italian	Italian	Italian	Italian	Italian

Source: B. R. Blishen, 1970: 123. Table VI. Reprinted from the *Canadian Review of Sociology and Anthropology*, Vol. 7: 2 (1970) p. 123, by permission of the author and the publisher.

white-collar immigrants from the United Kingdom tended to be upwardly mobile in Canada, while, conversely, the children of white-collar immigrants from Europe tended to fall in status relative to their fathers. (Richmond, 1968.)

Canada's immigration has altered in the late 1970's and 1980's. The number of non-European — and therefore non-''white'' — immigrants has increased. (See Table 2-7.) As non-European immigration has increased, so too has visible prejudice and discrimination. Especially in large urban centres, such as Toronto, discrimination against ''visible'' minorities has become a matter of significant public issue. One recent estimate suggests that ''white'' Canadians are three times more likely to be hired in Toronto than are ''black'' Canadians. (*The Citizen*, Janary 22, 1985.) These findings from a major survey by Frances Henry clearly indicated a preference in job interviews for ''white'' Canadians or immigrants. Especially for women, the ''wrong'' ethnic background is a marked disadvantage.

Table 2-7: Immigration by World Area, 1966–1970 and 1976–1980

Area	1966–1970	1976–1980
Europe (incl. U.K.)	65.1	32.2
Africa and Middle East	2.2	5.3
Asia and Pacific	11.1	36.4
United States	11.4	9.5
Latin America and Caribbean	10.2	16.6
Total	100.0	100.0

Source: Canada, November, 1981, p. 41. Total immigration to Canada 1980 was 143,117. (Canada, 1981: 43.) Reproduced by permission of the Minister of Supply and Services Canada.

Sexual Inequality

Contributing to the complexity of structured inequality are the effects of gender. Men have traditionally been expected to participate in the labour force and compete for occupational success, where women have not. Social expectations in fact discourage female participation. Accordingly, estimations of the class character of societies have characteristically taken male status as indicative of the standing of the entire family. To the extent that females have not been highly represented in the labour force, or in corporate or political positions of power, the emphasis upon male status as indicative of class structure has been realistic. But the last two decades

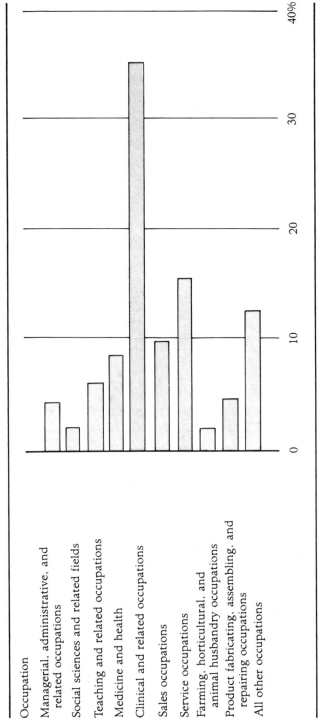

Figure 2-6 Percentage Distribution by Selected Occupation Major Groups of Women in the Experienced Labour Force,[1] Canada, 1981

Occupation

Managerial, administrative, and related occupations

Social sciences and related fields

Teaching and related occupations

Medicine and health

Clinical and related occupations

Sales occupations

Service occupations

Farming, horticultural, and animal husbandry occupations

Product fabricating, assembling, and repairing occupations

All other occupations

[1] The experienced labour force is derived by deleting from the total labour force persons 15 years and over who have never worked or worked only prior to January 1, 1980.

Note: Data based on 1971 labour force definition.

Source: 1981 Census of Canada. National Series, Vol. 1, Catalogue No. 92-920.

Source: Canada, September, 1984:6. Reproduced by permission of the Minister of Supply and Services Canada.

Figure 2-7 Labour Force Participation Rates of Women 15 Years and Over, Canada, Provinces, and Territories, 1981

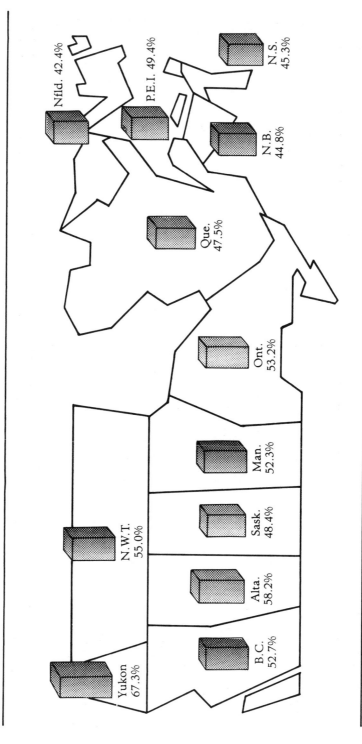

Source: Canada, September, 1984:7. Reproduced by permission of the Minister of Supply and Services Canada.

Table 2-8: (A) Percentage Distribution of Selected Major Occupation Groups for Female Experienced Labour Force and (B) Percentage which Females Form of the Total Population in the Experienced Labour Force for Each of These Groups, 1971 and 1981, Canada

	Percentage Distribution		Females as a Percentage of Occupation Group	
	1971	1981	1971	1981
Managerial	2.20	4.33	15.7	24.9
Professional, Technical, and Cultural	19.91	19.77	48.1	51.4
Teaching	7.99	6.22	60.4	59.5
Health Related	9.19	8.62	74.3	77.6
Other	2.73	4.93	17.3	29.2
Clerical	35.59	36.42	68.4	77.7
Sales	9.38	10.00	30.4	40.8
Service	16.96	16.01	46.2	52.3
Other	15.96	13.47	12.9	15.0
All Occupations	100.00	100.00	34.5	40.3

Note: Excludes occupations not stated.
Source: Canada, April 1984: 10. Reproduced by permission of the Minister of Supply and Services Canada.

Table 2-9: Women 15 Years and Over and Women in the Labour Force, Canada and Provinces, 1981

	Women 15 Years and Over	Women in the Labour Force
Canada	9,457,690	4,898,890
Newfoundland	198,190	83,980
Prince Edward Island	46,080	22,775
Nova Scotia	326,965	148,130
New Brunswick	261,935	117,270
Quebec	2,548,385	1,211,205
Ontario	3,405,425	1,878,300
Manitoba	396,435	207,335
Saskatchewan	359,225	174,005
Alberta	818,265	476,240
British Columbia	1,074,820	566,570
Yukon	8,020	5,395
Northwest Territories	13,945	7,665

Source: Canada, September 1984. Reproduced by permission of the Minister of Supply and Services Canada.

have been marked by a revolution of female social participation, in formal education (see Chapter 3) and in participation in the labour force. To put it tersely, social and legal emphases now stress full female access to every sector of occupational and decision-making achievement in Canada. But there is an enormous catch-up factor, in that attitudinal and organizational barriers do deter female participation. Part of the structure of inequality is the under-representation of females in high-status positions in our society.

In greater numbers than for any other occupational category, women fill clerical positions — the female analog of male "blue collar" or labour roles. Although they are represented in professional positions, these are for the most part the traditional female jobs of teacher and nurse. Of 526,055 "professional" women in 1971, 181,000 were teachers and 205,000 were nurses. (Gunderson, 1976: 113.)

Table 2-10: Average Annual Earnings, Canada, 1978 and 1979

Earner Group	Women	Men	Women/Men
All earners, 1979	$ 7,673	$14,981	51.2
Full-time workers, 1979	11,741	18,537	63.3
Full-year workers by occupation, 1978			
Managerial	13,250	24,337	54.4
Professional	13,484	21,865	61.7
Clerical	9,592	14,403	66.6
Sales	7,193	16,456	43.7
Service	6,372	13,258	48.1
Primary occupations (1977)	4,230	9,805	43.1
Processing and machining	8,698	16,271	53.5
Fabricating	8,179	15,728	52.0
Transportation	10,424	15,575	66.9
All occupations	10,008	17,404	58.0

Sources: For 1979, calculated from Statistics Canada, *Income Distribution by Size in Canada, 1979* (Cat. no. 13-207), Ottawa, 1981, Tables 70 and 72. For 1978, Labour Canada, Women's Bureau, *Women in the Labour Force 1978-79, Part II Earnings*, Ottawa, 1981, Tables 1A and 2B. Cited in Armstrong and Armstrong, 1983.

Recent data suggest that earnings for women are increasing as more women enter the labour force. Statistics Canada estimates that between 1967 and 1981 women's incomes have increased almost 45 percent in contrast to a 25 percent increase for male workers. But the average male earnings were $18,200 as opposed to only $9,700 for women. (Canada, March 1984: 7.)

As more women have gone to work, the importance of women's contribution to family income and life style has increased. In 1967, women earned 10 percent of family income, and, by 1981, the proportion was 19 percent. (Canada, March, 1984: 11.) By 1981, two-earner families represented 60 percent of all Canadian family units. (Canada, March 1984: 10.)

Ethnic origin, gender, and the structure of inequality must also be understood in this respect. While Canadian women may be making gains in entry to the labour force, and earning incomes as a consequence, there are particular barriers for immigrant women of non-English or non-French origins. Not only do such women contend with traditional family values that relegate them to the home, they also live in language ghettos. Confined to the home, they are less likely to develop English or French fluency. Moreover, they lack access to government language-training courses. The courses are only available if a woman is entering the labour market and in a job sector where the language is required in order "to perform the job." Traditional job areas for immigrant women, such as textile factories, do not require the language facility that qualifies for government courses. (*The Globe and Mail*, June 3, 1985.) When immigrant women do work, therefore, it tends to be in low-paying domestic work or in dead-end factory jobs.

It is clear that, in this period of our history, the nature of female participation in Canadian society may be characterized as having subordinate status. Insofar as the majority of women in Canada are still "employed" only in the home, and are thereby in a relationship of dependence upon a male income-earner, the social status of women is a reflection of their husbands' class standing. On the other hand, those women participating in the labour force are found disproportionately in clerical positions, and under-represented in high-status professional occupations, as well as in positions of ownership and power not well reflected in occupational statistics. And their lower incomes are viewed as supplementing family income rather than as primary or equal income. In sum, therefore, women as a group occupy lower-middle class status in Canadian society. The surge in female participation in the labour force is relatively recent, and the next several decades will reveal whether that general aggregate status is maintained.

The Economic Elite

The extent of inequality in Canada cannot be seen entirely in labour force statistics such as we have been using, for these exclude the enormity and the concentration of wealth and power. Thus, in addition to his analysis of ethnic stratification in Canada, a second major aspect of John Porter's work consisted of an analysis of that minority of Canadians who held pre-eminent power in Canadian society, the counterparts of those whom C. Wright Mills had characterized in the United States as the "power

Table 2-11: Women 15 Years and Over Who Worked Full-year (49–52 Weeks) Mostly Full-time in 1970 and 1980, by Occupation and Average Employment Income (in Constant 1980 Dollars), Canada

	Average Employment Income		
	1970	1980	Percentage Change
All occupations	$10,687	$13,677	28.0
Managerial, administrative, and related occupations	15,489	18,712	20.8
Occupations in natural sciences, engineering and mathematics	15,117	18,414	21.8
Occupations in social sciences and related fields	16,048	17,627	9.8
Occupations in religion	8,011	11,910	48.7
Teaching and related occupations	16,060	20,782	29.4
Occupations in medicine and health	12,532	16,652	32.9
Artistic, literary, recreational, and related occupations	13,699	15,329	11.9
Clerical and related occupations	10,474	12,559	19.9
Sales occupations	8,855	11,930	34.7
Service occupations	7,509	9,606	27.9
Farming, horticultural, and animal husbandry occupations	5,731	7,522	31.3
Fishing, hunting, trapping and related occupations	. . .	. . .	. . .
Forestry and logging occupations	. . .	15,517	. . .
Mining and quarrying, including oil and gas field occupations	. . .	18,653	. . .
Processing occupations	9,330	11,794	26.4
Machining and related occupations	9,906	11,881	19.9
Product fabricating, assembling, and repairing occupations	8,400	10,429	24.2
Construction trades occupations	12,276	15,423	25.6
Transport equipment operating occupations	10,450	13,463	28.8
Materials handling and related occupations, n.e.c.	8,941	11,277	26.1
Other crafts and equipment operating occupations	9,878	12,409	25.6
Occupations not elsewhere classified	9,200	11,377	23.7

. . . Non-zero counts less than 250, and corresponding averages and percentage changes are not shown.

Source: Canada, September, 1984. Reproduced by permission of the Minister of Supply and Services Canada.

élite.'' (Mills, 1959.) Porter analyzed the men of power in business, labour, politics, federal bureaucracy, mass media, universities, and religion. Ultimately, the structure of the economic élite was to attract the attention of the public and social researchers, perhaps inevitably, for the concentration of economic influence appeared of such magnitude as to shape the very character of Canadian society. (Porter, 1965.)

In the bulk of the analysis, Porter concentrated upon Canadian-owned corporations. He suggested that 985 Canadian residents, holding directorships in 170 ''dominant'' corporations, banks, and insurance companies, constituted the economic élite. (1965: 234–263.) This would mean, putting aside non-Canadian ownership for the moment, that 985 individuals dominate and control Canada. He finds a family continuity in the social background of these people, suggesting that the élite is virtually closed; or, to put it differently, that the upper sector of the Canadian stratification system extends across generations. (Porter, 1965: 275.) Of those people constituting this élite, 118 were trained in engineering or science and 108 in law. (275–277.) Generally, professionals and persons with backgrounds in finance dominated the élite, numbering 607. (Porter, 1965: 380–381.) Members of the élite were not necessarily university-trained. A group notably excepted from formal university training were heads of banks. (279.) In ethnic background, over 90 percent were of British background, only 6.7 percent were French Canadian. (286.) In all, only 18 percent of the élite group were estimated to have been of working-class origins, while 37.8 percent were of upper-class origins. (Porter, 1965: 390.)

In another investigation that followed up on Porter's work, Clement (1973: 260) found much the same situation: the élite remain Anglo-Canadian. Clement found they had much the same background in training as Porter had discovered, with some increase in law backgrounds. He established that the élite had become further closed to entry, with 59.4 percent of the élite coming from upper-class backgrounds, 34.8 percent from middle-class backgrounds, and only 5.8 percent from working-class backgrounds. (Clement, 1973: 284–285.)

Another window on the concentration of wealth was offered by Newman's work (1979). He identified twenty Canadians, nine with headquarters in Toronto, whose wealth exceeded $100 million — the very tip of the stratification pyramid. These are persons with monies acquired through inheritance and from their own firms, such as Bata Ltd. and Eaton's of Canada, money that of course does not show up in occupation-based analysis of stratification.

A recent series in the *The Sunday Star* highlighted the concentration of wealth in Canada by examining eight corporate conglomerates that control about 80 percent of the 300 companies listed on the Toronto Stock Exchange. (Francis, 1984.) Powerful and wealthy Canadians such as Weston, Black, Bronfman, Thomson, Reichmann, Desmarais, and approximately fifteen others, are sufficiently powerful to shape the lives of millions of Canadians.

"This? Oh, this is just a little something to keep us off the endangered species list."

Source: Reprinted by permission from *The Citizen*, Ottawa.

In a modern world of corporations, the facts of ownership, power, and wealth are complicated. But even if one puts aside literal ownership of property and wealth, there are enormous concentrations of power and income. The chief executive officers of major Canadian corporations enjoy fabulous annual incomes. With bonuses, dividends, and salaries, the incomes of such managers defy the experience of most Canadians. (See Table 2-12.)

In addition to Canadian economic power, there is the matter of non-Canadian control of corporations operating in Canada. Porter acknowledged the growing importance of non-Canadian corporations. Aside from the absentee decision-making such ownership represents, it means that the profits of Canadian corporations are to a significant degree being acquired by non-Canadians, in Porter's estimate equalling more than half the profits. (Porter, 1965: 269.)

As Clement points out, however, Porter's data related to a unique period of Canadian economic history. The period immediately after World War II, and especially 1948–50, where Porter's analysis concentrated, was one of industrial boom and relative independence in Canada. The British were out, and the Americans not yet in. (Clement, 1974: 52.) In his work, using up-dated information, Clement stresses the very marked increase in non-Canadian corporate make-up. He found that Canadians were active and in control of financial corporation (banks and insurance companies) and utilities, but not in industry. (Clement, 1973; 1975.) Overall, in firms of $25 million in assets or more, Clements found 62 percent of the directors to be outside of Canada, as contrasted to Porter's estimate of 27 percent. (Clement, 1974: 25.)

Table 2-12: Canada's High-Income Managers, 1983

	Company	Salary
Jack Gallagher	Dome Petroleum/Former Chairman	$3,457,175
Bill Richards	Dome Petroleum/Former President	1,408,611
Edgar Bronfman	Seagram/Chairman	1,237,360
Philip Beekman	Seagram/President	1,002,931
Angus MacNaughton	Genstar/Chairman	963,397
Ross Turner	Genstar/President	963,397
Walter Light	Northern Telecom/Chairman	904,000
Malcolm Taschereau	Dome Mines/Former Chairman	867,807
Edward Fitzgerald	Northern Telecom/President	850,000
Howard Macdonald	Dome Petroleum/Chairman	687,861
Jean de Grandpré	Bell Canada Enterprises/Chairman	658,000
John Stoik	Gulf Canada/President	623,075
P.J. Urso	McIntyre Mines/Chairman	570,000
David Culver	Alcan/Chairman	569,189
Fred Burbridge	Canadian Pacific/Chairman	560,995
Donald McIvor	Imperial Oil/Chairman	516,150
William Daniel	Shell Oil/President	513,834
Victor Rice	Massey-Ferguson/Chairman	512,952
George Albino	Rio Algom Mines/Chairman	500,300
Robert Campbell	Canadian Pacific Enterprises/Chairman	450,152
Arden Haynes	Imperial Oil/President	433,000
Roland Routhier	Texaco Canada/President	417,966
Charles Baird	Inco/Chairman	409,000
John Scrymgeour	Westburne Industries/Chairman	401,333
John Beddome	Dome Petroleum/President	392,644
William James	Falconbridge/President	366,870
L.M. Rasmussen	Husky Oil/Chairman	363,466
William Cummer	Westburne Industries/Vice-Chairman	356,165
Philip Dunoyer	Total Petroleum/Chairman	355,000
C.M. Knudsen	MacMillan Bloedel/Vice-Chairman	350,592

Source: *The Toronto Star*, June 3, 1984. Reprinted with permission —
The Toronto Star Syndicate.

Clements attributes this pattern to Canadian government policies, including tariffs, and the mercantilist tradition in Canada which profited from American-based industrialization (1974), much as Teeple argues that traditional mercantilists and government policies encouraged American industry in Canada. (Teeple, 1972: 21.)

In general, corporate power in Canada, both foreign- and Canadian-controlled, was viewed by Porter as influencing government to the degree that the government protects their interests, or, as Porter more generously put it, the economic environment is "stabilized." (Porter, 1965: 270–271.) In the light of such evidence, and of theoretical views suggesting that economic power shapes a society, the economic concentration found by Porter and Clement indicates a well-defined ruling class. Many social scientists have stressed that economic power is the basis of political power. Even social theorists insisting upon the "relative autonomy of the state" suggest that an economic élite within a ruling class not only controls the economy but also influences government and the nature of a society. (Mills, 1959; Miliband, 1969; Anderson, 1973; Panitch, 1978.) In discussing conflict and change in Chapter 5, we shall consider further the influence of economic interests.

Government and Bureaucratic Elite

Access to political decision-making is also class-bound. The class bias in political achievement has been established through Canadian history. Ward demonstrated that MPs elected from 1867 to 1945 clearly tended to come from middle- and upper-class occupations. Law in particular has been a dominant occupation in political careers. (Ward, 1950; Forcese and de Vries, 1977.) In more recent analysis, Forcese and de Vries find that the class pattern has persisted, with 60.5 percent of all candidates for Parliament in 1974 holding high-status occupations, while 76.9 percent of those elected were upper-status. (Forcese and de Vries, 1977.) The proportions were almost identical in 1972 (60.5 percent and 75.7 percent respectively). Also, for both Parliaments, the high-status advantage was true for all regions and for the three major political parties, especially the Liberals and the Progressive Conservatives. (Forcese and de Vries, 1974; 1977.) Reporting similar findings, Presthus calculated five class levels on the basis of education and occupation, and estimated that 71 percent of MPs were from the upper two classes. (Presthus, 1973: 275.) Similarly, Richard van Loon found that cabinet ministers in the period from 1867 to 1965 were overwhelmingly from professional backgrounds. (Cited in Manzer, 1974: 241.)

Given that persons of Anglo-Canadian background have been over-represented in high-status occupations in Canada, it follows that Anglo-Canadian representation in politics has also been high. By formal structure, however, the system of political representation ensures that non-British

Canadians will indeed be represented. Therefore the ethnic concentration such as it exists in the economic sector has not been so pronounced politically, especially with regard to French-Canadian representation. French Canadians have always been well represented in formal politics, including cabinet positions federally. But other ethnic groups who are numerically fewer than the French Canadians of Quebec do not do as well, because they tend to have less access to the higher-status occupations, such as law, which tend to be requisites for federal electoral success.

The ethnic pattern of privilege is clear when we go on to examine the composition of the bureaucratic élite in the federal public service. In the federal bureaucracy, top positions at the deputy minister level are predominantly filled by Anglo-Canadians, despite publicized efforts to emphasize the employment of French Canadians. Other ethnic groups are "scarcely represented," except for Jews. (Porter, 1965: 442.) Beattie also found that the career success of federal employees at middle levels of employment was related to ethnic background, to the detriment of francophones. (Beattie and Spencer, 1971; Beattie, 1975.)

In his work, Porter found that his bureaucratic élite of 202 persons were largely university educated (78.7 percent), and tended to be English Canadian, although the 13.4 percent French Canadian were largely in top-rank positions. (Porter, 1965: 441–442.) In the public service generally, there is bound to be a pattern of upper-middle class persons occupying important bureaucratic positions. This would have to be as a matter of definition; researchers indicate or measure class using education and income; and hiring practices of the meritocratic public service require educational qualification as a prerequisite for executive or career appointments. Ethnic bias enters in light of a pattern of ethnic selection or over-representation in achieving university-level education in Canada, favouring those already having high status and British-Canadian origin, as we shall discuss in Chapter 3. Thus, in terms of class background, Porter calculated that, although only 18.1 percent of the bureaucratic élite could be described as upper class, 68.7 percent were of middle-class background. (Porter, 1965: 445–446.) Presthus similarly calculates that 97 percent of the bureaucratic hierarchy consisted of persons of the upper three class levels in his framework, that is, upper-through-middle-class background. (Presthus, 1973: 275.) In more recent research, Olsen's analysis of the class background of the "state élite" confirms the above findings. Examining federal cabinet ministers, provincial Premiers, Supreme Court Justices, provincial Chief Justices, and high-ranking federal and provincial high ranking bureaucrats, he found an overwhelming tendency to middle-class background. With the exception of Quebec, the "state élite" also tended to be of British ethnic origin. (Olsen, 1977.)

Because the bureaucratic élite is, by definition, dependent on educational attainment, it seems more open than the economic élite, with its persisting family affiliations. Yet to describe the bureaucracy as open would assume not only fully-objective hiring practices, but also that the Canadian educational system had been producing adequate personnel. Fundamentally, to speak of the bureaucracy as open would require one to assume that the educational system is equally accessible to all Canadians. In fact it is not, as we shall see in Chapter 3.

The Poor

We may close our overview of the structure of stratification in Canada by recalling the subordinate, opposite extreme of the Canadian élite—that is, the impoverished in Canada. In the rural areas of the country, in the small towns, particularly the old small towns, and in the old inner city of slum housing, we find Canada's poor. In the rural areas, they reside in substandard residences, often engaged in subsistence farming or fishing or trapping. These are the families of the rural Maritimes, of rural Quebec and northern Ontario, and the West. They are often native peoples on reservations, where their communities constitute semi-colonial territories governed by provincial and federal bureaucrats; or increasingly, as in the inner city of Winnipeg, they are "welfare Indians." Even disregarding the enormous wealth of some families in Canada, and mitigating the figures given in national averages, the enormity of poverty in Canada is striking. Public data indicate that, in 1980, the average Canadian family income was $29,484 annually. But 17.2 percent of Canadian families earned less than $20,000. (Canada, April 1984: 46.) We stress that this is family income, and not individual income. The average individual income was $7,740 (men = $10,770; women = $4,710). Table 2-13 summarizes over-all Canadian poverty levels by family size and area in 1974 and 1984.

The best available data suggest that the distribution of income in Canada has been very stable for decades. In 1951, the lowest quintile earned 4 percent of total Canadian income, and, twenty years later, the proportion remained 4 percent. Similarly, in 1951, the biggest income group earned 43 percent of the total income, and, by 1981, this most privileged income group of families and unattached individuals still earned 42 percent of it. (See Figure 2-8.)

Contrast such economic conditions to the suburban lives of professionals, and the basic inequities of Canadian life are starkly painted. For example, in 1980, the average self-employed physician in Canada earned an income of $56,539. (Canada, April 1984: 22.) Thus, even excluding big-business money, the extent of economic inequality in Canada is profound. What this means in terms of real lives rather than anonymous numbers is impossible to portray in words or figures.

Using 1961 data, Podoluk defined poverty operationally on the basis of a study of 2,000 randomly selected families. She found that the average

Table 2-13: Poverty lines: 1974 and 1984

Family Size	Size of Community									
	500 000 or more		100 000–499 999		30 000–99 999		1 000–29 000		Rural (farm and non-farm)	
	1974	1984	1974	1984	1974	1984	1974	1984	1974	1984
1 person	$ 3,456	$10,238	$3,235	$ 9,723	$3,142	$ 9,121	$2,890	$ 8,432	$2,512	$ 7,571
2 persons	5,008	13,508	4,690	12,820	4,554	11,961	4,189	11,098	3,644	9,895
3 persons	6,391	18,068	5,985	17,123	5,810	16,004	5,347	14,886	4,648	13,250
4 persons	7,601	20,821	7,117	19,787	6,909	18,498	6,357	17,206	5,527	15,316
5 persons	8,496	24,263	7,955	22,972	7,724	21,423	7,108	19,960	6,181	17,810
6 persons	9,328	26,500	8,734	25,037	8,480	23,402	7,801	21,767	6,783	19,444
7 or more	10,228	29,167	9,574	27,617	9,297	25,812	8,552	24,004	7,437	21,423

Source: National Council of Welfare (March 1975; 1984) and March 1985

Table 2-14: Income Deciles of Canadian Families, 1970 and 1980.

Year	Lowest Decile	Second Decile	Third and Fourth Decile	Fifth and Sixth Decile	Seventh and Eighth Decile	Ninth Decile	Highest Decile
1970	1.5	3.8	12.5	17.7	23.6	15.2	25.8
1980	1.5	3.8	12.3	17.8	24.0	15.5	25.1

Source: Adapted from Table 4, Canada, May 1984.

Figure 2-8 Share of Income

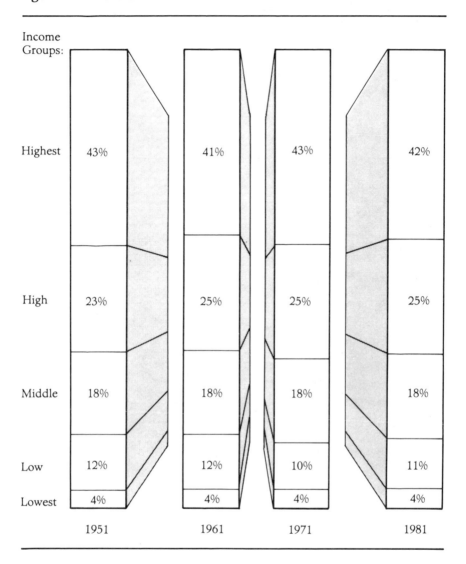

Income Groups:

	1951	1961	1971	1981
Highest	43%	41%	43%	42%
High	23%	25%	25%	25%
Middle	18%	18%	18%	18%
Low	12%	12%	10%	11%
Lowest	4%	4%	4%	4%

Source: Canada, March, 1984:6. Reproduced by permission of the Minister of Supply and Services Canada.

Canadian family spent about half its total income on subsistence items —
that is, food, clothing, and shelter. On this basis, she suggested that a
family spending 70 percent or more of its income on such staples was at or
below the poverty level. This measure indicated that more than 25 percent
of Canadians were impoverished. (Podoluk, 1968: 185.) More recent esti-

mates are similar, suggesting that families and unattached individuals in the bottom 10 percent of the income hierarchy consumed 60 percent of their income on food, clothing, and shelter in 1978. The proportion of income consumed on these staples — without any reference to their quality — steadily declines as one moves up the income hierarchy. The most privileged 10 percent spend 32.7 percent of their income on such basics. (National Council of Welfare, March 8, 1984.)

Figure 2-9 Profile of the Lowest Income Group, 1981

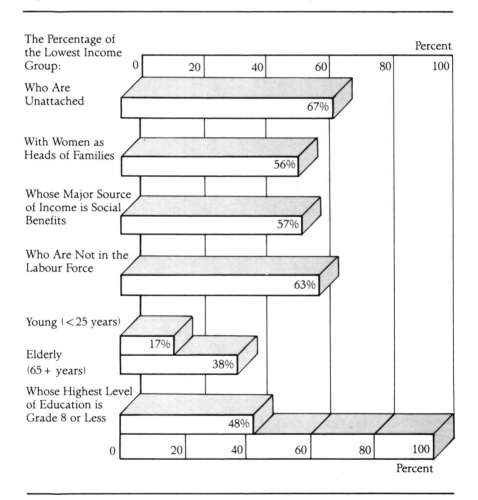

Source: Canada, April, 1984:15. Reproduced by permission of the Minister of Supply and Services Canada.

Women are especially handicapped in contending against poverty. Unemployed women receive lower unemployment benefits, and are unemployed longer than men. Especially, women in the age group 25 and older are apt to experience career interruptions including loss of job, marriage breakdown, and the burden of child custody. Single women and women heading single-parent families are overwhelmingly coping with income levels below the poverty line. Unattached males in the labour force received about one-third more total income than do their female counterparts. Considering income levels of single-parent families, whether the head of the family is employed or unemployed, the average income of a lone-parent family headed by a male was $23,243 in 1980. For families headed by females, the average income was $13,790. (Canada, May 1984: 3.)

Table 2-15: Unemployment Rate by Sex and Age, 1966–1977

Age	Sex	1966	1971	1973	1975	1977
15–24	Male	6.2	12.1	10.1	12.6	14.9
	Female	4.8	9.8	9.2	11.5	13.9
25-up	Male	2.6	4.3	3.4	4.3	4.9
	Female	2.7	5.0	5.4	6.5	7.4

Source: Table 5-5, p. 90, *Perspectives Canada III*, Ottawa, Ministry of Supply and Services, 1980. Reproduced by permission of the Minister of Supply and Services Canada.

Table 2-16: Percentage Distribution by Income Groups of Male-headed Lone-Parent Families and Female-headed Lone-Parent Families, 1970 and 1980.

	Male		Female	
	1970	1980	1970	1980
Less than 9,999	30.4	19.9	53.6	46.7
10,000-19,999	38.9	28.5	30.9	30.5
20,000-34,999	23.4	34.6	12.4	17.6
35,000 and over	7.3	17.0	3.1	5.3

Source: Adapted from Canada, May 1984.

There is another important variable in the structure of inequality: age. Canada's elderly exist in a precarious state of dependency upon meagre pensions. Women, especially, with longer life expectancies and less likely to have been employed and to have pension incomes, constitute a stratum of impoverished seniors.

Senior Canadians, whether living on pensions, or, like most elderly women, without pensions, have incomes that are barely at subsistence levels. (See Figure 2-9.) Elderly women are the most impoverished Canadians, exclusive of native peoples. In 1981, the average income for single women aged 65 was $7,444, with more than half the women in this age group receiving less than $5,610. (*The Toronto Star*, June 3, 1983.)

Most of the poor live in urban areas, for that is where most Canadians live. Relative to the size of the rural population, however, rural poverty is massive. About 21 percent of the total population live in rural areas, but 45 percent of Canadian poverty is in rural areas. (Canada, 1971: 18.)

The largest number of poor people live in Ontario and Quebec, the most populous provinces. But, as a proportion of the population, the highest incidence of poverty is in the Maritimes (Canada, 1971: 18), and it is higher among Francophones than Anglophones.

The greatest degree of poverty found in any group is that experienced by the native peoples of Canada. Lately, with some assistance from the federal government, Indians and Inuit have been pressing economically-significant land claims. But these publicized successes merely serve to underline the miserable existence of the bulk of the native peoples. Native Indians, the Inuit, and the Métis, who even lack treaty rights, have been relegated to the lowest rung on the Canadian stratification hierarchy, a consignment, as we noted earlier, analogous to that of the outcastes or untouchables of Indian society. Their indigenous cultures were all but wiped out by Anglo-European territorial expansion and trading, and even today their northern lands are designated for hydroelectric or other development such as the James Bay project in Quebec. Compensation may be negotiated, and its inadequacy debated, but it is generally true that the native peoples have not been allowed to compete on their own terms or those accorded most Canadians.

The greater tragedy of poverty is that it is institutionalized; there is inequality of condition, but there is also inequality of opportunity. The prospect in contemporary Canada of a child from a working-class family achieving social mobility to middle-class status is very slight, although that is precisely what is supposed to happen in Canada, largely through the universal system of education. The future of the educational system is the topic of our next chapter.

Conclusion

Canada is a nation of economic extremes. The pattern of relative advantage points clearly to regional, rural-urban and ethnic disparities. Generally, the Atlantic region seems to have the least share in Canadian affluence, and major metropolitan areas in Ontario, Alberta, and British Columbia seem the most prosperous.

It appears clear that Canadians operate at two levels of consciousness. On the one hand, because the majority of Canadians live well and are insulated from extremes of wealth and poverty, there persists the notion that classes do not exist in Canada. Yet, in their every-day lives, Canadians are acting in ways that acknowledge a class awareness, satisfied in the belief that such differences are not fixed and will be overcome in time through the upward mobility of individuals.

The basic structure of Canadian social organization consists of class-related distinctions. In Canadian towns we find stark relations of control and dependency; in Canadian cities and regions, we find clear patterns of hegemony and economic superiority. And running through this structure is a persisting pattern of distinction by ethnic background and by gender. British Canadians dominate Canadian business and bureaucracy, with the result that top levels of Canadian wealth and power seem ever more closed to non-charter group Canadians. Such chances as do exist for mobility are slight, and are distributed differentially by rural-urban residence, region, and ethnic background. And where there is mobility, it is mobility into the middle class, and not the upper-class élite or ruling class. Generally, the structure of inequality is stable. Income levels may change, and may arguably constitute an improvement in the lives of all Canadians. But the relative distribution of advantage is persistent in wealth, power, prestige, and the benefits into which these may be translated.

CHAPTER 3

Social Class and Opportunity

The Myth of Equal Opportunity

The idea of a classless Canadian society has been, as we noted in Chapter 2, a persisting conviction of middle-class Canadians. What this belief seems to express is the idea that such inequities as do exist in Canada are surmountable, and the reflection of personal ability and subsequent success or failure. That is, the mythology is that of equal opportunity to compete for unequal rewards, a situation only realized in a genuine frontier situation or in the ideal meritocracy. It is not equality that is being celebrated, but fair competition to be unequal.

Although Canada shares the North American belief in the existence of such equal competition, the myth has perhaps been made more of in the United States than it has in Canada. The open American frontier, with settlement preceding government authority, contributed to the image of the United States as a fabled land of opportunity. So too, perhaps, the notoriety of criminals and freebooters — whether outlaws, gangsters, or robber barons — enhanced the American myth. In contrast, it has been argued that Canadians, never experiencing anything comparable to the American revolution or the American "wild" West, have always been more tolerant than Americans of inequality, and less impressed with fables of mobility. (Lipset, 1963: 25.) In this vein, Gad Horowitz suggests that English Canada has always stressed a more conservative, less egalitarian orientation, one emphasizing "aristocratic responsibility." (Horowitz, 1960: 19–21.)

Consistent with these differing American and Canadian orientations, the school systems seem to have had different definitions and effects in the two North American nations. In the United States, education was early defined as a means to mobility, to a degree, perhaps, less ambiguously than in Canada. But more than that, education in the United States included a political socialization stressing a definition of "Americanism" and American individual and national success. In Canada, education has been élitist, the pastime of the privileged. As Neatby argues, the American and Canadian school systems, superficially similar (except in Quebec), operated from different philosophies: in the United States there was a notion of "progressive education" and "training for citizenship," while in Canada until the 1960s the orientation was not to the Canadian nation and success, so much as to the British Empire, and to continuity and tradition rather than to change. (Neatby, 1972: 12.)

Yet, in Canada, as in the United States, there has been an illusion of limitless potential for economic benefit, vested in vast lands and material resources available for exploitation. True, historically, Canada tended not to be the first choice of immigrants, perhaps because it was perceived to be "too English." Through much of its history, Canada has been a stepping-stone to the United States, land of "success" for immigrants landing in Canada as well as for the Canadian-born. In both nations, too, the myth of boundless riches was tarnished somewhat by the drastic poverty and disruptions of the Great Depression. (Neatby, 1972.) For many Canadians, memories of the 1930s linger on, with bitterness only somewhat moderated by nostalgia. But even these "dust bowl" days of the decade of the 1930s are viewed, in retrospect, as an aberration, rather greater in duration than originally prophesied, but only a temporary disruption of economic growth. Moreover, even in the Depression, many North Americans were inclined to ascribe poverty or non-success to the individual, although, as we shall see in Chapter 5, there was significant opposition to government policies. Certainly in "good times" the myth of equal opportunity, founded on an ethic of Protestant individualism in both Anglophone Canada and the United States, led to the blasé rationalization that if an individual was not successful, it was his own fault, and not to be blamed on social conditions. Thus, French-Canadian poverty and meagre representation in business were ascribed to flaws in individual character and, collectively, of the ethnic group, rather than to the nature of Anglophone influence and power, the role of the Catholic Church, or of traditional Quebec educational institutions.

Perhaps in the current decade we are less inclined to ascribe success or failure exclusively to individual effort or the lack of it. We begin to realize, for example, that unemployment and under-employment can also trap the highly educated. Yet, we are still inclined to be rather glib and proud over our own achievements, although critical and cynical, perhaps, about the successes of others awarded executive privileges and what are thought of as "rip-offs." When we view the unemployed, we are still inclined to speak of the "lazy, shiftless" poor, living on welfare. We encounter reports of native Indian poverty, or perhaps stumble upon "undesirable" neighbourhoods, and resort to the notion that native people are "drunken, lazy, and just no good, or else they wouldn't live like that." In each such instance, we respond to the superficialities of the situation, secure in our own relative prosperity, rather than evaluate the social conditions that bring about and support such individual behaviour and often prevent any alternative. That is, we still judge an individual and are inclined to attribute his status according to pure achievement. In point of fact, Canadians tend to inherit the social-class status of their parents.

A key factor in the chain of social conditions that link the social status of a family, the opportunity provided for children, and the social class of mature children is that of formal education.

Education and Mobility Opportunity

Expansion

The North American ethic of democratic equality is committed to universal literacy, and, more recently, with the growth of affluence and technological expertise, to a notion of universal education offered to the fullest extent of an individual's abilities. To some degree, these notions are now shared in one form or another by all of the industrialized world.

The drive to maximal education tends not to be viewed in the classical sense of making a better-rounded individual, as Cardinal Newman expressed it in his famous essay *On Education*. Nor is it premised on the aristocratic concept of training an individual to make use of his leisure time. Rather, to some extent, the notion has been accepted in the United States, and, perhaps less clearly articulated, in Canada, of education for better citizenship. Even more dominant is the idea that the formal educational system is the principal mechanism of training people in the skills required by and for industrial/commercial expansion, at the same time providing opportunities for social mobility in Canadian and American societies. Thus the 1950s and 1960s in the United States were characterized by massive government financial assistance to school systems, particularly with a view to servicing minority groups such as urban blacks and Puerto Ricans.

In Canada, critics pointed up the élitist nature of Canadian education, insofar as Canada educated to the university level only a very small proportion of her population. In 1961 only about 8.5 percent of the labour force had any post-high school education, nor did this necessarily include a university degree. (Porter, 1967: 114.) Critics further noted that very few Canadians acquired graduate degrees: we tended to import our professionals. (Porter, 1965.) By the 1960s we had accepted as our own the American definition of education as a development of national human resources, the key to continued economic development and prosperity, and a means of extending opportunity to all without any direct intervention in the distribution of wealth and privilege. The period 1950 to 1970 witnessed an incredible expansion of educational institutions in Canada, supported by all levels of government and ultimately all taxpayers, with the burden carried by urban taxpayers in rapidly growing cities. The federal and provincial governments increased support for all levels of education between 1950 and 1970. Meanwhile, the proportion of total costs met by student fees decreased.

Figure 3-1 Total Expenditures on Education as a Percentage of Gross National Product, Canada, 1950–1979

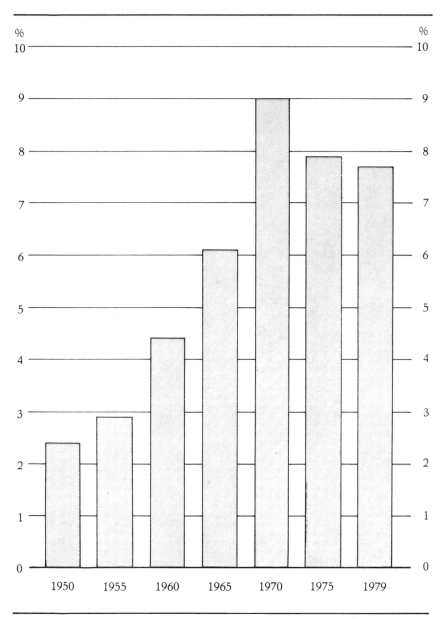

Source: *Education in Canada, 1981*. Reproduced by permission of the Minister of Supply and Services Canada. Ottawa: Statistics Canada, 1982.

In the 1950s, the emphasis was upon education as good social invest-ment. Therefore education was stressed and supported, heading to increased university participation. Besides, part of the expansion in higher educa-tional institutions was simply demographic, for, by the late 1950s, the schools were dealing with the children of the post-war "baby boom." These were the young people reaching the universities during the 1960s. Also, many more young women began to attend universities. Thus, all levels of education, from primary through university, expanded drastically.

This created an enormous demand for physical plant. Particularly coupled with rural to urban migration, there was a burst of school building in city suburbs. At the same time, universities were building new facilities, and entire new universities were created, particularly in Ontario.

Necessarily, of course, in addition to buildings, qualified personnel were required. But because of the prior pattern of educating a very small per-centage of Canadians to post-high-school levels, such trained personnel were not available. School teachers and university professors had to be imported, characteristically from the United Kingdom and the United States. Because of the prior underdevelopment of Canadian education, middle-class positions as educators now were being filled by non-Canadians.

Over all, the competition for skilled educators, whether Canadian-born or immigrant, worked to the advantage of wealthy, urbanized central Canada, and to the disadvantage of rural regions, especially Quebec and the Maritimes. Central Canadian teachers and university faculty have generally been better educated and better paid, thereby enhancing that area's recruitment advantage, and, arguably, its quality of education.

The Schools

The push to increased education did mean that school attendance became universal. By 1961, universal school attendance of youths to age 15 was all but realized, especially in Ontario.

When one compares school populations aged 15 to 17, it is apparent that a regional variation in quality of education and existing privilege is opera-tive. In this age group, the lowest proportion of continued school atten-dance is in Canada's least industrialized and urbanized provinces. The lowest attendance proportions are found in the Atlantic. Thus the "drop-out" phenomenon is concentrated in the least prosperous areas of Canada, reinforcing the existing pattern of unskilled labour and lower-status occupations. The pattern of educational participation is even more pro-nounced in Ontario's favour when one examines the participation of Canadians older than 17 or beyond compulsory education. (See Table 3-1.)

School attendance rates among the ethnic populations also indicate the variable utilization of education. Jewish and Chinese young people have the highest attendance rates and native peoples the lowest. (See Table 3-3.)

Table 3-1: School Attendance Rates (per 1,000 population) by Age Groups, Canada, Provinces and Territories

School Attendance By Age Groups	Can.	Nfld.	P.E.I.	N.S.	N.B.	Que.	Ont.	Man.	Sask.	Alta.	B.C.	Yukon	N.W.T.
						— Rate per 1,000 Population —							
Attending Full-time													
15 and over	117	118	128	122	117	118	122	107	109	111	103	107	104
15–17	785	724	800	800	769	791	806	768	766	742	774	722	545
18–21	369	274	420	397	357	372	430	321	313	279	312	253	197
22–24	132	76	101	109	97	131	157	111	98	117	123	102*	78*
25–49	24	17	19	21	16	22	24	23	21	28	28	24*	25
50 and over	4	3	2*	2	3	6	3	2	2	2	3	12*	7*
Attending Part-time													
15 and over	58	30	34	33	29	57	63	47	45	60	70	46	26
15–17	12	15	15	9	8	10	11	11	13	16	19	27*	21*
18–21	62	44	43	36	34	54	64	60	51	72	94	45*	32*
22–24	99	55	73	60	49	96	111	89	78	97	118	60*	41*
25–49	84	41	50	50	44	85	94	71	70	79	98	58*	29
50 and over	17	4	8*	9	7	15	21	12	15	17	22	11*	8*
Not attending													
15 and over	825	852	838	845	853	825	814	846	846	828	827	847	870
15–17	203	260	185	191	223	199	183	221	222	243	207	251	434
18–21	569	682	536	567	609	574	506	619	636	649	595	699	774
22–24	769	869	828	832	854	774	732	800	824	786	759	839	882
25–49	892	941	931	930	939	893	883	906	909	893	874	918	945
50 and over	979	993	990	989	990	979	976	986	983	981	975	977	987

* Rates based on fewer than 250 persons in the numerator.
Source: Canada, April 1984. Reproduced by permission of the Minister of Supply and Services Canada.

Table 3-2: Canadian Educational Enrolment, 1951–1984

	Actual		Preliminary	Projected
	1961–1962	1971–1972	1981–1982	1983–1984
		Thousands		
Total full-time enrolment	4,591.8	6,298.7	5,698.4	5,594.1
Elementary-secondary	4,409.8	5,801.9	5,023.0	4,905.2
Kindergarten	157.4	335.5	397.9	399.6
Grades 1–8	3,357.4	3,759.7	3,042.5	3,014.4
Grades 9 and up	895.0	1,706.7	1,582.6	1,491.2
Full-time post-				
secondary	182.0	496.8	675.4	688.9
College	53.4	173.8	273.9	276.9
Male	16.5	94.1	133.7	134.6
Female	36.9	79.7	140.2	142.3
University	128.6	323.0	401.5	411.9
Male	95.6	206.6	218.8	219.5
Female	33.0	116.4	182.7	192.4
Undergraduate	121.3	287.1	354.6	363.6
Graduate	7.3	35.9	46.9	48.3
Total part-time university				
(Credit courses)	..	155.4	252.8	268.6
Male	..	86.2	106.4	110.7
Female	..	69.2	146.4	157.9
Undergraduate	..	137.4	220.6	235.0
Graduate	..	18.0	32.2	33.6
Total full-time academic				
staff (teaching and non-				
teaching)	187.1	313.0	326.0	323.7
Elementary-secondary	173.9	271.3	271.0	267.4
College	4.4	14.1	21.1	21.8
University	8.8	27.6	33.9	34.5

Source: Canada, September 1982. Reproduced by permission of the Minister of Supply and Services Canada.

The Universities

University enrolments swung up through the 1950s and 1960s as did educational enrolment generally. "Instant universities" were built, non-Canadian faculty recruited, and increasing enrolments were projected by university administrators into the indefinite future. Undergraduate university enrolments are estimated to have increased by 331 percent from 1945–46 to 1964–65. However, by 1977, enrolments had stabilized, and had even begun to decline.

Table 3-3: Full-time and Part-time School Attendance Rates (per 1,000 population) by Age Groups for Selected Social and Cultural Characteristics

Selected Social and Cultural Characteristics	Full-time Attendance		Part-time Attendance	
	15–19	20–24	20–24	25 and over
	—Rate per 1,000 population—			
Canada Total	659	186	89	58
Place of Birth				
Canada	655	180	86	57
U.S.A.	716	258	88	58
United Kingdom	701	207	114	59
Other Europe	641	174	93	40
Africa	799	382	161	117
Asia	716	304	138	99
Ethnic Origin				
British	664	183	89	58
French	647	162	76	54
German	624	165	96	49
Italian	704	243	114	37
Ukrainian	648	169	99	49
Native Peoples	487	105	50	37
Dutch	651	179	97	58
Chinese	772	414	158	108
Jewish	823	483	130	73
Scandinavian	642	155	97	53
Religion				
Roman Catholic	656	177	84	55
Ukrainian Catholic	687	219	85	41
Mainline Protestant	662	181	89	54
Eastern Orthodox	697	239	96	40
Jewish	829	472	131	74
Islamic	708	265	125	104
Hindu	728	261	136	115
Sikh	688	153	89	51
Buddhist	704	319	155	101
No Religious Preference	619	205	109	97

Source: Canada, April 1984. Reproduced by permission of the Minister of Supply and Services Canada.

Yet, today, the provinces have begun to question the value of higher education — especially in British Columbia. And our federal government has claimed that its transfer payments for education have been diverted by the provinces. Politicians, businessmen, and academics have returned to a more élitist notion — including a "user pay" concept that demands higher student fees, and actively seeks lower student enrolment.

Table 3.4: University Graduates

| | Actual | | Estimated | Projected |
	1961–62	1971–72	1981–82	1983–84
	Thousands			
Graduates				
Secondary school	73.7	232.9	300.2	269.6
Post-secondary				
College diplomas and certificates	22.2	47.7	69.8	72.6
Male	5.0	21.8	30.4	31.5
Female	17.2	25.9	39.4	41.1
Bachelor's and first professional				
degrees	22.8	72.4	85.2	90.3
Male	16.5	43.9	42.2	44.8
Female	6.3	28.5	43.0	45.5
Master's degrees	2.4	10.3	13.0	13.4
Male	2.0	7.7	7.8	7.9
Female	0.4	2.6	5.2	5.5
Doctorates (earned)	0.32	1.7	1.8	1.9
Male	0.29	1.5	1.4	1.4
Female	0.03	0.2	0.4	0.5

Source: Canada, September 1982. Reproduced by permission of the Minister of Supply and Services Canada.

Middle Class Education

By the 1970s, far more of the educable population than ever before were attaining some post-secondary education. For example, the number of persons with completed university degrees in 1974 had more than doubled as against 1950.

The improvement in the proportion of better-educated Canadians has led some observers to conclude that mobility opportunities in Canada must therefore have been improving. According to this view, since more education means access to better and higher-status jobs, and since there are more people getting higher education, this must translate into more people getting better jobs and acquiring improved social class. However, this optimistic interpretation overlooks two rather obvious features of the education explosion — an upgrading of job qualifications for the middle class, and a considerable increase in the number of middle-class young women taking university degrees.

It is clear that increased university access has essentially been true for only the Canadian middle class. This privilege is so marked as to constitute a regressive system of publicly-funded education. Upper- and middle-income groups benefit, but lower-income groups also pay for a system which they do not utilize. In effect, "the relatively poor groups tend to subsidize the relatively rich." (Mehmet, 1978: 45.)

An illustration of middle-class advantage that is now beginning to reach the universities is the current emphasis upon French immersion education. Intended to enhance a genuine and well-intentioned concept of bilingualism, in effect immersion programs have essentially been exploited by the relatively privileged. The middle-class children graduating from such programs and pursuing their language skills in universities will have the job benefits that one might reasonably expect to be associated with bilingualism, particularly in the public sector. Current enrolment suggests that provinces such as Quebec, Prince Edward Island, New Brunswick, Manitoba, and Ontario promise to be at the forefront in institutionalizing this middle-class advantage. (See Table 3-5.)

(i) Upgraded job qualifications

There has been a redefinition of job requirements; many positions requiring university-qualified personnel in the 1950s and 1960s were positions requiring high school credentials in the 1940s and earlier. This is not to deny that with industrial growth some new skilled positions not previously part of the labour structure have come to be, requiring educated personnel. But what has also occurred is a general upgrading in the educational credentials required for positions even where such credentials have nothing to do with the task at hand. Therefore, by stratum, there has been less mobility would appear to be the case. A head of a family would hold middle-class status, for example, by virtue of an executive position in some firm; yet that parent might well have only a Grade nine education. However, that middle-class man's sons would now require, and probably obtain, a university degree to hold down the same kind of job and the same social-class status. There has been educational upgrading, but no intergenerational social mobility. Increased educational spending and enrolment constitute an educational inflation (Karabel, 1972), and fail to alter the basic character of relative inequality. As increasingly high levels of education have come to be demanded, the consequence has been that "particular qualifications 'buy' ever-decreasing amounts of occupational status and income." (Richardson, 1977: 424.)

Table 3-5: Elementary and Secondary Student Enrolment in French Immersion Programs, 1982-83 *

Province	School Population[a]	Students in Immersion	%
Newfoundland	142,394	819[b]	0.6
Prince Edward Island	25,203	1,644	6.5
Nova Scotia	174,505	869	0.5
New Brunswick	99,684	8,759[b]	8.8
Quebec	136,429[b]	17,472	12.8
Ontario	1,694,528	53,982	3.2
Manitoba	194,287	7,580	3.9
Saskatchewan	200,643	3,287[b]	1.6
Alberta	440,174	12,122[d]	2.8
British Columbia	498,836	7,756	1.6
Yukon	4,524	128[b]	2.8
Northwest Territories	12,760	102	0.8
DND Schools (Europe)(c)	2,687	408	15.2
Total	3,626,654	114,928	3.2

[a] Excludes pupils enrolled in French-language schools
[b] Figures provided by Department of Education
[c] Students in DND (Department of National Defence) immersion classes in Canada are included in provincial enrolments.
[d] Estimate (80 percent of students in schools where French is the language of instruction)
* Latest national statistics available.
Source: Statistics Canada except where noted. Prepared and published by *The Toronto Star*, June 16, 1985.

(ii) Female educational achievement

In addition, from that middle-class family, not only would we be apt to find male children attending universities where their parents did not, but also female children. Much of the influx into universities in Canada in the 1950s and 1960s was female enrolment. Where before World War II a girl was not usually expected by her parents to attend university, by the 1950s and 1960s female attendance was more and more taken for granted. Today, glancing about any classroom in any Canadian university, particularly in Faculties of Arts, you would find approximately 50 percent of the class consisting of females, where prior to World War II the proportion would have been far less, around 20 percent. Whereas, in 1920–21, only 20.4 percent of bachelor and first professional degrees were taken by women, by 1968–69 the proportion was 37.2 percent. (Manzer, 1974: 202–203.)

Table 3-6: Educational Attainment of Persons 14 Years and Over[1]

	Actual			Projected		
	1951[2]	1961[2]	1972	1974	1980	1985
Secondary or less	92.9	90.0	82.0	80.2	74.2	68.3
Post-secondary:						
Non-university	2.8	4.5	8.4	9.4	12.8	16.0
University	4.3	5.5	9.6	10.4	13.0	15.7
Total post-secondary	7.1	10.0	18.0	19.8	25.8	31.7
Total	100.0	100.0	100.0	100.0	100.0	100.0
Total persons 000's	9,759	12,047	15,992	16,706	18,708	19,840

[1] Includes high school and university graduates currently in the system.
[2] Includes only persons 15 years and over in 1951 and 1961.
Source: *Perspective Canada*, 1977: 93. Reproduced by permission of the Minister of Supply and Services Canada.

Considerable as the change has been, it should additionally be noted that the female access to the professions has not increased to the same extent; in law, in 1921, only 3.7 percent of the total number of graduates were women, and by 1961 the proportion was still only 5.2 percent. Female careers in medicine fared somewhat better, compared to law; in 1921 4.4 percent of the medical school graduates were women, and by 1961 the proportion was 7.9 percent. (Calculated from data reported in Porter, 1964: 117.) Current female enrolment in programs of law and medicine is approximately 28 percent of the total enrolment in the two professions. (See Table 3-7.)

Professional schools aside, there has been a change in established role definitions that had previously relegated females to secretarial and nursing schools, if they received post-secondary education at all. This change appears in statistics pointing up higher university enrolments. Since the 1960s, females from middle-class homes were competing to a greater degree with middle-class males.

There was, therefore, not as great a change in educational achievement by social class in Canadian society as statistics on university enrolment at first glance suggest, if the composition by gender is not distinguished. Middle-class young women were attending universities in greater numbers than they were in the 1940s, and in a sense inflating the statistics. That is, the increase in educational enrolment did not mean expanded opportunities for all classes. It is in considerable proportion middle-class females and not working-class persons who are accounting for the increase.

It is vexing to note, additionally, that higher education for middle-class women has not translated into a proportionate improvement in the participation of middle-class women in the occupational workforce. Once edu-

Table 3-7: Female Full-time Undergraduate Enrolment as a Percentage of Total Full-time Enrolment, 1978–1979 and 1982–1983

	1978-1979 (%)	1982–1983 (%)
Arts	53	55
Science	38	38
Commerce and Business Administration	32	40
Education	66	68
Engineering and Applied Science	8	11
Dentistry	18	24
Medicine	33	40
Nursing	97	97
Pharmacy	63	65
Household Science	98	96
Law	34	42
Veterinary Medicine	42	51

Source: CACSW, March 1985. Calculated from Statistics Canada, *Education in Canada: A Statistical Review for 1982–83* (Ottawa: Supply and Services Canada, June 1984), Catalogue No. 81-229, pp. 59–60. Reproduced by permission of the Minister of Supply and Services Canada.

cated, women have still been tending to enter the labour force in the traditional female professions, especially teaching and nursing, and white-collar semi-clerical roles. (Manzer, 1974: 223–234; Gilbert and McRoberts, 1975.) Despite their education and their middle-class status, with its correlated Anglo-ethnic origins, Canadian women entering the labour force still tend to be excluded from high-status jobs in the professions and corporate and government bureaucracies.

Table 3-8: Total Post-Secondary Education Population as a Percentage of Female Population 18–24, 1951–1977

1951	4.6
1961	8.2
1966	10.8
1971	14.6
1976	18.0
1977	18.2

Source: Canada, 1980, 1981. Reproduced by permission of the Minister of Supply and Services Canada.

Figure 3-2 Percent of Bachelor's and First Professional Degrees Awarded to Women, Selected Specializations, Canada, 1970 and 1980

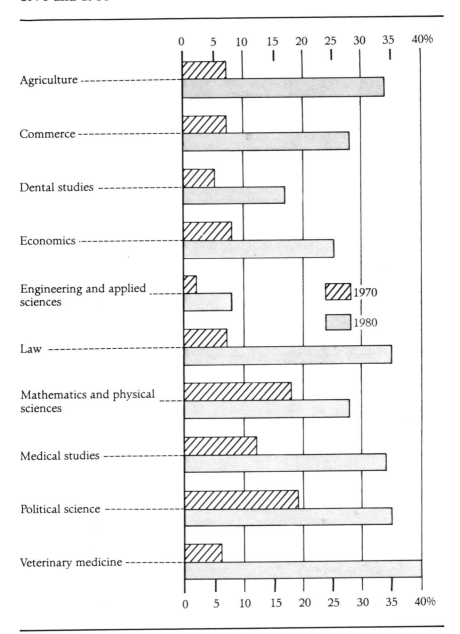

Source: *Education in Canada, 1981.* Reproduced by permission of the Minister of Supply and Services Canada. Ottawa: Statistics Canada, 1982.

Figure 3-3 University Full-time Participation

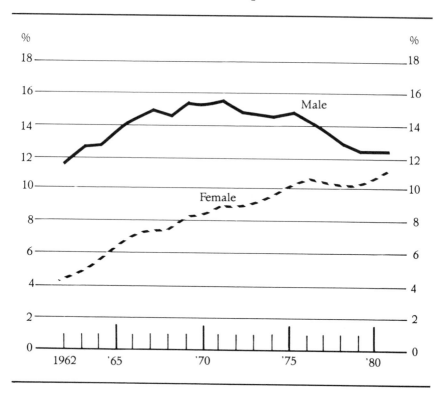

Note: Total full-time enrolment related to the 18–24 age group.
Source: Warren Clark, "Can Universities meet Challenge of Increasing
Participation?" *University Affairs*, February, 1982. Reproduced by
permission of the Minister of Supply and Services Canada.

It is also ironic that as female students began to reach equality in many
sectors of the university, government financial support of the universities
declined steadily, especially in Ontario. (See Figures 3-4, 3-5, and 3-6.)
This is in contrast to support given other public sector services, such as
health services. Grants by student enrolment, capital grants, monies for
library acquisitions all suffered after the 1960s.

Undoubted mobility opportunities have existed in Canada, throughout
the 20th century. But they have not been as numerous as some interpretations would suggest. Serious social barriers to mobility have persisted, and
Canadians have not been proceeding equally through the educational
system. The very institution that was meant to secure mobility has not
provided equally for all social classes. A basic indication of this is the
extent to which people aspire to higher educational levels, and higher
occupational levels, than their parents. We shall see that aspirations as well
as achievements are inherited by class.

Figure 3-4 University Part-time Participation

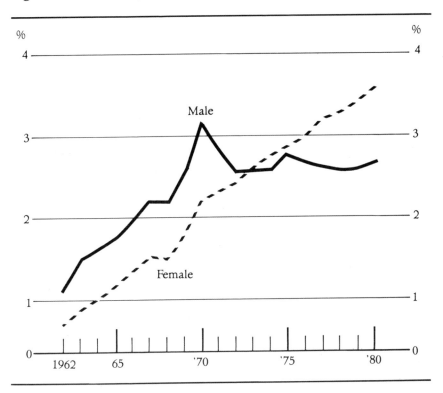

Note: Total part-time enrolment related to the 20–39 age group.
Source: Warren Clark, "Can Universities meet Challenge of Increasing
Participation?" *University Affairs*, February, 1982. Reproduced by
permission of the Minister of Supply and Services Canada.

**Table 3-9: Percentage of University Degrees Awarded to Women,
Canada and the United States**

		1962 (%)	1970 (%)	1976 (%)
B.A. and first Professional Degree	Canada	27.8	38.0	44.6
	U.S.A.	38.7	41.8	44.9
M.A.	Canada	18.1	22.0	29.9
	U.S.A.	32.8	40.1	45.3
Ph.D.	Canada	8.1	9.3	15.5
	U.S.A.	10.7	14.3	22.9

Source: From Table 15.17, p. 303 *Perspectives Canada III*, Ottawa Ministry of
Supply and Services, 1980. Reproduced by permission of the Minister of Supply
and Services Canada.

Figure 3-5   Index of Expenditures per Client Served in Ontario, 1973–74 to 1983–84 (in Constant Dollars)

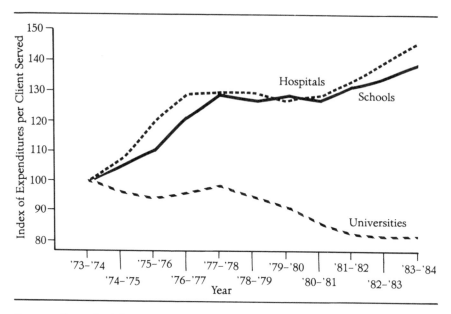

Source: Council of Ontario Universities, "Briefing Notes," Toronto, May 1985.

Figure 3-6   Index of Operating Grants Per Full-time Equivalent Enrolment, 1974–75 to 1984–85 (Canadian Average = 100)

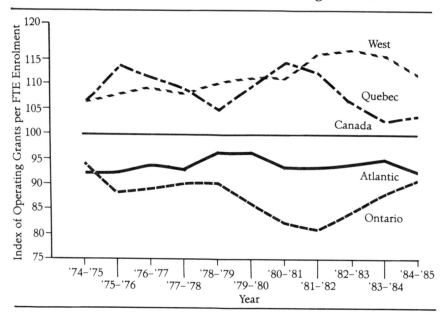

Source: Council of Ontario Universities, "Briefing Notes," Toronto, May 1985.

Figure 3-7 Index of University Expenditures on Library Acquisitions, 1970–71 to 1983–84

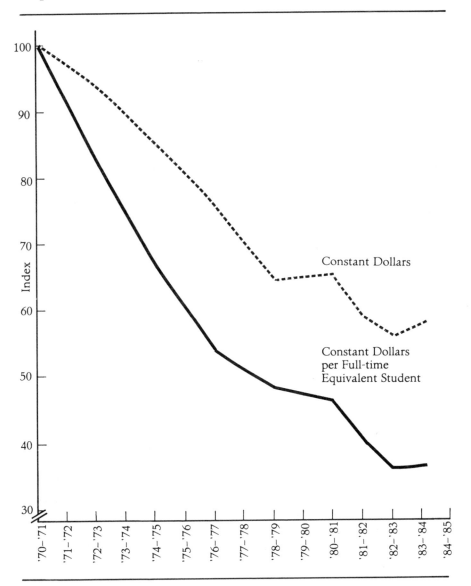

Source: Council of Ontario Universities, ''Briefing Notes,'' Toronto, May 1985.

Table 3-10: Female Enrolment as a Percentage of Total Post-Secondary Enrolment, by Level

Year	Non-University	University			Total Post-Secondary
		Undergraduate	Graduate	Total	
1961	69.1	26.2	16.4	25.7	38.5
1966	55.3	33.7	18.0	32.4	38.3
1971	45.9	37.7	22.6	36.0	39.5
1976	49.8	43.7	30.6	42.3	45.1
1981*	51.9	48.9	39.0	44.0	48.3
1982**	52.9	51.7	38.6	50.1	50.8

Sources: Calculated from, CACSW, March 1985. Canada, Statistics Canada, *Perspectives Canada III*, H.J. Adler and D.A. Brusegard, eds. (Ottawa: Supply and Services Canada, April 1980), Catalogue No. 11-511, Table 4.11, p. 79.
* Statistics Canada, *School Attendance and Level of Schooling* (Ottawa: Supply and Services Canada, January 1984), Catalogue No. 92-914, Tables 2-1, 2-2.
** Statistics Canada, *Education in Canada: A Statistical Review for 1982–1983* (Ottawa: Supply and Services Canada, June 1984), Catalogue No. 81-229, Tables 2-6, pp. 58–64.

Aspirations and Class

Stratification is a structural feature of societies, in the sense that it consists of distinguishable collectivities or groups of people dependent upon property or upon labour for their incomes, these relations being perpetuated over generations. There are also, of course, attitudinal components of a stratification system. We know, for example, that persons from different social classes will tend to have different attitudes regarding sexual behaviour, aggression, cleanliness, or promptness, to cite a few examples. So, too, they will have different attitudes and expectations regarding educational and occupational "success."

In Canada and in the United States numerous studies have explored young people's attitudes to educational and occupational achievement. Indeed, few areas of sociological interest have generated as much empirical research. The assumption of researchers has been that attitudes influence and serve as indicators of actual behaviour. Thus the level of education to which a boy or girl aspires or expects to achieve, and the kind of job aspired to and expected, affect the extent of education and kind of job actually obtained.

But, of vital importance relative to the egalitarian myth, these aspirations are not randomly distributed in the population. Rather, stated aspirations are indicative of and correlated with social class. Working with a Toronto sample of 108 children in public schools, Baldas and Tribe found clear evidence that, by the age of eleven, children had developed accurate conceptions of social class. Moreover, by that age, they classified people in terms of inequality, and showed well-developed expectations of lower-class failure and higher-class achievement. (Baldus and Tribe, 1978.)

Research in Canada has confirmed that aspirations are principally a function of the social class level of one's family, and rural versus urban residence — not altogether unrelated factors. (Siemens, 1965; Pike, 1970; Breton, 1972; Rocher, 1975.) Thus one is more likely to aspire to and expect to achieve a university degree if one comes from a middle- or upper-class family as opposed to a working-class family. Conversely, one is more likely to wish and expect to drop out of the educational system before completing high school, or immediately upon completion, if one comes from a working-class family as opposed to a middle-class family. Reflecting educational aspirations, middle-class youth are more likely to aim for high-status occupations like that of medical doctor or lawyer. (Siemens, 1965; Pike, 1970; Gilbert and McRoberts, 1974.)

Similar patterns of aspiration have also been noted with respect to native peoples, who must be thought of as a sub-group within the larger Canadian lower-status population. In an Alberta enquiry, for example, researchers found that only 9.8 percent of native students aspire to some post-secondary education, as contrasted to 50 percent of non-native students. (Alberta, 1971: 114.) Such attitudes translate into school conduct and attendance. One estimate puts the figure of native children dropping out of schools in Regina at 90 percent of the native children (Tenszen, 1985.) To the native children, school is a white, middle-class, alien, and hostile environment.

Social class, aspirations, and gender are also related. Boys have tended to have slightly higher occupational aspirations than do girls, even when from similar class backgrounds. (Porter, Porter, and Blishen, 1979: 90–99.) Traditional role stereotypes influence aspirations, as Brinkerhoff demonstrated in a study of Calgary high school girls. (Brinkerhoff, 1977.) But recent data suggest very similar educational aspirations for boys and girls. (See Table 3-11.) Girls' aspirations are influenced by the occupational status of their mothers and fathers. (See Tables 3-12 and 3-13.) The lower the socio-economic status of a student's family, the less likely the student is to aspire to university education, and this relationship is especially pronounced for girls.

The relationship between social class and aspiration persists even among students with high intelligence quotients. Gilbert and McRoberts report that in an Ontario sample of Grade 12 students, working-class male and female students in the university-prep or five-year stream in high school tend to plan for something other than university education, whether to enter the labour force or go on to some other form of post-secondary education. This is in contrast to the university-level aspirations

Table 3-11: Educational Aspirations of Male and Female Students in a CACWS Study

	Female	Male
University	55.9% (52)	50.0% (11)
College*	30.1% (28)	27.3% (6)
Paid job after high school	14.0% (13)	22.7% (5)
Total**	100.0% (93)	100.0% (22)

* Includes art colleges, secretarial colleges, polytechnical institutes, CEGEPs, and community colleges.
** Ten students were too uncertain of their future plans to be included in this table.
Source: CACSW, March, 1985. Reproduced by permission of the Minister of Supply and Services Canada.

Table 3-12: Daughter's Educational Plans, by Mother's Occupation in a CACWS Study

	Daughter's Educational Plans				
	University (%)	College (%)	Job (%)	Total (%)	Total number of girls
Mother's Occupation					
Professional	82.4	11.8	5.9	18.5	(17)
Sales, Clerical or Service	58.1	32.3	9.7	33.7	(31)
Housewife	53.3	26.7	20.0	32.6	(30)
Manual Labour	21.4	57.1	21.4	15.2	(14)
Total %	55.4	30.4	14.1	100.0	
Total Number of Girls	(51)	(28)	(13)	—	(92)

Source: CACSW, March 1985. Reproduced by permission of the Minister of Supply and Services Canada.

of middle and upper-class students of the same IQ range. (Gilbert and McRoberts, 1974: 13–14; 32–33.) In both streams, fewer girls than boys intended to acquire additional education. (Gilbert and McRoberts, 1977: 39.)

In a Manitoba survey of rural and suburban high school students, it was found that within each of the upper and middle classes, students with higher IQs (male and female) tended to aspire to higher levels than did students with lower IQs. But within the working class, higher IQ was not related to higher aspirations; that is, working-class students with high IQs tended not to have aspirations higher than other working-class students, nor aspirations as great as less "intelligent" middle- and upper-class students. What seemed to affect higher aspirations among working-class students was teacher encouragement. (Forcese and Siemens, 1965: 23–24.)

Table 3-13: Daughter's* Educational Plans, by Father's Occupation, in a CACWS Study

| | Daughter's Educational Plans | | | |
	University	College	Work after High School	Total
Father's Occupation				
Higher Status**	75.5%	18.4%	6.1%	55.1%
	(37)	(9)	(3)	(49)
Lower Status	32.5%	45.0%	22.5%	44.9%
	(13)	(18)	(9)	(40)
Total	56.2%	30.3%	13.5%	100.0%
	(50)	(27)	(12)	(89)

* Includes only female students who gave information about their father's jobs.
** Higher status includes professional, managerial, and technical positions.
Lower status includes sales, service, skilled and unskilled labour, farmer, retired, or unemployed.
Source: CACSW, March 1985. Reproduced by permission of the Minister of Supply and Services Canada.

Home and School Environment

Intelligence quotients are shaped by environment. The low IQ is itself a class or cultural disadvantage. (Mohs, 1982.) But even the working-class child with a high IQ score tends to be unlikely to aspire to continued education. In a major study of 150,000 secondary school students from all provinces, Breton found that the working-class student with a high IQ was less apt to want to go on to post-secondary education than the middle- and upper-class students with high IQs. (Breton, 1972: 140.)

Some observers are quite happy to ascribe differential achievement by social class to the intelligence of students, noting that working-class children have lower IQs. The implication is, of course, that such IQ scores are adequate measures of intelligence and indicate hereditary differences. According to this view, it is because of lesser intelligence that working-class students do less well, and it is why they and their families are, in fact, working class. A literal interpretation of IQ test scores permits such a view, for consistently, in fact, working-class children do less well on IQ tests, even where some attempt has been made to standardize for class and ethnic background. But sociologists find contrary data more convincing, and take the view that IQ tests are very imperfect and crude indicators of innate ability, as distinct from social experience. IQ tests reflect middle-class experiences and learned abilities, including symbolic manipulation. Working-class children do less well because the tests do not measure working-class meanings and skills, and because they are usually administered in a middle-class setting—the school. The middle-class person whose "native tongue" is English, or French in Quebec, will do better. Thus, deriving from his examination of such IQ bias against Mexican-American children, the American sociologist John Garcia refers to the administration and reliance upon IQ tests as the "conspiracy of the ruling class," for they serve to perpetuate dominant class definitions of performance and existing inequities. (Garcia, 1972; Kerchoff, 1972: 73–74.)

Similarly related to the IQ bias is the matter of school preparation. The middle-class child, before entering school and throughout his school years, lives in a supportive and compatible environment. Prior to school he will acquire verbal and reading skills, either by deliberate emphasis or merely as a normal feature of day-to-day living. There are books and magazines, papers, pens, and pencils all readily available in the middle-class home and used by the parents, and their use by the children is taught and encouraged. The parents will themselves be quite well educated and literate, and will hold down jobs where intellectual activity is required, thereby standing as role models for the children. In fact, more than simply having occupational role models, the upper- and middle-class child will frequently have deliberate tutoring by parents or professionals. Increasingly formal pre-school training is becoming the norm. Nursery schools, pre-schools, and kindergartens are costly advantages not routinely available to working-class families, while those already privileged use them to provide their children with an accelerated instruction in school-related skills and familiarity with the school environment. (Kerchoff, 1972: 60–79.)

Other features of home environment that interact with the school situation relate to nutrition and health. There are data indicating that working-class children suffer from nutritional deficiencies and illness to the extent that school attendance and performance are impaired. (National Council of Welfare, March, 1975: 21–22.) Also, once in the school system, the working-class child is more apt to attend older, inner-city schools, with poorer facilities, equipment, and perhaps teaching staff than in the suburban schools of the more privileged.

In addition, influencing the attitudes of their children, it is quite common for working-class parents to be suspicious of and even hostile to schools. Thus, not only do working-class households lack the tools of education, but they also lack supportive attitudes. In fact, a working-class child who too strenuously attempts to succeed at school activities will meet not only the ridicule and opposition of peers, but often also of parents. At the same time, teachers may react negatively to the behaviour of the working-class child. In research done in an Ottawa primary school in 1972, Richer found that in classrooms that were traditional and teacher-dominated, working-class children received significantly less than a proportional share of teacher contacts and attention. In contrast, however, in open-style classrooms, working-class children received more than their proportional share of teacher interaction. Richer suggests that in the open environment, the more aggressive working-class child was able to demand and initiate attention, where he was not able to do so in the closed classroom. (Richer, 1974.) Yet, of course, such open-concept classrooms are few in number in our school systems.

Home environment and school environment interact to reinforce non-achievement for the working-class child, and high performance for the middle- and upper-class child. There is differential advantage from the time children enter first grade. The middle-class child will perform in the expected manner, for he has already been taught to do so. The middle-class child comes to be viewed as more intelligent, and is rewarded accordingly, by school and by parents. But the working-class child, also performing as expected and consistent with learned experience, does not do well and is "stigmatized" as a failure. This definition is passed on, in teacher conversations and school records, and is also communicated to the child, who comes to view himself as a failure. Failure comes to be a self-fulfilling prophecy.

The problem is evident among immigrant populations. Immigrants often have difficulties with the schools, reflecting their cultural attitudes. If a child from an immigrant family comes from a cultural environment that does not stress education or complex concepts, the school will be perceived as hostile. Moreover, the child's effort in school will not be reinforced by parental effort at home. Immigrant children therefore experience early streaming into non-academic programmes, a feature much remarked of schools in the city that is Canada's largest recipient of immigrants, Toronto. (Ferri, 1985.)

Similarly, children of immigrants may find themselves caught between school and home. The modern expectations and values of school will contradict traditional values of parents, and the school therefore is viewed by the adults as threatening. This is probably more pronounced for girls, who are expected to work in the home. Thus, for example, Portuguese, Greek, and Italian immigrants intimidated by the schools, in part because of a language gap, blame the schools for their children's behaviour problems. (Perez, 1976; D'Antini, 1976; Kinkopoulos, 1976.)

The schools, as we have previously argued, capitalize upon the entering advantage of middle-class students, not from some conscious and malicious conspiracy, but simply from a privileged, class ethnocentrism. Our schools are operated by middle-class school boards, administrators, and teachers. In Anglophone Canada these people are characteristically of British-Canadian background. In a sample of high school teachers in Hamilton, Jones found that the majority of teachers came from families of above-average socio-economic status, and most were English or second-generation Canadian. (Jones, 1963, 537.) They quite naturally expect behaviour consistent with their own middle-class children, not working-class nor especially slum children. The absence of designated traits often elicits disapproval and punishment of an overt sort, as well as a more subtle biasing of teacher attitude and behaviour.

Negative self-concept and low educational aspirations are well-established characteristics of working-class children obliged to compete in a school environment alien to their home and neighbourhood experience, and in which they are at a distinct competitive disadvantage relative to middle- and upper-class children. The latter bring relevant pre-training, experience, and affirmative attitudes to school, while working-class children bring behaviour, skills, and attitudes that are either not recognized or are punished in the classroom. Not only is self-blame taught in schools, it is taught by the prior victims of the industrial system, the parents of working-class children. (Rubin, 1976: 55.) The schools socialize and in a real sense incarcerate working-class individuals, with legislation setting mandatory school attendance whether functional learning occurs or not. In the latter regard, one of the school's social functions is to reduce the level of formal unemployment (Braverman, 1974: 439–440), acting as "caretaker of the hidden unemployed."

The class origins of students may also become overt class conflict on the playing fields or in the corridors of Canadian schools. An example is to be had from an Ottawa school (Allen, 1980: 3), where parents complained to school board officials about conflict between the "vocs" or vocational program students and the general or academic program students. In this instance, the "vocs" were accorded lower prestige, as is usual in Canadian schools. There was a prevailing pattern of taunting and harassment of the "vocs" who were labelled as trouble-makers and inferiors. As well, they were relegated to inferior physical locations such as seating at the rear of the school bus or assignment to portable rather than permanent school buildings.

Given the range of obstacles and assistance to social mobility in Canada, such as living conditions and support in the home or the qualifications of teachers, variations in aspiration by social class, including such influences as region, and rural versus urban residence, are quite unremarkable. Working-class children are in a very real sense socialized to aim much lower than their middle-class counterparts. This socialization is vested in the every-day experiences of the various classes, and serves to maintain the system of social stratification.

Socialization occurs in the home, among peers, in the neighbourhood or community, and in the schools themselves. Working-class and middle- or upper-class parents will have different attitudes toward formal education and different skills to impart to their children. Similarly, there are different economic demands and pressures amongst the working-class, to earn money rather than to study; education may be free, but not all implements are. More important, the income that families forego while their children attend school may be perceived as vital to the standard of living of a working-class family. The middle-class advantage extends to the classroom. Rather than neutralize or overcome family (class), neighbourhood, or regional influences, the school crystallizes them and reinforces them.

Rural students experience situations similar to the urban working class in the "alien" nature of the school environment. They, too, feel pressure to "work" and earn money while having fewer models of high-status roles or occupations, and fewer opportunities to deal in abstractions. Their teachers may have less training than urban teachers, and the schools may have poorer facilities. Where the facilities are comparable to urban schools, as in the "consolidated" schools, they are often utilized only at the expense of additional hours spent in busing to the school. Consequently, lower aspirations are also characteristic of rural students.

In the classroom, the working-class child is less likely to perform up to middle-class-dominated school expectations, either in skills or in decorum — each related to home experience. Poorer performance, and perhaps early failure, become self-perpetuating, for the child becomes labelled as "not too bright," a "failure," and perhaps a "trouble-maker." Eventually, as the child perceives this teacher attitude, also shared by his middle-class peers, his or her self-image becomes consistent with the label, as do aspirations and achievements. In aspiring to low levels, the student with poor grades, usually from the working class where there is less preparation and support to earn good grades, is simply conforming to the expectations of family, friends, and teachers. (Forcese and Siemens, 1965: 23.)

Even given the ideal school situation of the genuinely unbiased teacher, and even given a student doing well academically, evidence suggests that working-class children tend to think that the teacher views them unfavourably. That is, whatever the teacher's actual attitudes, the lower-class child perceives the teacher to be hostile, thereby affecting the student's self-image and attitude to school. (Davidson and Lang, 1960: 107–118.)

Also relating to self-image and aspirations are teacher attention and encouragement. The teacher is, in effect, being rewarded by the "good" student who does what is expected and makes fewer demands, including disciplinary demands. In turn, therefore, the "good" student is further encouraged by the teacher, whereas the "poor" student, usually from the working class, is further neglected despite needing greater assistance, thus reinforcing inadequate performance. The student who is not receiving any rewards or benefits in the school is then apt to turn to non-academic pursuits in order to win acceptance of peers or school authorities; these activities might be athletic or delinquent. The import of teacher and school influence was identified by a Manitoba survey of senior high school students (Forcese and Siemens, 1965) and similarly in a Halifax study. In the latter it was concluded that school environment, including teacher attitudes (as perceived and in fact) and student sub-cultures, were more important than family environment in influencing continued school attendance. (Or, 1970.) This is so in the sense, also, that extraordinary teacher encouragement and support may overcome the handicaps of class background.

It is ironic that it is the working-class children who can benefit more from teacher support, yet they are least apt to receive it.

> . . . the teacher's influence upon lower-class children is potentially much greater than her influence upon middle-class children. The latter generally receive assistance and encouragement at home, and are thus better able to be academically successful *in spite* of the kind of teaching they experience. (Kerchoff, 1972:74.)

Failing exceptional support at home or at school, working-class children tend to drop out of school as early as the law permits, often failing to complete high-school matriculation and only infrequently going on to post-high-school programs, especially university, thereby rarely moving on to occupations bringing high prestige and high income.

Class, Aspiration, and Achievement

There is no question but that formal educational opportunity is critical insofar as Canadian employers have come to emphasize academic credentials as indicators of suitability for employment. Educational institutions have come to serve as gatekeepers to "success"; the emphasis is, in effect, upon gate-keeping, rather than facilitating mobility. Significantly, where formal education may permit some mobility, it does not secure equal opportunity for all classes in Canada. Some working-class students make it through the schools and universities, but, generally, educational institutions have served the function of perpetuating the relative advantages of middle- and upper-class persons, ensuring that they will inherit the class standing of their fathers.

In work done for the Ontario Economic Council, Mehmet followed the 1974 body of full-time male students graduating in bachelor degree programs in Ontario universities. His analysis of parental tax support and differential student achievement suggests that the present university educational system in Ontario is regressive. Despite student aid for poorer students, children of high-status parents disproportionately win access to high-status educational streams, especially in law, dentistry, or medicine, "where the current selection procedures tend to favour student applicants from well-to-do families in general, and in particular from families in which the father himself is a lawyer, dentist, or physician." (Mehmet, 1978: 46.) He concludes that "the principal net gainers from the university system are the middle and upper-middle groups at the expense of the lower-income groups. In this sense the university system is a large public expenditure program in which the relatively poor group tend to subsidize the relatively rich." (Mehmet 1978: 45.)

When we examine the extent to which aspirations and expectations are in fact realized, we find success most probable among middle- and upper-class students. Note that this means that, while working-class students are less likely to have high aspirations in the first place, even given high aspirations, they are less apt to fulfil them.

For example, one of the few studies that followed up on reported aspirations by checking achievements was conducted in Manitoba. There it had been found that working-class students were less likely to aspire to university. In the follow-up it was found that only to a slight extent did more of the high-aspiration upper- and middle-class students go on to university than high-aspiration working-class students. Yet this was not a matter of comparable achievement. The researchers were of the view that the pool of high-aspiring working-class students was too small for a greater class distinction in achievement to show up. That is, the bulk of working-class students had already fallen out of the educational system, with the result that the few lower-class students remaining were something of an élite. (Siemens and Jackson, 1965: 18–19.)

Clearer findings are reported from a large research project under the direction of Bernard Blishen and John Porter. Students in Ontario were surveyed near the end of their Grade 12, in 1971, and then re-questioned more than a year later in the fall of 1972, by which time they should have completed Ontario Grade 13, the final year of high school. When they were re-contacted, it was found that of the 2,119 students reached, 59.9 percent had left school without completing Grade 13. (McRoberts, 1973: 6.) Not all of these entered the labour force. But, in the original survey in 1971, only 25 percent of the students had expected to enter the labour force, whereas by 1972, 47.7 percent had actually done so. Only 29.5 percent of the total follow-up sample had gone on to university, where in the original survey, 40 percent had expected to do so.

When these results were examined by social class, it was found that twice as great a proportion of middle- and upper-class students had entered university as had working-class students. (McRoberts, 1973: 33–34.) If we consider the structure of the Ontario high school system at the time of the research, we find that it consisted of four-year and five-year streams. The latter, since it included Grade 13, in fact constituted a "university-prep" within the high schools. Notably, there is a disproportionate class representation in each of the two streams. Middle- and upper-class students cluster in the five-year stream, to the extent of more than three quarters of the middle- and upper-class students, while working-class students are approximately evenly divided among the two streams. (McRoberts, 1973: 24; Porter, Porter, and Blishen, 1975: 58–60; Gilbert and McRoberts, 1974: 42.) The data are reported in Table 3-14.

The disproportionate class representation persists even when IQ is controlled. Although a relatively high number of working-class students of high IQ were in the five-year stream, at the same time, even upper- and middle-class students of low IQ were in the five-year program in high proportion. (McRoberts, 1973: 25.) (See Table 3-15.) Moreover, when it came to "cashing in on" the five-year program, even among the high IQ students, only 33.2 percent of lower-status students entered university (68.3 percent completed Grade 13), in contrast with 65.2 percent of upper- and middle-status students entering university (87.7 percent completed Grade 13). (McRoberts, 1973.)

Table 3-14: Student's Program by Father's Occupational Status*

				Status			
Program	I	II	III	IV	V	VI	Total
5 — year	86	83	74	69	51	51	65
4 — year	14	16	26	30	43	49	35
Number	(178)	(212)	(289)	(534)	(1,021)	(299)	(2,530)

* Source: Reprinted with the permission of B.R. Blishen and John Porter, from their study of Ontario High School Students.
Cited in: Gilbert and McRoberts, 1974; 1975.
Marion R. Porter, John Porter and Bernard R. Blishen, *Does Money Matter?*
Prospects for Higher Education: Toronto, Institute for Behavioural Research, York University, 1973. Reprinted with permission of Carleton University Press, Inc.

It should be remembered that we are not assuming IQ scores to be a literal measure of intelligence or an objective and valid measure of mental ability. As we have discussed, short of the extremes of genius and idiocy, IQ tests may better be considered a measure of social advantages and learned social responses appropriate to the middle-class schools of the

Table 3-15: Proportion of Ontario Grade 12 Respondents in Five-year Program, by Social Class and by IQ

Mental Ability	Class		
	Upper	Middle	Working
High	94.7	86.2	79.8
Moderate	79.4	79.8	56.6
Low	66.0	50.3	38.5

Source: McRoberts, Hugh A., ''Follow-up Grade 12 Students from the Blishen, Porter Study of Educational Aspirations.'' Ottawa: Department of Sociology and Anthropology, Carleton University, 1973.

dominant ethnic group. Thus such tests, by their nature, reduce the number of working-class students who score highly. However, the previous data demonstrate that even if working-class students manage to do well against the middle-class definition of intelligence, they are still relatively unlikely to go on to higher educational and occupational achievement. Such findings are indicative of the role of schools in the stratification system. Educational attainment is determined by family status. Occupational attainment is, in turn, determined by educational achievement. (Boyd et al., 1985.) In a simple sense, therefore, education is not so much a means to class mobility; rather, it mediates and reinforces family advantage. The consequence of the interaction between social class, home, school, aspirations, and achievement, is the retardation of working-class mobility and the maintenance of middle- and upper-class advantage.

By whatever the indicator, data suggest that children inherit the social classes of their families in Canada. Rather than overcoming such inheritance, the school system reinforces it. Given the existing environmental and educational restraints, the extent of working-class mobility is inevitably slight. For example, in his study of a working-class neighbourhood in Toronto, Crysdale found that very few children of manual workers improved upon their father's occupational status. He estimated that about two out of five may have jobs superior to their fathers', but these are usually still within the same social class level. Moreover, about the same number of sons actually occupied lower positions than their fathers, or were downwardly mobile. (Crysdale, 1968: 2.) In general, therefore, there was no class mobility; where there was improvement in occupational position across generations, it was not so much in terms of higher status jobs as in better wages, fringe benefits, and greater job security, while still at the level of manual occupations. (Crysdale, 1968: 296.)

Even where mobility occurs, for persons from the lower classes and economically deprived regions, there are traditional occupations that are reserved for working-class achievers. For example, teaching, social work, and particularly nursing have been defined as middle-class occupations offering opportunity to working-class persons. As such, they are viewed as the least desirable middle-class vocations for middle-class persons. Moreover, having taken up such professions, working-class persons are more apt to make careers of them, as opposed to leaving them after a brief time for improved positions. This pattern was demonstrated in a study of nursing careers in Halifax, where nurses of middle-class origins did not persist in their careers to the extent of their colleagues of working-class origins. (Hoare, 1969.)

Generally, therefore, success, even where it is attained by the person of working-class family, is limited. Relatively few persons escape their class of origin, and, when they do, it is characteristically by way of the less prestigious and less financially rewarding professions.

Conclusion

The key to whether a modern industrial society is open and extends opportunities for mobility sufficient to overcome ascribed social class membership is the educational system. If working-class persons are succeeding in schools and universities, we have indication of an open-class system. (Parkin, 1972: 111.) The educational system would then be functioning in keeping with the meritocratic ideal and an egalitarian ethic. But, in Canada, the educational system has not been working in such a fashion. By region, by ethnic group, and by social class, the probability of academic success and occupational entrée are unequal. Upper- and middle-class students are permitted to meet the meritocratic definition of equal competition; working-class students are not.

The remarkable and rare entrepreneur aside, occupational success has increasingly become dependent upon educational screening. Education was to have been the means of overcoming the inheritance of social class. However, as presently constituted, the educational system favours the already privileged, and screens out the already disadvantaged. Rather than defeating stratification, formal education is a cause of persisting and increasingly rigid stratification. Especially as educational systems are élitist, stressing narrow criteria of performance, and, in particular, limiting access to universities, it is inevitable that education will serve more to maintain social class advantage than to overcome stratification. The existing educational system and the class system are inextricably intertwined and mutually reinforcing. As educational institutions have expanded, the benefits have not so much reached the working class as benefitted the middle class. One is given no choice but to "make it" in the school system if one is to secure superior status. But as the means to meritocratic egalitarianism, educational organization has acted to secure meritocracy for the meritocrats, or middle-class status for the middle-class.

CHAPTER 4

Class, Life Style, and Behaviour

Class as Reality

Whatever the inadequacies of measurement, it is clear that social classes are not mere artefacts of definition. They are real and integral aspects of Canadian society. Intrinsically economic, they are meshed with sexual, ethnic, and regional differentiation. The classes that exist in Canada may be estimated by resorting to information on the labour force or education such as we have been doing, although it must be recalled that such data do not fully express the extent of poverty or the magnitude of inherited corporate wealth. However, these data do reflect the relative economic advantages in Canadian society, in that educational qualifications and occupational roles have been associated with varying levels of economic return. Such economic acquisition is translated into degrees of prestige and power, but is no less fundamentally economic for that.

The essential reality of class consists not merely of existence, but also of persistence. The advantages of one generation are passed to the next, and wealth and power are consolidated. This is particularly so of the closed upper class of owners, persons who maintain control of major industrial resources and corporate wealth, including Canada's major financial institutions. This economic élite has become increasingly impenetrable. But we have stressed rather more the inheritance of middle-class advantage, for this is a more salient, if no more important, dimension of stratification for the majority of Canadians. The élite may be closed to the aspirant to mobility, but so, too, is the middle class of professional and managerial occupations and remuneration increasingly closed to working-class mobility. Especially instrumental in this regard is the educational system. To a large extent the upper-class child may be safely indifferent to formal academic credentials, for his career, wealth, and security are ensured by virtue of the family's ownership of industrial property and massive capital accumulation. But the non-propertied person lacking inherited wealth depends upon a professional or white-collar career, the bases of which are educational credentials. Education secures and maintains a middle-class occupation, including middle-class position better than one's parents.

The working-class individual, we have seen, tends to be unable to compete for educational certification and middle-class occupational standing. Just as the middle-class person tends to be incapable of achieving upper-class status because of the enormity of inherited relative disadvantage, so too, in structural position and learned skills, is the working-class individual unable to overtake the inherited advantage of the middle class. Sheer economic difficulties and learned attitudes militate against successful competition in middle-class-dominated educational institutions and career sectors. Thus, inherited wealth and learning opportunities secure the perpetuation of social class. Classes do not consist of individuals differentially achieving on the basis of ability, but of individuals inheriting the advantages or disadvantages of their parents before them.

Canada, we are told, is an affluent society. Most people reading these remarks are likely to be of the privileged middle class and in quest of a credit against the requisite university degree. We would share a relative satisfaction with our life styles and prospects, and some pride in our society. We would perhaps take satisfaction in the conviction that no one starves to death or dies of untreated disease in Canada. But unfortunately such a conviction, although literally correct, would require qualification. Even in terms of such fundamentals as food and health care, class in Canada is not just a matter of some people having too much and others too little.

The ''welfare state'' secures basic sustenance, shelter, medical care, and a measure of security for all Canadians, administrative malpractice aside. But this is by no means the same as all Canadians being well fed and adequately nourished, well and adequately sheltered, or well and adequately cared for medically. Nothing could be less true. And, even if it were, as we shall take up in Chapter 5, the existence of welfare programs in conjunction with the existence of class structure both concedes and contributes to the greater rigidity of that class structure, however humane such welfare programs might be.

Quality of Life

i. Health Care

It is readily apparent that some Canadians spend virtually all their income in order to secure food, clothing, and residence, while others have an income large enough to enable them to consume a massive volume of luxury items. In Chapter 2 we noted definitions of poverty that were dependent upon income level and proportion of income available for non-necessities. Canadians who exist at or near the subsistence level as defined in our society may be markedly richer than people in many nations, but they are no less deprived in contrast to their more privileged fellow citizens, or deprived in relation to some national ideal.

A fundamental indicator of class disparity is quality of health care. The poor eat less nutritious foods and are not as well cared for, medically. In 1969 Antoine Paquin worked in a lower-class area of Montreal. Among the 222 elementary school children he studied he found alarming indications of malnutrition and its consequences. Of the children, 21.3 percent were inadequately nourished, 22 percent underdeveloped in weight and height, 27.5 percent retarded in physical-mental coordination, 39.11 percent had a history of diabetes in the family, and 20 percent a family history of tuberculosis. (National Council of Welfare, March 1975: 11–12.) In 1971, other research in eight schools in working-class areas of Montreal found ''more than half of the 3,424 children examined to be physically ill. More than 10 percent were so ill that they required hospitalization.'' (National Council of Welfare, March 1975: 12.)

Medical treatment is guaranteed to Canadians under provincially administered health care programs. Yet medical and hospital facilities are still not equally available to all Canadians. Nor are rehabilitative aids and programs, or drugs. The latter, in particular, are not covered by government insurance programs except under stringent welfare conditions, a deficiency particularly to the handicap of the working poor and the aged. For the poor — especially the rural poor — seemingly minor factors such as cost and difficulty of transportation, or time lost from work, in order to reach physicians, hospitals, rehabilitative centres, or pharmacists, are significant deterrents.

Generally there is sufficient reluctance and difficulty amongst the poor in obtaining quality health care that middle- and upper-class persons actually utilize medical facilities and services to a greater extent than do working-class persons. Not only will the upper classes more often seek and receive medical attention by virtue of attitude and access, they are more often able to secure specialized medical treatment. Ultimately, combined with poorer nutrition and poorer working and residential conditions, a consequence for lower-income Canadians is a more uncomfortable and often painful existence, and earlier deaths.

Data from Ontario and Saskatchewan indicate that, with medicare, working-class persons use hospitals more than do higher-income-class persons. The latter, however, make more use of visits to the offices of physicians. (Manga, 1978; Beck, Horne, 1976.) Overall, upper-class persons receive greater medical assistance, as they are more apt to secure specialized and higher-cost medical treatment. (Beck and Horne, 1976; Manga, 1978.)

Similarly, dental treatment is not universally available in Canada. Access to dental care and to quality treatment increases drastically with the class level of Canadians. Class variation in dental care is especially pronounced in the absence of any comparable program of dental insurance and the very high cost of dental treatment.

Table 4-1: Average Family Medical Benefits in Ontario by Income Class, 1974

	Income Class				
Average dollar benefits	$0-3,399	$4,000-7,999	$8,000-13,999	$14,000-19,999	$20,000+
	$159,37	$145.93	$202.07	$257.01	$253.79

Adapted from: P. Manga (1978) 139.

We know generally that health care is *not* available equally to all Canadians, despite state-administered "insurance." Even the cost of the "insurance" is lower to the more privileged. Premiums in Ontario, for example, are demonstrably regressive in that, for example, a family with an income of $14,000 pays as high a premium as a family with an income of $50,000. Moreover, Canadians with higher incomes tend to benefit from significant employer contributions to the cost of premiums. (National Council of Welfare, 1982: 43–45.) A similar pattern emerges in most of Canada's other provincial jurisdictions. In part because of the prevailing notion of medical entrepreneurship and careerism that brings physicians disproportionately to cities, and the limited encouragement for medical practitioners in rural or frontier regions, urban middle- and upper-class residents receive superior care. To a degree comparable only to lawyers, Canadian physicians are allowed almost unfettered control over the sale of their services — controlling entry into the profession and the content of training, setting standards of conduct, and, through "over-billing", controlling even the price of their labour, despite health insurance medical scales. The state does not direct the location of qualified personnel, nor the volume of patients "treated" by physicians. In this medical system of laissez-faire, the bulk of medical personnel locate in lucrative urban markets. The skilled personnel are in the cities, as are the quality facilities. Consequently, rural residents and native peoples suffer from high rates of infectious diseases and less adequate treatment, as do working-class persons in cities. Dental care is similarly affected. These variations relate to the regional and the rural-urban differences that we have previously outlined. There are far more doctors and dentists, for example, in urban areas. By major region, British Columbia and Ontario have the greatest number of physicians and dentists relative to their population, while the Maritimes (Nova Scotia excepted) and the Yukon and Northwest Territories are least well served. Also poorly served is Saskatchewan, still largely a rural province and perhaps also still suffering the effects of a medical exodus in the 1960s, a topic we shall take up in Chapter 5. Overall, the industrialized and prosperous regions of Canada have the bulk of the medically-qualified personnel. Similarly, when we examine individual expenses for dental services, we find the greater expenditures in the economically developed regions of Canada, reflecting in part the higher costs of such services, but, more basically, the more frequent utilization of dentists. Noteworthy is the stability of relative expenditures over the decade from 1961 to 1971 (Table 4-2).

The availability of medical and dental treatment is not merely a matter of the number or accessibilty of physicians and dentists. Also pertinent is the availability of specialized medical skills. Here the advantage is to the urban industrialized regions of Canada. (Rosenberg, 1979; 1983.) A medical or dental career is most lucrative in the cities, as well as more prestigious within the professions. That alone would serve to attract specialists. But, in addition, specialization requires a considerable population and elaborate facilities, including instructors; for the latter, the teaching hospitals of the large metropolitan centres are vital.

Table 4-2: **Expenditure per Person on Dentists' Services**[1]

Canada	1961	1966	1971
	6.39	7.02	8.07
Newfoundland	1.98	2.20	2.79
Prince Edward Island	3.93	4.43	4.70
Nova Scotia	3.48	4.59	4.66
New Brunswick	3.43	3.69	4.21
Quebec	3.97	4.61	5.08
Ontario	8.55	9.36	10.70
Manitoba	6.65	6.26	7.58
Saskatchewan	5.27	5.49	5.36
Alberta	7.00	7.88	8.97
British Columbia	9.85	9.87	11.70

[1]Annual expenditure in constant 1961 dollars.
Source: *Perspective Canada*, 1974: 57, Table 3.36.
Reproduced by permission of the Minister of Supply and Services Canada.

Medical care may be guaranteed to all Canadians, but ease and promptness of treatment, and expertise, are not equally guaranteed. The regional distribution of skilled personnel and the varying attitudes of the members of the social classes make for a disparity of health care services.

Another important feature of health care services in a class society is the patient's dependence upon the physician. In the most general sense, a patient has no check, no warranty, no means of "quality control" over a physician's services. Particularly among the under-educated lower class, there is little inclination or encouragement for checking into medical services. Where there is apparent abuse, the recourse to civil suit is unlikely, even for more prosperous Canadians. A medical professor, T. David Marshal, argued at a meeting of the College of Family Physicians of Canada, that it is all but impossible to win a malpractice suit in Canada. In part, he suggests, this may be because of the class affinity of trial judges and doctors when a suit actually comes to court, as well as the high cost of court proceedings. (*The Gazette*, September 18, 1978, p. 5.)

Table 4-3: Patients per Doctor, 1981

Canada	646
Newfoundland	853
Prince Edward Island	844
Nova Scotia	673
New Brunswick	958
Quebec	619
Ontario	626
Manitoba	660
Saskatchewan	
Alberta	765
British Columbia	558
Yukon	768
Northwest Territories	1,097

Source: *The Sunday Star*, November 15, 1981 and Mr. Robert Croft.

To some degree, the differential access to quality health care is reinforced in such aspects of the legal system as the unlikehood of winning malpractice suits. Inequality is also attributable in some instances to corporate and government negligence or indifference. For example, failure to respond promptly to threats of mercury poisoning among the Indian population, or of lung disease among miners, illustrates social-class disadvantage in which corporations and government share a responsibility. A well-documented example is to be had in Elliot Leyton's moving account of the incidence of silicosis and lung cancer among the fluorspar miners of St. Lawrence and Lawn in Newfoundland. Leyton's account starkly portrays the agony of working-class employees, the miners, who not only suffered agonizing and early deaths, but also the cover-ups and opposition of government and corporate authorities in apparent collusion. Their ''dying hard'' was the outcome of an industrial system quite literally exploiting its working-class employees to the point of death. By Leyton's estimate, since the mines opened in 1937, at least one hundred men have died as a direct consequence of the exposure to silica and radiation, and another hundred are dying. ''One household in every three has a dead or dying miner in the towns of St. Lawrence and Lawn.'' (Leyton, 1975: 11.)

Of Canada's population, the native peoples suffer more than any other group from disease, poor nutrition, and inadequate health care. A good

Table 4-4: Mortality

Age	Indian	Non-Indian
1–4 years	3.1	0.8
5–19 years	1.9	0.7
20–44 years	6.0	1.5
45–64 years	15.7	9.0
85 + years	57.0	55.0

Deaths per 1,000 population in each age group 1973–76 average.
Source: *The Sunday Star*, September 25, 1982.

indicator of relative advantage is the rate of infant mortality. Over the previous six decades, the populations of Ontario and the Western provinces have enjoyed higher life expectancies at birth than the Canadian average. In contrast, Quebec and the Atlantic provinces have been characterized by life expectancies below the national average. (The exceptions are the men of Newfoundland and the men and women of Prince Edward Island.) (Nagnur, 1982: 19.) For Canada as a whole, the infant mortality rate in the years 1961–1963 was 28.6 deaths per 1,000 population. For native Indians the rate was 65.5 per 1,000, and for the Inuit the rate was 178.9. (Canada, 1965: 52.) Despite steady improvements, disparities persisted in the 1970s, especially for the Inuit. Or, if we take the incidence of tuberculosis as our indicator of quality of life and health care, we find enormous variations. The Inuit, in 1971, suffered a rate of tuberculosis approximately 30 times as high as non-native peoples, and Indians a rate approximately 7 times as high. Incredible as these statistics are, they are down sharply from the rates of 1965, when the Inuit rate of tuberculosis per 100,000 population was 846 as contrasted with the total Canadian rate of 25 (Table 4-5).

Table 4-5: Tuberculosis among Inuit, Registered Indians, and other Canadians

	Total Canada	Inuit	Indian	Other
	— Rate per 1,000 Population —			
1965	25	846	163	22
1966	23	882	181	20
1967	23	1,020	161	20
1968	22	810	177	21
1969	21	1,093	166	18
1970	18	672	125	16
1971	18	496	122	17

Source: *Perspective Canada*, 1974: 43, Table 3:14.
Reproduced by permission of the Minister of Supply and Services Canada.

Periodically, an incident comes to light that illustrates a basic prejudice that exacerbates poor health care for native persons. An appalling instance of ethnic- and class-related arrogance and disregard occurred recently in Manitoba. A native Indian woman admitted to St. Boniface General Hospital (Winnipeg) for exploratory surgery, awoke from her operation to the realization that the surgeon had strung her sutures with approximately 30 beads. The woman said: "The doctor played with my body. Nurses laughed at me. When I went down for x-rays, everybody wanted to see what the doctor did to me and laughed." She went on to explain her frightening helplessness and her frustration at being "in such a big place with so many white people who laughed at you." And she speculated: "If they could do that to me, what could they do to little Indian children who couldn't speak for themselves?" (The Canadian Press, December 10, 1980.) Another example documented in a federal government enquiry into circumstances in Alert Bay, a town in northeastern Vancouver Island, highlights the class-related discrepancy in health care available to Canadians. The report documented a record of drunkenness and incompetent performance of medical routine by the town's only physician, as well as at least one and probably three deaths as a consequence. Although a jury at the inquest found the physician negligent in the death of one 11-year old Indian girl who died of a ruptured appendix, he was cleared by the College of Physicians and Surgeons. The federal government report later concluded that the College was more intent upon protecting its members than in protecting the public. (The Canadian Press, April 27, 1980.)

Interacting with health care attitudes and accessibility to physicians are the environmental effects of work and home. Working-class persons generally suffer reduced health and longevity. Community health research conducted by Montreal General Hospital that surveyed 200,000 people in Montreal found clear indication of poor health, greater anxiety, and shorter lives among lower-income residents of Montreal in contrast to upper-income persons. The working-class neighbourhood of St. Henri revealed a life expectation of 66 years, while in upper-class Westmount the life expectancy was 76 years. Also reflecting environment, heart disease and cancer were much higher in St. Henri and another working-class neighbourhood, St. Louis-du-Parc. (The Canadian Press, June 3, 1985.)

ii. Basic Expenditures

In addition to physical health, there are other indicators of the differential well-being of Canadians. The extreme illustration is once again the plight of Canada's native peoples. In part reflecting mental health as a function of quality of environment, but also specifically relating to environmental conditions themselves, native Indians are more apt than other Canadians to die a violent death. (See Figure 4-1.)

Figure 4-1 Violent Deaths per 100,000 Population

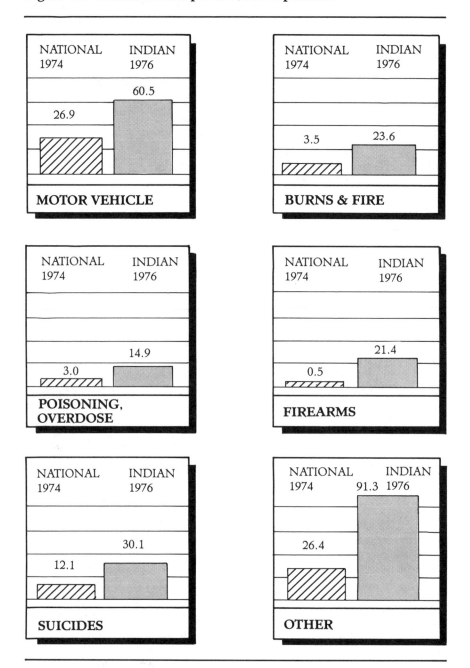

Source: Communications Branch, Indian and Northern Affairs Canada.

Looking at the overall Canadian population, regional variation in the quality of shelter is a factor that we know to be related to social class. For example, in 1968, the percentage of homes with flush toilets, including those shared with other families, was 84.4 percent for those with household average incomes of under $1,000 per annum, as contrasted to the national average of 94.3 percent. Also, for this same low-income group, the incidence of central heating by furnace was 63.7 percent, while the national average was 76.9 percent. What is not apparent in these figures is that lower-income homes are also older, and they are more crowded. (Canada, 1968: 42.) Thus, added to sheer income deprivation are tangible and fundamental differences in the quality of life, in terms of facilities that middle-class Canadians take for granted and that we would expect to be universal in an affluent welfare state.

Table 4-6: Some Living Standard Measures in the Atlantic Provinces and in Quebec

	Atlantic Provinces		Québec	
	1971	1979	1971	1979
GDP per capita (71 constant dollars)	2,465	3,121	3,304	4,338
	1971	1976	1971	1976
Persons per housing unit	3.9	3.5	3.6	3.1
% of Households with:	1970	1980	1970	1980
Electric Refrigerators	92.8	98.9	99.6	99.9
Automatic Washing Machines	26.3	54.6	45.6	74.2
Automobiles	70.6	76.9	72.2	77.2
Telephones	84.1	89.0	94.5	97.9
Television Sets	94.0	98.1	97.7	98.6

Source: Bank of Montreal *Business Review*, December 1981.

When we go on to consider non-subsistence items, such as eating in restaurants, the consumption of wine, and the enjoyment of travel, art, and entertainment, the differences in Canadian life style are, of course, magnified. Naturally, the expenditure and consumption related to such commodities increases with income level. (*Perspective Canada*, 1974:10.)

Regional variations in family consumption are also evident. The amount of disposable income varies by region, demonstrating the previously-remarked pattern of greater income in urban areas and in industrialized provinces such as Ontario. The great contrast is with the Maritimes, as we have already seen in connection with other criteria. It should be additionally noted that this greater non-subsistence spending also means greater spending on security-related items, such as supplementary health care insurance, dental insurance, life insurance, and pension plans. The purchase of such security is a basic advantage of well-to-do Canadians, and often is a routine "fringe benefit" of employment and not a cost against salary.

We need not be too literal in examining such expenditures. Volume of consumption is not synonymous with quality of life or some concept of "happiness." But to the extent that there are systematic regional and class differences in non-subsistence disposal incomes, we may reasonably infer that some Canadians are better able to enjoy and to fulfil their lives than others.

The two basic material items against which quality of life may be estimated are housing and food. We have already seen some data indicating that the facilities and the quality of housing are markedly variable, as we all know from our own personal observation. Whether renting or owning, housing is the major expenditure of the poor. It must be noted also that home ownership is class-related. In rural areas, most people, whatever their income class, own a home. In 1969, 79.2 percent of the rural poor owned a house, as against the general proportion of 81.0 percent. But amongst the urban poor, the ratio begins to sharply decline. The overall rate in 1969 was 53 percent, and for the lowest income quantile, 37.6 percent. In Canada's eleven largest cities, home ownership in the lowest income quantile was only 23.6 percent. (National Council of Welfare, April, 1974: 18.) In general, the poor spend a larger proportion of their incomes on housing, and receive in return poorer housing, than do middle-class Canadians.

Table 4-7: Number and Percentage of Home-Owner Families Living Alone and Paying 35 percent or more of their Income on Shelter. (Showing Average Family Income, Canada, 1981)

Type of Family	Number paying 35% or more of their income on shelter	Percentage paying 35% or more of their income on shelter	Average Family Income $
Husband-wife with Children	246,780	10.0	33,154
Husband-Wife Empty-Nest	45,845	6.5	23,486
Male Lone-Parent	6,675	13.3	26,892
All Families	389,480	10.1	30,325

Source: Canada, April 1984. Reproduced by permission of the Minister of Supply and Services Canada.

Table 4-8: Number and Percentage of Renter Families Living Alone and Paying 35 percent or more of their Income on Shelter. (Showing Average Family Income, Canada, 1971 and 1981)

Type of Family	Number paying 35% or more of their income on shelter		Percentage paying 35% or more of their income on shelter		Average Family Income $	
	1971	1981	1971	1981	1971	1981
Husband-wife with Children	84,445	94,380	9.9	14.4	8,956	22,560
Husband-Wife Empty-Nest	28,925	36,950	19.0	16.1	7,861	19,604
Male Lone-Parent	30,220	5,970	9.3	20.0	9,635	20,577
Female Lone-Parent	69,790	132,775	47.6	49.2	4,815	10,741
All Families	217,335	315,890	14.5	19.8	8,570	20,243

Source: Canada, April 1984. Reproduced by permission of the Minister of Supply and Services Canada.

The poor in Canada are obliged to live in sub-standard housing, often paying exorbitant rents. The amount of public, rent-controlled housing available for the poor is utterly inadequate. In 1985, in Toronto, a three-year wait was estimated for applicants to subsidized housing. (June 17, 1985.)

Senior Canadians are a major element of Canada's impoverished population. A recent survey by the National Council of Welfare suggests that the pension income of 27 percent of the aged population of Ontario is below $7,200. Sixty-one percent of seniors receive less than $12,000 per annum. (*The Toronto Star*, June 18, 1984.) In the absence of adequate state-supported residence or nursing homes, merely finding affordable housing is increasingly beyond the means of many elderly Canadians.

Similarly, food is the second major household expense, and again the poor must spend a greater proportion of their incomes and, in many instances, even pay more for items of the same or lesser quality as contrasted to middle-class costs. This is true also of expenditures on clothing and household items generally, especially durables. The poor rarely have the option of shopping around. They often purchase items, especially food, in low-volume stores with high costs. Suburban stores are not accessible to them, and that is where the major chains locate. Because of their inability to pay cash for major purchases, i.e., refrigerators, television sets, or

Table 4-9: Ranked-Order Average Monthly Shelter Costs for Home-owner and Renter Families Living Alone, Canada, 1981

Average Monthly Shelter Cost $	Type of Tenure and Type of Family		
443	Owner	Husband-Wife	Childless
426	Owner	Husband-Wife	With Children
348	Owner	Male Lone-Parent	
331	Renter	Husband-Wife	With Children
325	Renter	Male Lone-Parent	
312	Renter	Husband-Wife	Childless
309	Owner	Female Lone-Parent	
306	Renter	Husband-Wife	Empty Nest
287	Renter	Female Lone-Parent	
225	Owner	Husband-Wife	Empty Nest

Note: Owner's shelter cost includes mortgage payment (principal and interest), taxes, utilities, fuel, and municipal services.
Renter's shelter cost (gross rent) includes cash rent, utilities, fuel, and municipal services. It should be kept in mind that some part of owners' shelter costs may be considered investment.
Source: Canada, April 1984.

automobiles, the poor must pay a price which is inflated through interest charges. Even utilities may cost more. "Because they are judged to be higher credit risks, security deposits of varying amounts are required from the poor as a matter of routine by telephone, gas, and electricity companies." (National Council of Welfare April, 1974: 38.)

In such a situation of high dependency upon local merchants and lenders, and spending as they do a much higher proportion of their incomes upon staples, the poor are far more vulnerable to inflation. Over the last decade of drastically rising costs, the major components have been housing and food. Obviously these are necessities that no one can forego. Hence, the low-income Canadian is directly penalized with each and every rise in price, without the protection enjoyed by the middle class, with their higher incomes, and their ability to save by comparison and volume shopping, and by paying in cash. (National Council of Welfare, April, 1974: 10–17.)

iii. Work

Variations in quality of life are not only detectable at the level of distribution and consumption. It must also be recognized that the quality of work-life differs fundamentally from class to class in stratified societies. As a general rule, it may be noted that within the range of working-class occupations, work is boring and beyond the control of the worker. It is also often dangerous and demeaning. In upper-middle-class professional occupations there is a measure of control over one's work, and a lack of the merely routine. There may also be a pleasant working environment.

From time to time, we conjure up an image of Dickensian England and the industrial horrors of unbridled capitalist exploitation. Clearly, Canadian industrial capitalism, restrained by law, and by trade unions, is more "civilized" than this. Yet the infamous "sweatshops" of the 19th and early 20th century industrial nation may yet live on in the Canada of the 1980s. In her book *The Seam Allowance*, Laura Johnson (1982) estimates that in several thousand immigrant homes one may find workers, usually women, making garments for "as little as $1.00 a piece." One may choose to see such a vast network of para-industrial labour as "mere" exploitation. But there are less equivocal horrors that derive from industrial exploitation and irresponsibility as, for example, when safety standards supposedly imposed and monitored by the state are patently inadequate, or are ignored with scant, if any, penalty. A New Democratic Party report estimates that half a million Canadians formally subject to the Canada Labour Code work in unsafe and unhealthy conditions. (The Canadian Press, 1982.)

In Canada, the number of work-related injuries per 100 workers actually appears to be on the increase rather than in decline. For example, in Quebec in 1977, 245 persons died in industrial accidents. Another 155,000 were injured and required time off work. (*The Gazette*, October 24, 1978.) Speculating that injuries are under-reported by 24–30 percent, Statistics Canada reports a rate of 10.22 injuries per 100 workers in 1969, and 10.57 in 1977. (*Perspective Canada III*, 1980: 68.) The frequency calculated on the number of disabling injuries per 100,000,000 hours worked (each worker is estimated at 2,000 hours working time per year) increased from 18.69 in 1969 to 24.30 in 1977. In terms of the number of persons, this translates into 289,841 disabling injuries in 1969, including 1,000 fatal injuries and 476,187 disabling injuries, including 819 deaths, in 1977. The number of non-disabling injuries increased from 504,587 in 1969 to 559,900 in 1977. (*Perspective Canada III*, 1980: 68.)

Such statistics are rendered more meaningful if we consider real examples of maiming or death. In Brandon, Manitoba, recently, a woman lost eight of her fingers in an industrial accident demonstrated in court to have been caused by the employer's failure to provide safety equipment for a machine being operated by the new employee, who had received scant minutes of training. In provincial court, the company was fined $500.00. (The Canadian Press, October 9, 1980.)

Martin O'Malley published a column in the *The Sunday Star* that was revealing of indifference to industrial danger, and illustrated the nature of worker risks. He described an inquest ignored by other reporters whose newspapers were uninterested in routine "industrials." A worker, badly mauled, had "died of asphyxiation and strangulation in the 'grinding room' at the Toronto Brick Company." (1980: 4.) The worker was a Greek immigrant, typical of those who man the unpleasant and often unsafe jobs of industrial Canada. The victim had fallen into a conveyor belt and had been pulled into the roller. Despite the Industrial Safety Act, the roller was not guarded or screened — until after the death.

Such industrial accidents are not part of a public consciousness, and not part of the approved calculus of state policy or propaganda. Thousands of Canadian workers are living out shortened lives and painful illnesses because of their job conditions, and, it would seem, because of incompetence and/or the willful negligence and disregard of employers and the state. The state has intervened in legislation and inspection, even with advertisements, but the intervention is sporadic and perfunctory, and the penalties trivial. Similarly, the media do not ferret out or emphasize the tragedies of industrial damage, in contrast to their attention to more sensational news content such as crime.

Industrial accidents are only part of the story. A related feature of the working-class work place is the high risk of industrial disease, a persisting manifestation of stratified industrial Canada. Although compensation boards acting for corporations and the state tend not to recognize the full extent of such human costs, as Leyton (1975) so poignantly demonstrates in *Dying Hard*, there is every reason to believe that the incidence of industrial accident and disease is massive.

We previously indicated the example of the fluorspar miners of Newfoundland, subject to hazardous levels of fibre and dying agonizing and impoverished deaths from cancer. (Leyton, 1975.) Throughout history, mining has been a notoriously hazardous and unpleasant occupation, and it is remarkable that it remains so today in Canada despite technological advances and protective legislation. One of Leyton's miners, fifty years old, dying of lung cancer and denied compensation, describes his "dying hard":

> "The Doctor said it's good for a little while yet, not too long. I figured then he only gave me a year. But I knows I'm getting worse. I can tell meself, with the breath, and the pains I has now. I has pains through the chest I never has before. And spitting up this blood, and this burning there in my stomach. And I don't have to walk at all, just lay down on the bed — and this'll grab me like cutting off the breath." (Leyton, 1975: 96.)

Probably the most significant Canadian example of industrial disease is cancer, such as the lung cancer that afflicts asbestos miners. (Montero, 1979: 227–248.) Research done in the 1970s offers the estimate that 60 percent of the asbestos miners at Thetford Mines, Quebec, those working 20 years or more, have defective lungs. The same x-ray data, when interpreted by another expert, put the estimate as high as 84 percent. (Tataryn, 1979: 36.) In Quebec, the asbestos companies "had maintained a policy of not telling workers they were suffering from asbestos-related diseases until the men became physically disabled." (Tataryn, 1979: 29.) In 1975 an 8-month strike occurred at Thetford Mines, not over salary, but over this health issue. The miners were striking in order to win effective dust control — operational measures long in place in mines owned by the same firm in other national jurisdictions, such as West Germany. (Tataryn, 1979: 53–54.) A tacit collusion of corporate and state indifference or ignorance had created a situation where Canadian workers were simply treated as expendable.

Similar health costs are found in other areas of Canada. Elliot Lake (Ontario) uranium workers have a high incidence of dust-induced lung cancer, by one estimate a rate three times the national average. (The Canadian Press, 1982.) So, too, Yellowknife (NWT) gold miners, who suffer arsenic poisoning and consequent cancer. In this latter instance, as in others, the victims are native people, an ethnic minority generally characterized by a degraded position in Canadian society. Another report, released by the Manitoba Federation of Labour, estimated that 350 workers die annually in the province from job-related cancer. (The Canadian Press, September 5, 1980.) A similar estimate was made by the director of the Saskatchewan government health and safety branch, suggesting that at least 25 percent of all cancer cases were work-related. (The Canadian Press, September 5, 1980.)

The inventory of blatant industrial diseases is considerable. Coal miners suffer from "black lung," textile workers from "brown lung," miners, factory workers, and shipyard workers die from asbestosis, while other factory workers, for example in automobile plants, suffer gas and fume poisoning and high noise levels, not to speak of limbs damaged or severed in industrial accidents. (Levinson, 1974: 77–78.)

Industrial production has also created vast quantities of noxious waste and pollutants that eventually harm persons other than a plant's own employees. In contrast to free-booting 19th century capitalism, there are today some restrictions imposed and enforced by state regulatory agencies. But state action to eliminate or regulate undesirable industrial by-products seems inconsistent and flimsy. Daily, we read of carcinogenic substances or industrial pollutants such as acid rain, by-products that corporations produce in disregard of legislation. The state and agencies such as the courts create an illusion of control; in 1985, several accidents involving PCB spills on public highways raised the question of adequate restrictions and penalties.

Noxious industrial substances affect workers in the first instance. They also affect workers' families, and entire communities. The incidence of death from cancer, for example, increases in areas of extractive industrial concentration. Major metropolitan areas such as Toronto and Hamilton have high rates, as do areas in northern Ontario and Quebec where environmental pollutants have concentrated. Similarly, the area around Halifax and much of Cape Breton in Nova Scotia have high rates.

The costs of industrial negligence and ignorance tend to be borne disproportionately by the more vulnerable working class. They are vulnerable because of exposure, and also because of less adequate nutrition and medical treatment. Generally, if one considers the relationship of social class to health, the negative consequence is inescapable. Put simply, "the poor die younger." A recent federal government report indicates that Canadian males in the lowest income quintile will die an average of six years earlier than those in the highest income group, while for women, the loss of life duration was approximately 3 years. (The Canadian Press, February 28, 1981.)

There are also diverse emotional consequences of work. Job satisfaction varies enormously with social class. Even where the working class task is physically satisfactory so far as working hours and environment are concerned, there is some probability that the job will be tedious, boring, and depressing. In most working-class jobs there is little discretion or job control. Close supervision will be stressed, and frequent inspections or threat of suspensions, rather than worker responsibility. Such has been a feature, for example, of the working conditions of the inside workers of the Canada Post Corporation. In most working-class jobs, it is difficult or impossible to control the pace of work, or to establish one's own agenda or timing, especially as technology is introduced to set the pace. In contrast to professional, middle-class jobs, workers are subject to mechanical and management imperatives. In the workplace, industrial employees are themselves "treated like a machine" (Levinson, 1974: 59) rather than like a person, are assumed to be irresponsible and uncaring, an assumption that comes to be self-fulfilling. Faced with dead-end, boring, and essentially non-responsible job assignments, workers may respond with pranks, on-the-job boredom-breaking games and fantasies, and petty sabotage. Other behavioural symptoms of unsatisfactory work include depression, insomnia, poor appetite, and alcoholism. (Horn, 1975: 92.) Describing the Lordstown, Ohio, General Motors Corporation plant, where every 36 seconds a worker must complete his assigned tasks as 101 cars come down the line every hour, Garson describes the sheer anomie of frustrated workers who must perform a pedestrian work routine without any control over work content or pace. (Aronowitz, 1974: 21–50; Garson, 1977: XII; 86–89.) Such frustrating and mindless employment is widespread. The working man's pleasure, beer, is itself produced at some cost to brewery employees. Adams writes of working in a Winnipeg brewery, amid noisy, "clanking" conveyor belts, the screaming foreman, the imperious line, the harried workers filling the cartons, a case every six seconds. (Adams, 1973: 27–29.) Working-class jobs, therefore, even if not dangerous, are often quite simply defeating, with the worker literally alienated from his or her product.

A related workplace practice is the deliberate theft of labour. An example from the United States may serve. In 1979, the United Auto Workers confronted General Motors with the charge that the Chevrolet plant in Flint, Michigan, had deliberately managed to build up to 1,600 trucks with unpaid labour. The superintendent's office contained an electrical switch that governed the speed of the assembly line. Assembly-line speed is specified by collective agreement, relating production to the number of employees. To evade this constraint, superintendents at the plant had for a period of about six months been increasing the speed of the line for twenty or twenty-five minutes in a nine-hour shift, thereby effecting the increased production. (American Press, 1979.)

Similar exploitation has occurred elsewhere in the auto industry and in other assembly-line industries, where the pace of the line and the trivial character of the task have induced enormous worker alienation. There are some imperfect data on work satisfaction. They indicate that the least satisfied workers are the semi-skilled and unskilled manual workers, and, thereafter, semi- and unskilled white-collar workers. Conversely, the most satisfied were managerial and professional employees, followed by the skilled blue-collar workers. Both these latter occupational groups enjoy a large measure of job control or autonomy, whereas unskilled and clerical workers have scant job discretion. (*Perspective Canada III*, 1980: 279; 289.) There are variations in income benefit and physical and psychological satisfaction, therefore, that relate to social class location. Unskilled workers, white-collar workers, skilled workers, professional and managerial employees in ascending order, approximately reflect in job satisfaction the relative disadvantages experienced by Canadians in the subordinate social classes.

Danger, injury, and illness are only the more tangible physical disadvantages of the occupational labour force in a class society. Most jobs are also boring and alienating, with workers putting in time without deriving any intrinsic satisfaction from their work. For this reason, Rinehart speaks of work as a ''social problem.'' (Rinehart, 1975: 2–6.) When alienation and subordination to often arbitrary authority is added to a physically unpleasant or unhealthy working environment, one finds as characteristic of modern class societies a fundamental inequity in the quality of working-class life as contrasted to that of owners, high-ranking managers, and self-employed professionals.

Class and Criminal Deviance

If working-class persons are socialized so as to expect to have consumer items of a given quantity, and then the means to the acquisition of such items are inadequate, then it is not remarkable to find them violating social expectations of behaviour, including those legally defined. Deprived persons might, for example, decide not to work at all, because work fails to gain them any advantages. Or they might go through the paces, in a sense, working to rule or to a minimum acceptable rate. Conceivably, too, they might resort to illegal means to acquire desired benefits. Many years ago, Robert K. Merton suggested that where the learned goals in a society exceeded the legitimate means of achievement for individuals or groups of individuals, people might retreat or withdraw, conform in a ritual-like manner, rebel against the system, or resort to deviant or non-legitimate means. (Merton, 1957.)

There is no clear evidence suggesting which of these is more probable. In fact, one might question whether the key assumption of learned goals is characteristically operative if we are thinking of working-class persons; rather, the ''culture of poverty'' may be taken in part to be the irrelevance of such goals. However, it is probably a safe assumption that working-class Canadians do, to some extent, value the consumer items to which they do not have access. Yet, of Merton's response alternatives, it is safe to note that rebellion is exceedingly rare, and conformity apparently common. Nor is there evidence to suggest that working-class persons are more apt to engage in criminal deviance than are middle- or upper-class persons. Rather, when they deviate, they resort to different and more conspicuous forms of deviance.

In fact, assuming the plausibility of Merton's model, it would predict middle-class criminal deviance more clearly than working-class deviance, at least insofar as crimes against property are concerned, as opposed to overt violence or aggression. It is precisely the middle-class person with high aspirations, as we have seen in Chapter 3, who, in order to realize these aspirations, may resort to illegitimate means. The ''relative deprivation'' of the middle class, as contrasted to the inherited subordination or ''culture of poverty'' of the lower class, may result in a greater incidence of criminal deviance — deviance of a form particularly suited to middle-class ''white collar'' opportunities. Also, for the same reason, as we shall go on to discuss, the middle class might better be expected to be the source of political protest and opposition than the more absolutely deprived working class.

It is commonplace in our society to think of crime, delinquency, drunkenness, drug use, and even gambling as working-class vices. The view that such deviance is dangerous and undesirable is reflected in our patterns of police enforcement and in our criminal code. In our society we stress the punishment of criminal actions that clash with middle-class conceptions of propriety.

The police, themselves recruited from working-class backgrounds, are organized and socialized to uphold middle-class values and laws. In legislation and enforcement, from the police through the judiciary, the predisposition is to think in terms of working-class deviance and middle-class respectability. For example, in subsidized housing communities, with their concentration of visible working-class tenants, the police generally expect trouble to occur, and often precipitate difficulties in a self-fulfilling way by a heavy-handed presence. (Forcese, Begin, Gould, 1978.)

The working-class individual engaging in criminal activity is resorting to behaviour that violates the property rights of middle-class persons, often by means of threatened or actual violence. It is the violence and the conspicuousness of the crime that prompt objections. The offences are straightforward, non-subtle, and highly visible, readily attracting the intervention of law-enforcement agencies. Robbing a service station, a store, a bank, a home, or an individual are rather conspicuous crimes, though they may be slight in terms of actual property loss. The public, with the ready aid of the media, are aware of such offences. They are clear-cut violations of Canadian law. Their straightforward nature permits straightforward police activity, judicial procedure, and punishment, and the offender, as a working-class person, lacks the influence or prestige to dispute prosecution or arrange intercession on his or her own behalf.

Contrast the nature of working-class criminal activity to that of the middle class. It is probably fair to say that every reader of this book has committed illegal acts of a criminal nature, whether smoking marijuana, indulging in Canada Customs violations, or committing some act of fraud or theft. But few will have been apprehended or punished and, therefore, few will have been stigmatized as criminal. The opportunities for middle-class crime are subtle, not highly visible, and not as subject to police supervision. Stealing supplies from the office, accepting gifts for business or government favours, and "padding" the expense account are not readily detected. Moreover, they are widely considered to be acceptable acts and are even budgeted for by employers. Similarly, more serious middle-class crimes, such as large-scale embezzlement or fraudulent stock deals, are rarely punished with severity, especially relative to working-class crimes involving far slighter monetary value. The several related factors are: less-detectable crime, less subject to police scrutiny or public indignation, and normative toleration of such middle-class illegalities, with only slight pressure for judicial follow-up.

In 1973, W.J. Fitzsimmons, a former deputy commissioner of the Royal Canadian Mounted Police, commented on the enormity of white-collar crime. In a press report he is quoted as remarking:

> Canadian business lost at least $2.5 billion last year through internal crime. . . . "Statistics Canada doesn't require companies to report losses because of white collar crime," Fitzsimmons said in an interview. He said that, in the United States, statistics show that 37% of business failures are the result of criminal action. (*The Gazette*, August 31, 1973.)

Thus, working-class criminal activity is more likely to be taken through the judicial system and appear in statistics; middle-class crime is not.

Similarly, delinquency, drunkenness, and drug use are the more visible and deemed punishable when engaged in by working-class persons. The working-class alcoholic is a "drunk" and the middle-class alcoholic a "good guy." Lower-class boys who engage in vandalism are delinquents, while middle-class vandalism is justified with the favoured expression, "Boys will be boys." The very simple point is that in a society dominated by the middle class, definitions of deviance and the imposition of sanctions are to the disadvantage of lower-class offenders.

Class and Attitudes to Punishment

Perhaps paradoxically, or perhaps reflecting an aspect of what Marx was pleased to call "false consciousness," the working class are more disposed to favour harsh punishment for criminal acts than are middle-class persons, even when working-class crime is in question. Working-class Canadians tend to express less satisfaction and patience with the paraphernalia of "due process." This was illustrated in the reactions of Ottawa residents questioned regarding the kidnapping and death of Pierre Laporte in 1970 and the federal government's response to this "October crisis" in enacting the War Measures Act, dormant since World War II. Working-class respondents in the survey, identified by education levels, tended to urge prompt and harsh retribution for the "persons responsible" for the death of Laporte, even in some instances suggesting torture of some sort. In contrast, middle-class persons urged restraint and careful prosecution and trial of those "responsible"; given the prospect of a guilty verdict, they were less inclined to suggest capital punishment. (Forcese, Richer, de Vries, and McRoberts, 1971.)

Table 4-10: Attitudes Toward Due Process and Punishment After the October Crisis, by Education

	Elementary School	Some High School	Finished High School	Some University	Finished University
By-pass due process	72	55	52	26	22
Treat as was Laporte	75	67	71	47	51

Source: Forcese, Richer, de Vries, McRoberts, 1971: 9.

Table 4-11: Support in a Canadian Community for Freedom of
Speech, by Level of Schooling, 1970

Level of Schooling	% Support for freedom of speech				
	Low	Medium Low	Medium High	High	Total
Grade school	40	35	14	12	101
Junior high school	37	33	20	10	100
High school	19	26	33	22	100
Some university	7	14	35	44	100
Completed					
one university degree	6	5	19	69	99

Source: Ted Harvey, "Attitudes Towards Free Speech in a Canadian
Community: A Study of Social, Political, and Psychological Correlates." Papers
presented at the Forty-Third Annual Meeting of the Canadian Political Science
Association, Volume 3 (mimeo), Table 5.

If we continue to take education as a rough indicator of probable social
class, there are other Canadian data that demonstrate the relationship
between class membership and social tolerance or liberal attitudes to civil
rights. Harvey found, in a western Canadian city, that support for freedom
of speech increased with educational level. In his sample, 69 percent of
those who had completed a university degree indicated high support, as
contrasted to only 12 percent of those with grade-school education. (Ted
Harvey, as cited in Manzer, 1974: 291.)

Other observers have remarked upon differences in attitudes or values
according to social class. In particular, less patience with due process, a
greater inclination to violent or aggressive behaviour and "strong" or
"tough" solutions to problems, and fatalism have been suggested as
characteristic of working-class persons. (Kluckhohn and Strodtbeck, 1961;
Lipset, 1965.) Summing up these attitudinal characteristics, the notion of
working-class "authoritarianism" has been offered by researchers. The
"authoritarian" is considered to manifest intolerance of minority groups
and of "unusual" behaviour, and to support "strong" leaders and extremist
candidates for political office. These attitudes are hypothesized to be
derivative of childhood socialization and perpetuated through generations
in the lower class through socialization. (Adorno *et al.*, 1958; Lipset, 1960;
Langton, 1969; Dawson and Prewitt, 1969.) For example, having lived in a
downtown working-class neighbourhood in Toronto, Lorimer and Phillips
remark upon the strict parental control manifest in direct and immediate
physical punishment, particularly by the father. (Lorimer and Phillips,
1971: 40.) Yet, apparently favouring strength and resort to force, a derivative
of everyday experience and socialization, it is precisely the working class

of our society who are most apt to experience such tactics from law-enforcement agents. In addition, and of considerable importance, it may be that such learned attitudes and responses to environment contribute to working-class religious behaviour and political behaviour, or its absence.

Class and Religion

An aspect of class behaviour relates to religion. The composition of church congregations is very distinct by social class, and represents a structural feature of Canadian society. But more important, and our reason for considering religion here, is the extent to which religious belief and affiliation relate to and reinforce classes and class behaviour.

Sociologists have distinguished religious affiliations by the degree to which they are organized as opposed to spontaneous; staid in membership acquisition as opposed to evangelistic; conventional and restrained in worship as opposed to emotional and spontaneous; ritualist and élitist in religious expression as opposed to mass-participatory. In each of the above pairs, the first of the paired modes tends to be associated with religious groups consisting of upper- and middle-class members, and the second with working-class members. (Goodall, 1970.) To take an extreme example, contrast the staid Episcopalian congregations of the urban upper-middle-class United States to the snake-handling religious ecstasy of congregations of rural working-class people in Tennessee. In a study of 27 "churches" in Lethbridge, Alberta, the spontaneity of lower-class sects contrasted to the formal proceedings of lower-middle-class churches, to the relative informality of middle-class church behaviour, to the semi-formality of upper-middle and upper-class churches. (Goodall, 1970.)

Gallup Poll data in 1985 suggested a decline in church attendance among Roman Catholics and Protestant denominations. The overall national attendance was 32 percent, consisting of a 43 percent attendance rate for Roman Catholics and a 29 percent rate for Protestants. In 1957, the overall rate had been 60 percent, with rates of 87 percent and 43 percent for Roman Catholics and Protestants respectively. (*The Toronto Star*, June 17, 1985.) The Roman Catholic rate conceivably would have shown a greater decline were it not for immigration to Canada from traditional Catholic countries, such as Italy and Portugal. The withdrawal from church activity tends to be a middle-class phenomenon. Conversely, fundamentalist religious movements appear to be gaining support, in contrast to the established churches, and are probably drawing upon lower-middle and working-class populations. (*The Toronto Star*, June 1, 1985.) Reported on the same day as the poll results was an assembly of 18,000 people in Maple Leaf Gardens, Toronto, for a service by television evangelist Jimmy Swaggart.

Evidence suggests that religious organizations in Canada clearly stratify by class composition. The Anglican, Presbyterian, and United Churches are characteristically upper-middle class in membership, as are Jewish congregations. Other Protestant denominations and the Roman Catholic Church are characteristically working class in membership. (Teevan, Jr. and Jackson, 1972.)

Canadian data indicate a hierarchy of denominations. In the top rank of actively religious persons are the Jewish and the Anglican (Episcopalian), with lower-class standing ascribed to the Roman Catholic Church. Based on a Toronto sample, Teevan and Jackson examined the mean income, education, and occupational standing of the heads of families attending various denominations. They report that Jews, Anglicans, members of the United Church, and Presbyterians are all well above the means levels, while the Lutherans, Baptists, Roman Catholics, and Greek Orthodox are below. (Teevan Jr. and Jackson, 1972; 5.)

Consistent with these findings, Allingham reports that, in Ontario, the Anglican Church consists of relatively homogeneous high-economic-status persons. The United, Presbyterian, and Baptist Churches are less homogeneous in the class standing of their members, although still tending to consist of relatively high-status persons employed in government and corporate administration, whom termed the "bureaucratic élite." (Allingham, 1962.) Overall, in rank order of members' status, Allingham listed the Anglican, Jews, Presbyterian, Greek Orthodox, Baptist, United Church, and Roman Catholic church. (Allingham 1962.) These findings correspond with the 1968 Toronto study of Teevan and Jackson, with the exception of the United Church, which the Toronto researchers found to rank in the top levels.

Table 4-12: Mean Values of Income, Education, and Occupational Level, by Religious Denomination (Male Household Heads), Toronto, 1968

Religious Affiliation	Income (N)		Education (N)		Occupational (N) level	
Jewish	$10,778	(54)	12.1	(61)	29.3	(63)
Anglican	8,873	(307)	11.4	(327)	39.2	(336)
United Church	8,793	(334)	11.6	(341)	39.0	(354)
Presbyterian	8,284	(102)	11.3	(112)	41.1	(115)
Lutheran	7,921	(57)	11.0	(59)	40.8	(63)
Baptist	7,622	(37)	10.7	(40)	39.6	(41)
Roman Catholic	3,928	(423)	9.3	(467)	53.6	(484)
Greek Orthodox	5,678	(45)	8.5	(47)	56.5	(49)
Total	8,100	(1,359)	10.7	(1,454)	43.9	(1,505)

Source: Teevan and Jackson, 1972.

It would be difficult to attribute ''success'' or class membership to religious belief or membership in any clear-cut causal sense. But it is the case that certain religions in Canada are associated with certain ethnic groups and social classes and therefore, insofar as class standing is inherited, so, too, is religious membership. Also, among persons active in religious denominations, those enjoying upward social mobility will associate themselves with the appropriately upper-status denominations. (Teevan Jr. and Jackson, 1972.) Generally, the point is that there exists a hierarchy of church rank in Canada, congruent with the class structure of Canadian society.

Religion, Class, and Politics

The ideologies of the several religions reinforce existing class attitudes, behaviour, and structure. Of particular import, this includes political behaviour and social change. Election data show that persons of Protestant affiliation will tend to vote for the Progressive Conservative Party, a reflection of class and ethnic membership. On the other hand, Jews and Roman Catholics will tend to vote for the Liberal Party. (Alford, 1963: 1965.) These data lump varying denominations together as Protestant, and are confounded with regional and ethnic effects, but there is some evidence to suggest that these patterns of voting by religion persist even when the effects of ethnicity and social class are controlled. (Anderson, 1966.) This would mean that religious affiliation may act to over-ride class economic interests.

Table 4-13: Party Support by Religion, 1962, in Pre-election Poll

| | Religion % | | | | |
	Protestant	Jewish	Catholic	Other*	Total
PC	47	19	24	27	36
Liberal	29	58	49	17	38
NDP	13	23	8	27	12
Socred	11	—	19	29	14
100% =	(1,187)	(47)	(915)	(41)	(2,190)

Source: R. Alford, ''The Social Bases of Political Cleavage in 1962,'': 273, in J. Meisel (ed.), ''Papers on the 1962 Election,'' Toronto, University of Toronto Press, 1964: 214. Permission granted by the University of Toronto Press.

Although aggregating the Protestant religious denominations suggests a Protestant conservatism, this is not altogether true. Methodists and United Church members were instrumental in organizing and supporting the Co-operative Commonwealth Federation (CCF), for example. Not only was J.S. Woodsworth a minister, but T.C. Douglas, who succeeded to the leadership of the party and the Premier's office in Saskatchewan, and was later national CCF leader, is a Baptist minister. Stanley Knowles, long returned to the House of Commons from North Winnipeg, is a United Church minister. (Crysdale and Beattie, 1973: 282.) In the contiguous tradition of rural protest and third party formation, Social Credit's William Aberhart was a Baptist minister.

In contrast, the Anglican Church and the Roman Catholic Church have been associated with opposition to the CCF/NDP. The Anglican Church of Canada has been the church of the upper-middle and upper classes of British origin and so has been acting class-consistently in its opposition. The Roman Catholic Church, the affiliation of French Canadians and working-status immigrants, has not been so class-consistent in its opposition to anything smacking of socialism or "Godless" communism. But in Quebec the Roman Catholic Church clergy of superior rank were histori-cally part of the economic and political establishment, as Rioux noted (Rioux, 1971), and closely allied with the provincial Union Nationale Party. In addition, the Roman Catholic Church has tended to be anti-union; Clark states that it was the church influence upon French-Canadian workers in northern Quebec and Ontario company towns that prevented the formation of labour unions in opposition to company influence, as we noted in Chapter 2. (Clark, 1971.) Part of the "middle class revolt" in Quebec that saw Jean Lesage's Liberal Party turn out the Union Nationale was also anti-church, as is present Parti Québecois support.

Despite the widely assumed notion that religion is becoming obsolete in our secular society, it is in fact the case that religious institutions continue to play an important role in socializing and influencing Canadians. One need not attend church regularly or frequently, nor even attend church at all as an adult, to have learned in childhood ideological outlooks that persist in influencing one's behaviour. At times these influences are to the detriment of class interests, but in other instances, as we have seen, they actively promote class awareness and interests.

i. *Political Participation and Social Class*

The works of Marx and Engels were concerned with the prospect of classes engaging in political action. The fundamental opposition was between capitalists who acted to protect their economic dominance, with the state as their instrument, and the workers who were being exploited. As they developed an awareness or consciousness of their shared economic predic-ament, the working class would become the vehicle of revolutionary change

Table 4-14   Winning and Losing Candidates by Occupation and Political Party, Canada, 1974

Political party	Electoral status	Law, social science	Managerial, natural science	Miscell. upper middle class	Total high status	Middle white collar	Skilled or semi-skilled	Primary Occupations	Other	Total low status	Total Total
Liberal	Winner	35	55	24	114	13	5	4	5	27	141
	Loser	26	43	22	91	13	3	11	5	32	123
	Total	61	98	46	205	26	8	15	10	59	265
PC	Winner	25	26	18	69	8	1	15	2	26	95
	Loser	37	59	30	126	26	6	5	6	43	169
	Total	62	85	48	195	34	7	20	8	69	264
NDP	Winner	3	4	7	14	1	1	0	0	2	16
	Loser	18	45	88	151	26	33	12	24	95	246
	Total	21	49	95	165	27	34	12	24	97	262
Social Credit	Winner	0	3	2	5	3	2	1	0	6	11
	Loser	2	3	22	57	29	25	15	15	84	141
	Total	2	6	24	62	32	27	16	15	90	152
Other	Winner	1	0	0	1	0	0	0	0	0	1
	Loser	6	46	51	103	37	58	7	60	162	265
	Total	7	46	51	104	37	58	7	60	162	266
Total	Winner	64	88	51	203	25	9	20	7	61	264
	Loser	89	226	213	528	131	125	50	110	416	944
	Total	153	314	264	731	156	134	70	117	477	1,208

Source: Forcese and de Vries, 1977.

in society, overthrowing the ruling class, the state, and class stratification. Only in such political action would the proletariat actually constitute a class in the full Marxist sense. Subsequently, Lenin seized on the notion of the "dictatorship of the proletariat," where the workers form the government and the state temporarily becomes their instrument until the day it "withers away" in the interests of a truly egalitarian and classless society.

Persons other than Marxists have expected corresponding relationships between political behaviour and social class, often with some similar expectation of "radical" action by lower-class persons. Yet actual behaviour seems to contradict such expectations.

It is a very well-established empirical generalization, extending through all the Western democracies, that working-class individuals have a low rate of participation in politics. This is true of memberships in political parties or related organizations, and even the simple action of turning out to vote. To put the generalization conversely, the higher the social class, the greater the extent of political participation, including fundamentally the greater probability of any political participation whatsoever. (Milbrath, 1965.) Middle- and upper-class persons, with good reason, view the political process as more efficacious than do working-class persons; that is, conventional political agencies are perceived to be useful and responsive to their interests. (Milbrath, 1965: 56.) In fact, middle-class persons have the education and the affiliations that make it easier to participate in politics, and to participate effectively. A matter as trivial as the proper and efficient conduct of meetings is often not part of the experience of working-class persons. Usually, they have little organizational experience. In their Toronto working-class study, Lorimer and Phillips reported that the only viable voluntary association memberships held by their respondents were in churches and labour unions. (Lorimer and Phillips, 1971: 75–76.)

In Canada, citing work undertaken by John Meisel, Manzer shows that, as social class level increases, so does the sense of political efficacy. (Manzer, 1974: 311–313.) Thus, working-class persons feel greater helplessness and, in a sense, fatalism, regarding their lives as unalterable. Working-class persons are markedly wary of politics and political representatives at all levels of government. They are suspicious of the perceived arbitrary powers of political officers, elected or appointed, and feel neglected and powerless, expressing the view that they simply "can't win." (Lorimer and Phillips, 1971: 78–84.)

ii. Class and Voting

This skepticism or apathy is expressed in failure to vote. Working-class persons are less likely to vote than are middle-class persons. (Milbrath, 1965; Lipset, 1960.) For example, in Toronto and Vancouver working-class neighbourhoods, researchers have estimated that approximately one-third of the eligible voters actually turn out at the polls. (Lorimer and Phillips,

1971: 75–76; Ewing, 1972.) The working-class vote, which some theorists expect to be radical and socialist, is rarely mobilized.

Marxist-oriented theorists would find such a failure deplorable and an indication of the absence of working-class consciousness, even while scornful of voting as effective political action at any rate. Others, however, have theorized that a low level of political participation on the part of working-class voters is desirable, insofar as it makes for a "stable" political system. Lipset has argued that working-class persons, because of their intolerance of civil rights and their preference for the strong leader, would be apt to bring about undesirable electoral victories, should they in fact vote. (Lipset, 1960.) Normally, when only middle- and upper-class voters turn out, conventional candidates are elected, candidates whom we have already seen in Chapter 2 to be themselves middle- and upper-class persons and members of established political parties. In Canada, the only notable departure from this pattern of higher-status persons becoming successful in politics is in the Social Credit Party, and, to some degree, the New Democratic Party. (Forcese and de Vries, 1975, 1977.)

In contrast, Lipset continues, when the level of voting turnout increases (probably indicative of an increase in working-class voting, since that is where most non-voters are normally to be found), there is greater probability of the election of persons whom Lipset characterizes as "extremist," those favoured by the working-class authoritarian. The extremist may be of the left or the right. Whether one accepts the designation "extremist" or not, what does seem to occur is greater support for candidates from the non-established parties, third parties such as the Social Credit in Canada.

This is related to the phenomenon of candidates' class standing declining as the various political parties' prospects in a riding or region decline. That is, the more marginal a party, the lower the status of that party's candidates. The greater the electoral prospects of a party, then the higher the status of their candidates. (Forcese and de Vries, 1974; 1977.)

A related expectation is that the working-class vote will tend to favour left-wing or socialist candidates, while the upper-class vote will be more conservative. In fact, some such relationship does show up in western Europe and in the United Kingdom. (Alford, 1963; Lipset, 1960.) But recalling all the while that the extent of working-class voting tends to be slight in the first place, such working-class voting as does occur is not so marked and consistent in left-wing preference as the assumption of lower-class preference for socialist polities would predict.

In the United Kingdom there is the well-known phenomenon of the so-called "working-class Tory," referring to lower-class support for the British Conservative Party. (McKenzie and Silver, 1967.) In Canada we similarly find support for other than the New Democratic Party in working-class ridings (as in David Lewis's 1974 defeat), as well as patterns of self-reported Conservative or Liberal party support by working-class persons. (Alford, 1963.) In Vancouver civic elections from 1958 to 1970, approxi-

Table 4-15: Trade Union Voting, Federal Election 1962

	Union families	Non-union families
Conservatives	26%	40%
Liberals	38	38
NDP	22	8

Adapted from R. Alford, "The Social Bases of Political Cleavage in 1962," in J. Meisel (ed.), "Papers on the 1962 Election," Toronto, University of Toronto Press, 1964: 211. Permission granted by the University of Toronto Press.

mately one-third of the working-class vote went to right-wing candidates. (Ewing, 1972.)

This is not to say that there are no indications of class preferences for specific parties. Some ridings, for example, are traditionally more likely to support one party than another, with neighbourhoods viewed as conservative or socialist strongholds. Especially in civic and provincial elections where riding boundaries are more apt to be coincident with class-segregated neighbourhoods, are such patterns evident. For example, analyses of 1941 and 1945 elections in Manitoba are able to distinguish patterns of ethnic and of class voting. (Taylor and Wiseman, 1977; Wiseman and Taylor, 1974.) Another good example that has extended from the civic to the federal level is to be found in North Winnipeg, where the left-wing radicalism of North Winnipeg is demonstrably class-based. (Stevenson, 1977.) At the level of civic elections, not only New Democratic Party but Communist Party candidates have been elected. At the federal level, this area has returned New Democratic Party members to Parliament since the pre-World War II period. For example, on the basis of several pre-election polls, Alford reports the non-existence of class support in keeping with the traditional left-right expectation. (Alford, 1963.) We may point to the New Democratic Party or the Progressive Conservative Party receiving distinguishable proportions of support from the working class or the upper class, respectively. But in neither instance is it true to say that a class majority supports the party presumed to be of the left or the right, or that it is working- or upper-class compatible. Rather, the Liberal Party established itself as the party of the centre, and consistently attracted a majority support, until 1985, apparently by appealing to all social classes, including gaining the greatest proportion of support given by the voting working class. (Alford, 1963; Alford, 1964: 211.)

Unlike elections in Australia or England, where class voting is relatively well established, Alford found that, in Canadian federal elections, regionalism is a better predictor of voting support. (Alford, 1963; 1964.) Porter also argues the import of regional voting in Canada. (Porter, 1965.) As we have previously emphasized, the major regions of Canada are themselves distinguishable ethnically and economically, and they have developed traditional voting allegiances. Thus, New Democratic Party support, federally and provincially, is stronger and more consistent in western Canada, where there is also support for Diefenbaker-style Progressive Conservatives. Ontario has been a stronghold of Progressive Conservative Party support, especially at the provincial level, where, until 1985, the "Big Blue Machine" lived on without being challenged for several decades. Quebec has consistently supported the federal Liberal Party, which remains a viable political force provincially with the demise of the previously powerful Union Nationale and the decline of the Parti Québecois. The Atlantic provinces have supported the two old parties, with a Liberal edge especially pronounced during the heyday of Joseph Smallwood's Liberal Newfoundland government. In the Atlantic region, CCF-NDP support has been rare and isolated. In Cape Breton there has been a long-standing pocket of CCF-NDP support in the mining communities, producing the election of federal representatives. And in a federal by-election in 1978, an NDP member was returned for the first time ever in Newfoundland.

It seems to be true, as we would argue, that, in Canada, class interests are being summed up in regional voting at the federal level. However, beyond the Canadian case, other reasons have been put forward to account for the absence of clearer class politics. As a general explanation intended to apply to European as well as to North American politics, Lipset argues that the left-right distinction is too simple to really show up in political behaviour. The distinction does not represent consistent class interests. He offers the distinction between the economic and the civil sectors, and suggests that the working class may support left-wing policies economically, but, in the light of working-class authoritarianism, right-wing or conservative civil or social policies are apt to be supported. (Lipset, 1960.) Therefore, it is the salient issues in an election campaign that will determine the direction of working-class response. Civil issues such as the abolition or retention of capital punishment in Canada invite a conservative working-class response, as does immigration policy in England. Conversely, an economic issue such as wage controls, a policy apt to be introduced by non-socialist political parties, will tend to elicit a pro-socialist working-class vote.

In addition, Lipset argues that where a two-party system has evolved, ideological and class cleavages tend to disappear from politics. In order to win, each party must generalize its policies and campaign promises in order to appeal to the greatest number of voters. (Lipset, 1960.) As a result, neither of the two parties becomes a viable class choice, at least not for the working-class voter. In a similar vein, Alford notes that American and Canadian political parties, unlike those in Australia or in England, have not attempted to develop class identities. (Alford, 1963.) In particular, except for the New Democratic Party in Canada, there are no firm labour-union ties, even where there may be expectations and a prior history of labour-union support as in the case of the Democratic Party in the United States — an exception that has failed the Democrats in recent presidential elections.

Historically, the New Democratic Party has been explicitly affiliated with labour unions, particularly dating from the 1930s and 1940s, when many socialists held important union positions and encouraged CCF support. (Horowitz, 1968: 54.) However, this affiliation and labour-union financial support have not been readily translated into electoral support of the New Democratic Party by rank-and-file union members. Alford sees Canada and the United States as societies in which the classes have not polarized politically. Moreover, the ruling class has effectively controlled the political process, alternating "competing political élites" from within the ranks. (Alford, 1967.)

We noted in Chapter 2 that members of the House of Commons and of the cabinet are largely of high social class. The only deviation from this pattern is in the "third" parties, especially the Social Credit. Much of the minor-party support is agrarian, small business, lower-middle class, and lower-status professional (for example, teachers). With the exception of such third-party influence and to some extent the Diefenbaker interlude in the Progressive Conservative Party, the upper classes have effectively monopolized conventional politics. (Forcese and de Vries, 1974.)

Pinard suggests that ruling-class control of politics has been a particular feature of Quebec political history. The ruling class has dominated decision-making positions and has gained lower-class support. He argues that "negative voting" — that is, working-class support for right-wing parties and the "conservative and nationalist" character of Quebec political movements — is a function of "élite mediation" of class interests. The upper class in Quebec controls the economic resources and enjoys a value consensus, unlike other societies where there may be conflicting élites within the upper class. Thus the Quebec governing élite, utilizing its control of economic power and the agencies of socialization, such as the church, has manipulated or "translated" working-class interests into terms consistent with upper-class values and interests. (Pinard, 1970: 107–108.)

Another argument is Lipset's view that Canada is a conservative nation. He states that, in contrast to the United States, Canada has grown out of a foundation in counter-revolution. (Lipset, 1963.) Similarly, although not agreeing that Canada is unmitigatedly conservative, Horowitz suggests that there is, in Canadian society, a sense of "aristocratic paternalism" in the attitudes of the ruling class, and in derivative welfare policies. (Horowitz, 1968.) Because of this genuine conservatism, with its hint of social responsibility, ideologically loaded, class-based politics have not been articulated in Canada.

However, in Horowitz's view, there is another side to the coin. Because of a clearly defined conservatism in Canada, as contrasted to the characteristic liberalism of the United States (conservatism and liberalism in the sense of European-based ideologies), there has also been room in Canada for a socialist alternative. That is, in the United States, the emphasis on a liberal centre has pre-empted the possibility of either a conservative or a socialist extreme. (Horowitz, 1968: 3–57.) But, unlike the United States, Canada has developed a socialist party and has returned that party to office in three provinces, as well as regularly sending a contingent to Ottawa. Lipset and Horowitz both attach importance to Canada's conservative Loyalist origins, but Lipset then sees Canada as inherently conservative, where Horowitz finds a genuine socialist sector among the range of Canadian ideologies. We shall consider each of these views further in evaluating whether there is a class-conscious working-class politics in Canada, after all, despite findings stressing the absence of class voting in Canada.

iii. Class and Political Movements

Thirty-six years ago, Lipset published an analysis of the emergence of a socialist party in the Canadian West. In 1968, in the preface to a new edition of his work, Lipset suggested that, in retrospect, he is of the view that he had not been dealing with a socialist party after all, merely an inherently conservative agrarian populism (1950; 1968). The CCF is rendered consistent with his over-all thesis of Canadian conservatism and greater American egalitarianism. (Lipset, 1963.) Also, in a sense, Lipset was consistent with more radical theorists — expressing the view that farmers, as property owners, could not be genuine socialists, and that the CCF movement was, like Social Credit in Alberta, merely a bourgeois populism. (Conway, 1978.)

Thus Peter Sinclair (1975) has insisted, as has Tom Naylor (1972), that the development of the Saskatchewan CCF must be understood to be similar to that of the Social Credit in Alberta. Sinclair observes that the development of both parties "is best explained by stressing how the populist elements in each were consistent with the petit bourgeois character of the most numerous class in each province." (Sinclair, 1975: 1.) This awareness of the class origin of the two protest parties then leads Sinclair, like Lipset, to the view that the outcome was not socialist in Saskatchewan. He writes: "When CCF leaders attacked capitalism, they were not attacking the idea of private ownership of productive property or the private accumulation of profit, [an idea] which is essential for a long-term commitment to Socialism." Rather, he continues, "To be against capitalism in Saskatchewan meant to be against monopoly exploitation; it did not mean to be against small-scale private enterprise, because this would have meant challenging the whole way of life of prairie farmers." (Sinclair, 1977: 6.) Hence, given a classic definition of socialism, and of the class position of farmers, one is led to the conclusion that both Social Credit and the CCF were merely populist protest parties, and not significantly distinguishable in ideology or policy.

A familiar manifestation of western opposition politics, whatever the ideological label, is the attitude to tariffs. (Conway, 1983.) Western Canadians have historically opposed tariffs, and thereby opposed central Canadian interests. Conversely, free trade has been a popular western Canadian concept. Free trade was an objective of the Progressive Party in the 1920s, and remains a western objective in the 1980s.

Some social scientists have persisted in the view that the CCF-NDP have constituted a genuine socialism, in contrast to the absence of such a party in the United States. As we remarked above, Gad Horowitz suggests that socialism has developed in Canada precisely because of Canadian conservatism (as opposed to American liberal centrism.) The élitist Canadian conservatives make room for and prompt the development of the counter-ideology of socialism in a kind of dialectic fashion. (Horowitz, 1968.) In addition, he argues that socialist ideology was imported to the United States by "aliens," that is, by persons who were non-English-speaking immigrants from Europe. The ideology was therefore itself perceived as alien and rejected as "un-American." In Canada, in contrast, socialism was imported principally by immigrants of the same ethnic background as the dominant social class; that is, Englishmen with Fabian and trade union experience. (Horowitz, 1968: 24–29.) This last point is very much consistent with Lipset's initial explanation of the rise of the CCF in Saskatchewan. (1950.)

The initial co-operative and protest movements of the Prairies were certainly not socialist in the European ideological sense. But agrarian populism evolved into the CCF party, and its socialist commitment developed through the ideological and organizational input of immigrants from the United Kingdom, as well as from Europe. These were persons with experience in working-class politics and often with affiliations with the working-class Methodist denomination, oriented to social problems. (Lipset, 1968: 43.) The first leader of the CCF was J.S. Woodsworth, a Methodist minister; M.J. Coldwell was experienced in British socialism and active in labour organizing. This kind of input was crucial, for, as the literature on social movements suggests, the leaders of the movement lend it a particular stamp. They turned Saskatchewan agrarian protest to a practical approximation, though not a theoretical realization, of socialism, however unlikely socialist farmers might appear. In contrast, American immigration to Alberta, as well as fundamentalist Baptist religious ideology, would have influenced and shaped the ideological character of Alberta agrarian protest, largely identical in structural origin to Saskatchewan political unrest, but becoming translated into support for conservative Social Credit. The conditions and sentiments of economic dissatisfaction and protest were transmuted into one direction or another by the nature of the persons actively organizing the protest movements.

In Saskatchewan, the leaders were ideologically committed to socialism, and attempted to shape the populist dissatisfaction of the farmers accordingly. In the course of building upon this dissatisfaction, there was necessarily a failure to implement traditional European theoretical definitions of socialist policies. In Alberta, as Sinclair argues, William Aberhart's charismatic appeal permitted the establishment of an authoritarian and right-wing political definition, building upon similar agrarian dissatisfaction. (Sinclair, 1977: 11–12.) Both, however, were reformist; what did differ, however similar their populist bases, was the ideological definition of the reform, and the intent of the leadership.

Generally, political protest movements in Canada have been based in rural communities; this is true for the Progressives, the CCF, Social Credit, and the Créditistes. And their support has been from a particular class of the rural population. The cross-national literature on social and political movements offers the generalization that the mass support for such movements comes from those segments of the population experiencing "relative deprivation." As a region, the Prairies were economically precarious. It was not a matter of impoverishment, but of "boom or bust." One year, depending on the crop, and world markets, farm income would be high, another year low. In 1930 the price of a bushel of wheat was $1.50, and in 1932 it was 38 cents, and actually less at the grain elevator. (Gray, 1966.)

James Gray relates the story of an Alberta farmer who had a good crop in 1932, but little cash to show for it. (As Gray notes, prairie farmers suffered not merely periodic crop failure such as agriculturalists have always experienced, but often inadequate cash returns even given good harvest. The fluctuation in the price structure, and its utter collapse in the 1930s, was the insufferable feature of prairie farming.) Thus, Gray's farmer

> ...harvested thirty-three bushels to the acre and took it to market when the price of No. 1 Northern was twenty-eight and a half cents at the elevator. That autumn had been cold and wet and much of the grain was tough and smutty. This caused the farmer's wheat to be discounted eighteen cents a bushel. Threshing and twine cost seven cents; hauling three cents a bushel. Thus a bumper crop returned its grower *one-half cent* per bushel.
>
> *The Winter Years* by James Gray. Reprinted by permission of Macmillan of Canada, a Division of Canada Publishing Corporation.

The rural population was constantly faced with uncertainty, and was frustrated in any attempt at rational planning and production. For example, investing in expensive farm equipment manufactured in the east came to mean brief use and subsequent re-possession. Farm debts, under the control of eastern Canadian chartered banks, were enormous. Resentment against the banks, railroads, and manufacturers, all located or controlled in the East, was inevitable, and persists to the present. The theory of relative deprivation suggests that, precisely because prairie farmers experienced occasional periods of prosperity, as contrasted, for example, to owners of smaller Quebec, Ontario, or Maritime farms, they were moved to "radical" or non-conventional action.

Within any region, the actively dissatisfied are not the people who have always been poor, or those who have been most deprived, but rather people who have experienced some better condition and have found their expectations of continued prosperity frustrated. Lipset (1968) reports that the initial support for the CCF in Saskatchewan came not from the poorest or most marginal farmers, nor the wealthiest, but those whom we might call middle-class farmers. They were perhaps not middle class by urban standards or definition, but, relative to their fellows, they were persons who were big enough to expect something better, rather than so poor as to despair or so wealthy as to be secure. The boom-or-bust feature of prairie single-crop agriculture, with its wild fluctuations in farm income, constituted the setting for middle-class farm dissatisfaction. The provincial and federal governments were viewed as the tool of eastern "big business" interests. In this setting, the CCF became the voice of the Saskatchewan farmer, growing from protest movement to political party to government in 1944 — the first socialist government in North America. That year happened to be the year of the highest farm incomes in Saskatchewan history. (Lipset, 1968: 131.)

The people who supported the new party through its emergence to the point where it formed the government were the middle-income farmers, with some support from the few workers in Saskatchewan's small cities. The middle-income farmers were those who had supported the Progressives 30 years earlier in the West, as did their fellows in Ontario, and were the people who have generally been the basis of rural protest movements. (McCrorie, 1971.) The same kind of people supported the non-socialist protest party in Alberta, leading to William Aberhart's formation of a new Social Credit government in 1935.

We may take one additional Canadian example in order to underline the rural middle-class basis of protest. Almost 30 years after the Social Credit victory in Alberta, Pinard found a similar pattern of rural protest in Quebec. (Pinard, 1971: 94–98.) We underline that the protest occurred after the war, when Quebec had moved out of its agrarian isolation and under-development. In the federal election of 1962, many observers were amazed by the support given the Quebec wing of the Social Credit Party of Canada, and their leader Réal Caouette. The Créditistes were supported by the solid middle-range farmer and the small town businessman and his employees. (Pinard, 1971: 250.) That is, support was from precisely the class of people who were neither mired in poverty nor rolling in affluence, the class of people who have supported third-party alternatives to the Conservative and Liberal parties throughout Canadian history.

We stress, therefore, the non-conventional aspect of such political support, in that it departs from "old" party lines. As protest movements, whether coming to be characterized as of the left or the right, they represent dissatisfaction and attempts at social change. This is not to deny, as Lipset does, that agrarian socialism is any less socialist than some industrially-oriented pure form. Without a doubt, CCF government support in Saskatchewan did not represent conventional socialism of European theory or experience. It was not a movement of industrial workers, but of small property-holders, farmers experiencing a fluctuating economy and acquiring facility in co-operative marketing. (Bennett and Krueger, 1968.) Their frustrations were little different from those of their fellow farmers across the Alberta-Saskatchewan border. But insofar as there was a distinctive socialist input from British and European immigrants, from the Methodist and United Churches, and eventually from the study groups formed by such people and well-attended through rural Saskatchewan, neither can it simply be dismissed as mere populism. The agrarian protest, objecting to eastern Canadian economic control and the insecurity of prairie agriculture, became socialist as much as any collectivity may be said to be so; that is, the party was socialist, and voters supported many of its principles.

Support for a socialist party is opposition to ruling-class interests in Canada, as was support for Social Credit and Diefenbaker "conservatism." It is not a matter of conservative versus socialist ideology, but of opposition radicalism versus upper-class advantage. The opposition may not be born of firm ideological conviction, consciousness, or cohesiveness. Macpherson insists that in the nature of the small landholder, the petite bourgeoisie, there is an "oscillation between conservatism and radicalism." (Macpherson, 1953: 226.) However that may be true, small landholders have been an enduring force of resistance and change in Canadian class society.

We may observe in these examples two exceptions to the apparent absence of class politics in Canada. First, we find that there has indeed been political opposition to the established parties and the class and regional interests that they represent, in the West and more recently in Quebec. The regions themselves act in a class-like manner. In addition, whether the anti-"establishment" protest is translated into "socialism" or "conservatism," it remains, nonetheless, the opposition of a subordinate segment of the Canadian population to superior class interests, protest not initially crystallized about any ideological conviction, but deriving from experiences in the regional, ethnic, class structure of Canada.

Voting for established parties is conventional and ritual political action in Canadian society. The extent to which Canadians express class sentiments in routinized voting cannot be taken as indicative of class consciousness. Rather, class-based politics, consisting of the actions of industrial and rural workers (among whom we include most individual farm owners), is expressed in non-conventional behaviour, as in the repudiation of the major parties. This has by no means been a consistent feature of Canadian politics, or even of regions such as the Prairies. But it has been frequent enough to suggest class-like politics where none is supposed to exist.

Conclusion

Previously, we had considered the structure of class stratification in Canada, and the opportunities for mobility. But class means more than differences in wealth or occupational choice. There are real differences in the benefits that we might consider fundamental to human existence, as well as the more obvious differences in the consumption of luxury items. The Canadian welfare state does secure basic sustenance, clothing, shelter, and health care for Canadians, but these benefits are by no means uniformly available. Rather, they are systematically associated in quantity and quality with urbanized middle- and upper-class existence. The class structure thereby enforces a discrimination in basic human benefits.

Class-related discrimination is also reflected in the nature of criminal deviance and the nature of law enforcement. Working-class deviance is necessarily conspicuous, and often violent. There are not the opportunities for hidden theft that are available to the middle-class person. In addition, police activity tends to concentrate upon lower-class persons, in part because of the aggressive public nature of their criminal deviance, but also because they are vulnerable to prosecution.

Ironically, as a function of environmental experience and expectations, working-class persons not only assume that they will be the objects of harassment and violence, but also are less tolerant of moderate punishment and due process than are middle-class persons. This working-class intolerance has been characterized as a working-class authoritarianism, and has been taken to account, in part, for working-class political conservatism in the sense of support for right-wing parties.

The nature of political action is of crucial import, for class interests and their realization are to be found in political action. Support for conservative politics seems contrary to working-class economic interests and a manifestation of false consciousness. Such behaviour also seems related to religious ideology. Some religions, such as the Roman Catholic, have consistently espoused conservative politics and have actively discouraged socialist sympathy on the part of their members, while, amongst the Protestants, the Anglicans have been class-consistent in their conservative inclinations. In contrast, other Protestant denominations, such as, in its time, the Methodist, seem to have articulated a class awareness and responsiblity inclined to socialist support.

The ideological input of religion, and of immigrants committed to ideological philosophies, has had considerable impact upon the character and development of political protest in Canada. Protest has related to the regional expression of class interests. Whether socialist or non-socialist, such protest movements as have developed are class-related, in the sense of recognition of a situation of shared relative deprivation, and a conviction that taking collective action is a means for rectifying that situation.

To a considerable extent, political protest and opposition have been agrarian, but we are of the view that, in the context of Canadian regional relations, such agrarian action is consistent with class interests and action. In an industrialized society, the large or corporate agriculturalists aside, the farmer, though an owner, is in an economic position akin to that of the industrial worker, and with perhaps less security. Rural interests are thus expressed in agricultural unions, co-operatives, and third-party support, just as labour has expressed its interests in labour-union organization. The opposition of interests between corporate industrial capitalists and the farmer is similar to that between industrial owners or financiers and the blue-collar or white-collar worker. This is an especially volatile incompatibility, as the agrarian interests are vested in a region's subordination to the metropolitan influence of industrialized Ontario. Class-based social action seeking the alteration of this dominance is the subject of our concluding chapter.

CHAPTER 5

Class Conflict and Prospects for Change

Class and Change

In the 19th century, Karl Marx and Friedrich Engels argued that the interests of capitalists and the interests of workers were inherently contradictory. Inevitably, class conflict would become overt, and the revolutionary victory of the workers would come to pass. For Marx and Engels, the concept of class was not just a description of the structure of economic control, but, more important, it was the key to a theory of social change. The working class, as a collectivity conscious of its relations to the property ownership of the capitalists, was to be the vehicle of societal progress, ultimately realizing full equality of condition in a communist society.

Although Marx offered no time frame within which the revolution would occur, many observers have delighted in noting the apparent failure of Marxist predictions. Instead of becoming more impoverished, workers in developed societies have shared in industrial prosperity to an extent Marx failed to anticipate, while the *lumpenproletariat* have been extended considerable welfare privileges. In the place of class polarization, a "new class" of white-collar employees and professionals has developed, and serves to insulate the working class from the upper class. Rather than fewer and fewer capitalists controlling the means of production, ownership has been dispersed in corporate structures and amongst their shareholders and managers.

These features of modern capitalist societies are factual enough; it is their interpretation that is open to debate. The possibility of class action persists insofar as there persists a basic opposition of interest between owners and workers. The working class may share in industrial benefits to some degree, but, especially according to the concept of relative deprivation, they do not share to the point of satisfaction, let alone equity. The unemployed may be supported by the state, using funds collected from wage-earners, but they are not, thereby, somehow rendered full and equal participants in society. The middle class may have acquired some measure of job security and consumer capability, but they have not gained any greater control over the economy. Formal ownership may have largely passed from individuals to corporations, but ownership is not any less concentrated. On the contrary, it is more concentrated, given the size of modern corporations whose effective ownership is vested in one or a few individuals possessing blocks of shares. Changes in class affluence have not altered the fundamental relations of production and control in western societies like Canada. Nor have such changes prevented a steady and gradual shift in the direction of employment-dependence. That is, every year fewer and fewer Canadians are self-employed; they have become wage workers. The class of owners is becoming progressively smaller, and the class of workers progressively larger. At the same time, industries are becoming less labour-intensive and more dependent upon capital-intensive technology. Employment for workers is all the more precarious, as a result.

It is not a matter of rescuing Marxist theory, but of recognizing the continued salience of Marx's descriptions, however much he may have failed to anticipate the massive potential of industrial societies to produce and distribute wealth and to defer and control class opposition. Whether the opposition of interests of which Marx spoke and which does obtain in altered form in Canada will result in overt conflict and significant change is far more open to question.

In western societies, and in Canada in particular, there obviously has always been class conflict, as manifested, for example, in strike activities. And, increasingly, union organization and the use of strike action are aspects of the working lives of white-collar and professional employees as well as of manual workers, perhaps suggesting the class polarization that Marx anticipated. In this chapter, concentrating in large part upon organized labour's relationship with employers and government, we shall consider the Canadian experience of class conflict and the prospect for action that might alter the Canadian stratification system.

The Working Class and Conflict in Canada

Much of our earlier discussion has stressed the stability of social stratification in Canada and implied the absence of any non-rural class consciousness. Yet Canadian history is replete with instances of overt conflict among social classes, conflict indicative of class consciousness and effective in generating such a consciousness. Often class awareness and conflict have been expressed simply as reciprocal hostility, as in the attitudes and comments of members of the working and upper classes, with the middle class characteristically echoing upper-class sentiment. Thus, working-class distrust and resentment of welfare agents, for example, and middle- and upper-class declarations of their own tax-paying virtue, are indicative of widely shared antagonisms. Likewise indicative of some class awareness, though usually ''false consciousness'' as far as a Marxist would be concerned, are the non-unionized Canadians' suspicion of unions, and their inclination to blame unions not only for disruptions in services, but for international economic trends such as inflation.

In our early Canadian experience, class hostility was most explicit during the initial phases of unionization, especially in the years immediately preceding World War I, through the war years, and into the Depression of the 1930s. During the Depression, for example, Canadians were certainly aware of differential privilege. The prosperous people who survived the economic disaster regarded the indigent with disdain, and were reciprocated with bitterness and hostility. Gray relates many such examples, as in the case of a group of relief-workers on a make-work project in Winnipeg, who were harassed by an indignant citizen, furious over the disposition of his tax money on "lazy bums." In turn, the "bums," persons who had lost their jobs, responded with threats of violence. (Gray, 1966: 45.) Often, as we shall go on to consider, the violence was more than a threat.

Additionally, the conflict of classes has been linked to ethnic bias in Canadian history. In 1918, for example, riots in Quebec City were a feature of French-Canadian working-class opposition to military conscription. (McNaught, 1970: 81.) The internment of Japanese Canadians on the west coast during World War II was an instance of the authorities acting against an entire ethnic group. Indian protests in the 1970s were class-related, whether they were expressed in blockading highways in British Columbia, occupying a park in Kenora, Ontario, or organizing a march to Ottawa that climaxed in a violent confrontation with the RCMP on Parliament Hill.

There is a long tradition of such ethnic/class distinction and conflict, as long as the history of contact among Indians, Europeans, Euro-Canadians, Anglo-Canadians, and non-Anglo immigrants in Canada. In World War I, the invocation of the War Measures Act led to several thousand arrests and summary deportations of immigrant workers who had failed to satisfy the Anglo-Canadian definition of loyalty. (Brown and Brown, 1973: 36.) Similarly, in the Depression, the government resorted to arrest and deportation of "aliens" as one means of reducing the number of unemployed.

Prejudice, discrimination, and the confrontation of ethnic minorities and government are aspects of class in Canada, and are explicit manifestations of conflict between the privileged upper or ruling class and working-class persons in Canada's "ethnic mosaic." Usually, thus far, the urban middle class as a collectivity has "opted out," although middle-class individuals have been crucial in organizing and taking part in opposition actions. The major foci of conflict have been labour and agrarian action. We have discussed agrarian protest in Chapter 4, and require only a few additional remarks as prelude to a brief description of related conflict involving the industrial worker. We will stress three major occasions of class confrontation in Canadian society: the Winnipeg General Strike of 1919; the "On to Ottawa Trek" of 1935; and the Saskatchewan Doctors' Strike of 1962.

Farm Protest Politics

When we looked at the pattern of agrarian protest and third-party support in Canada, we found it pronounced in the Canadian West. But Quebec and Ontario rural residents have also perceived themselves to be in fundamental disharmony with urban Canada, supporting "third parties" such as the Progressives or the Créditistes. In 1974, farmers across the nation protested against the prices they were getting, most dramatically in Quebec, where calves were slaughtered and buried in outrage.

Donald Creighton, a conservative Canadian historian, has suggested that radical political action in Canada has been a fluctuation, though not a synthesis, of labour and agrarian radicalism. (Creighton, 1972: 160.) Thus, in the wake of labour action and the Winnipeg General Strike, the agrarian Progressive Party emerged, eventually to provide the setting for the emergence of a prairie socialism and the CCF. The Progressive Party was a rural party, expressing the interests and frustrations of people on the Prairies and in Ontario who perceived themselves as lacking in influence and their proper share of national resources. Because it was more particularly related to regionalism and social class, W.L. Morton views prairie support for the Progressives as a manifestation of protest against the colonial status of the West in its relations to eastern business interests. (Morton, 1950: 164-65.)

The Prairies, locus of most radical farm politics, have also been the source of considerable labour-union radicalism. The two forces have underlined regional cleavage in Canada.

Labour Protest Politics

In Canada, the history of labour-union organization and activities has been the most explicit example of class conflict. We find working-class unionists pitted against upper-middle and upper-class managers and employers. Strikes have always been a direct expression of class conflict. Today, when we are well past the initial phases of labour-union organization, we take for granted that strikes are pacific withdrawals of service, with perhaps only an occasional picket-line skirmish. Modern large-scale labour violence, even what appears to have been organized as such, as at the James Bay hydroelectric project in 1974, nowadays seems extraordinary. Similar violence, however, was once routine in North America, with strikers on the one side, and the police and strike-breakers hired by employers on the other. For example, the Royal (Canadian) Northwest Mounted Police were frequently brought in to break up strikes, particularly in the Canadian West around the time of World War I. (Brown and Brown, 1973: 38–45.) In this regard, it is interesting to note the argument that the

Winnipeg General Strike may have saved the Royal Northwest Mounted Police from disbandment, for it established an important strike-breaking role for them. (Brown and Brown, 1973: 45.)

The last quarter of the 19th century and the years prior to World War I were filled with class conflict in Canada. The years 1876 to 1914 saw troops called out 33 times to control and put down strikes in Ontario, Quebec, and the Maritimes. (McNaught, 1970: 80.) Between 1900 and 1919 there were more than 2,000 labour conflicts. In 1919 alone there were 336 strikes and lockouts, involving 150,000 workers in 1919 alone. (Creighton, 1972: 159.) In this period there were at least 35 incidents of violence. (*Labour Gazette*, 1965: 20.) After the war, labour action intensified as the veterans returned. In 1914 trade-union membership in Canada numbered 166,000. By 1919, membership was approximately 378,000. (Creighton, 1972: 158.)

During this period, the overt conflict of classes was unmistakable; a marked difference between western and eastern labour became apparent, in no small part attributable to European settlement in the West and the immigration of British settlers with socialist and labour-union experience, as we noted in describing the development of the CCF. Robin states that the West was far more radical than the East. (Robin, 1968: 160.) S.D. Clark suggests that both labour and agrarian protest in the West were manifestations of western Canadian opposition to "eastern dominance." (Clark, 1950: vii; Creighton, 1972: 159.) The cleavage became especially apparent in 1918, at the national Trades and Labour Congress meeting in Quebec City. (Robin, 1968: 160.) At this time, the western inclination toward political education of workers and political action surfaced as a minority view; eventually, two western socialists were ousted as officers, and a new Congress president was elected. The new president, Tom Moore, was a personal friend of the American unionist, Samuel Gompers. (Robin, 1968: 160–162.) Moore's election highlighted a persisting split in the character of Canadian labour: eastern labour organizations have been internationalist — that is, affiliated with American unions — while western unions have often been stubbornly nationalist, even when formally affiliated with American-based unions.

In the West, at the Western Labour Conference held in Calgary in 1919, the notion of One Big Union (OBU) grew up, amidst statements of support for "Russian Bolsheviks." (Robin, 1968: 175; Penner, 1973: xiii.) The concept of the OBU was dear to the socialists, who reasoned that it would be a means to class consciousness, and that the strike would be the means of political action. (Robin, 1968: 175–176.) The OBU was never to be realized; nor was there ever a consensus about the concept, even in the West. (Robin, 1968: 177.) But it set the mood for events in Winnipeg in 1919.

Winnipeg was a centre of strong support for the OBU concept and generally the centre of labour protest in Canada. (Robin, 1968: 168, 191–192.) One of the causes of protest was an Order in Council passed by the federal government on October 11, 1918, restricting speech, association, publications, and above all, the right to strike. (Robin, 1968: 166.)

i. Winnipeg, 1919, and After

The Winnipeg General Strike began on May 15, 1919, and lasted until June 25. (Penner, 1973: xxv–xxvii.) It featured labour on the one side and the Winnipeg Citizens Committee, consisting of businessmen and professionals, on the other. Special police, the RCMP, and the regular army ultimately confronted the strikers in the streets of Winnipeg.

The upper class perceived the situation to be a challenge to authority, a presage of revolution. The workers and labour leaders saw it as a matter of gaining recognition of unions and collective bargaining as a means to improved working conditions and wages. There is little doubt that neither side really understood the other, an apt illustration of the varying perceptions and ideologies of social classes. The political authorities, such as Mayor C.F. Gray, seemed to be bewildered by events, which appeared to be running out of control, obliging a resort to force. The newspapers were consistently opposed to the strikers, characterizing them as aliens and communists. On the other hand, to the strikers, the authorities were selfish and ruthless exploiters. In May, the Citizens Committee started to publish *The Winnipeg Citizen*, wherein strikers were portrayed as agents of lawlessness and foreign revolution, in statements of the following sort:

> Lawlessness and disorder are rampant throughout the city all day and every day. Men and women are wantonly assaulted on the streets. (Balawyder, 1967: 1.)

> The citizens of Winnipeg have been fighting . . . against a determined effort to establish Bolshevism and the rule of the Soviet here and then to expand it all over the Dominion. . . . (Balawyder, 1967: 19.)

To the present day, establishment historians persist in viewing the strike as a violent and deplorable aberration. Labour is held accountable, rather than their class opponents, or the mounted and armed police who charged the strikers on "Bloody Saturday." For example, Donald Creighton's acclaimed history of Canada's first century devotes only one page to the strike, and refers to it as the "Winnipeg riot." (Creighton, 1972: 60.)

The strike was called in sympathy with construction and metal trades workers who were striking for an eight-hour day. (Balawyder, 1967: 1–3.) At its peak, the strikers effectively withdrew all services, from transportation, milk and bread deliveries and postal deliveries, to the services of firemen, telegraphers, and civic employees, including policemen. (Balawyder, 1967; Penner, 1973.) On the first day, 27,000 workers were out. (Balawyder, 1967: 3.) At its peak, there were 35,000 strikers in a population of 175,000, whereas, on the day the strike began, Trades and Labour Council membership numbered only 12,000. (Penner, 1973: x.)

So far as the unions were concerned, the strike consisted, not of demonstrations and "lawlessness", but of simple withdrawal of services. However, an additional ingredient in the situation consisted of the presence of servicemen returned from the war. Numerous parades were organized by soldiers caught in unemployment on their return from abroad. On June 21, one such parade was attacked by armed special police, mounted police, and members of the regular army, in the effective climax of the strike. At least one marcher was killed and about thirty were injured. (Penner, 1972: x; Balawyder, 1967: 5.)

Civic and federal authorities co-ordinated their responses, and acted to confront rather than negotiate with the strikers. On May 26, the Winnipeg Citizens Committee voted to fire all civic employees who went out on strike. On June 5, the federal government passed an amendment to the Immigration Act, allowing the deportation of British-born immigrants, so that the government could arrest and be rid of some of the leaders of the strike. (Robin, 1968: 181.) On June 9, all but 16 members of the Winnipeg police force were fired for failing to sign a promise not to strike, an action leading to the formation of the special police force on June 10. (Balawyder, 1967: x.) June 17 saw the arrest by federal authorities of 12 strike leaders, including J.S. Woodsworth. (Balawyder, 1967: 4.) Then, after the violent confrontation of June 21, soldiers and police patrolled the streets of the city, fully armed with pistols and machine guns. The police attack of June 21 effectively destroyed support for the strike, and on June 25 it ended. (Balawyder, 1967: 5.)

The labour radicalism of the West, the activities and strategies of the socialists, the decision to form the One Big Union were the background events of the strike. That it was a characteristic western event is evidenced by the fact that most of the international unions, which, as we have noted, were strongest in eastern Canada, opposed the strike. (Robin, 1968: 184.) The autonomous unions of the West were strongly influenced by British socialist officers, who, in turn, were influential in the strike. (Penner, 1973: xix.) For reasons of immigration and background, and because of the circumstances of western Canada and its more or less colonial relationship to eastern Canada, the manifestations of class consciousness and class conflict, urban and agrarian, were viable in the West to an extent not true of the East. The strike was broken, but the class bases of the strike lived on in the city. Bercuson summarizes:

> "The Winnipeg general strike was a manifestation of the continuing class division that has marked the history of the city for over half a century. The events of May and June, 1919, were preceded and followed by growing splits in society and were largely products of those divisions. The strike was the most traumatic of events which contributed to class memory and polarization, but it did not initiate these psychological attitudes. Class consciousness was a strong factor in Winnipeg prior to the strike, laid the foundation for labour's political successes in the 1920s, and was largely responsible for the continuing division of Winnipeg into those whose parents or grandparents were

strikers, and those whose forebears were members of the Citizens'
Committee.''

Bercuson, David, *Confrontation at Winnipeg*, Montreal, McGill-
Queen's University Press, 1974: p. 199.

In the years after the strike, labour organization in Canada grew, although
it did not resort to dramatic confrontation like that of 1919. Creighton
states that the strike marked the deflation of radical labour politics.
(Creighton, 1972: 60.) But Canadian labour was active and aggressive
throughout the 1920s. In terms of Canadian autonomy, Abella suggests
that up to and peaking in 1935, Canadian unions were at their strongest,
with about one-half the union membership in independent Canadian unions.
In 1921, the Canadian Catholic Confederation of Labour was founded and
was characteristically nationalist through the 1930s. In 1930, the radical
Workers' Unity League came into being, to a large degree under communist control. (Abella, 1973: 2-3.) With the exception of the Catholic Federation, largely active in Quebec, the Communist Party of Canada was active
in union leadership, especially in the Workers' Unity League.

Abella notes that the Communist Party was ultimately instrumental in
the destruction of independent Canadian union activity, in that, in 1935,
the Party ordered the disbandment of the Workers' Unity League in favour
of affiliation with the Trades and Labour Congress, an affiliate of the
American Federation of Labour. The Communist objective was a united
labour front. (Abella, 1973: 3.) After 1935, American affiliates came to
dominate. In larger part, in addition to the Communist Party decision, this
was due to the actions of Ontario labour organizers rather than the work of
the Americans themselves. (Abella, 1973: 2; 5; 216.) The model of the
American unions and their apparent successes proved too attractive, though,
as Abella notes, it is questionable whether they ever played more than a
role of offering moral support in aid of Canadian workers. Certainly they
never aided them financially, for Canadian dues went south to a greater
degree than financial aid came north. (Abella, 1973.) Despite American
union affiliation, one unique feature of the Canadian unions persisted: a
flirtation with socialism and eventually the foundation of a socialist party,
the CCF-NDP. Horowitz suggests that even the Trades and Labour Congress never repudiated socialism in the unequivocal manner of the American unions. (Horowitz, 1968: 58.) But affiliation with American unions
was effectively to prevent formal, explicit, labour affiliation with the future
CCF-NDP. (Horowitz, 1968: 235.)

The year 1936 marked the entry of the Congress of Industrial Organization (CIO) to Canada, at the instigation of Ontario labour leaders. (Abella,
1973: 210.) In 1937, the CIO was organizing steel workers in Nova Scotia,
and also found itself in a dramatic confrontation in Oshawa, Ontario.
(Abella, 1973: 5; 21-22.) The United Auto Workers' strike against General
Motors of Oshawa established the CIO as a powerful labour organization
in Canada. (Abella, 1973: 21-22.)

From this period, only in western Canada did marked nationalist labour sentiment crop up, especially in British Columbia unions, where movements to secede from American-based unions occurred periodically. (Abella, 1973: 111–138.) Also, western labour radicalism would live on even within the Canadian Congress of Labour, the result of a 1939 merger of the CIO and the All Canadian Congress of Labour. The latter included a remnant of the One Big Union movement (Abella, 1973: 44), a dream that finally collapsed during the Great Depression.

ii. Depression and the On to Ottawa Trek

The Depression set the stage for a dramatic confrontation between workers and the authorities. Throughout the decade of the thirties numerous incidents took place between the unemployed and the police. The railroad police of the Canadian Pacific Railway established a particular reputation for viciousness among the unemployed "riding the rails."

The specific policy of the Depression that elicited both working-class and middle-class bitterness related to the creation of relief work camps. On October 8, 1932, the work camps were created by Order in Council of the federal government. (Horowitz, 1973: viii.) They were set up and administered by the federal authorities, actually operated by the Army, and, by 1934, contained 25,000 young men. After four years of operation, at least 115,000 men and as many as 170,000 men had occupied the camps at one time or another. (Gray, 1967: 147; Sherlock, 1985.)

The camps were the objects of middle- and upper-class abuse because they were make-work projects, and deemed a waste of public funds. Yet they were created not only to occupy the unemployed and remove them from urban centres, but also to satisfy middle-class values, in that they did require labour rather than provide welfare simply on the basis of need. For the unemployed workers, they were the supreme insult and degradation. The camps existed in isolation, spawning boredom, with a reservation-like administration that did not allow camp inhabitants to form any organizations or to have any grievance procedures, while the wages paid were 20 cents a day. Bitterness was inevitable. (Gray, 1967: 147–148.)

On April 4, 1935, 1,500 relief camp workers moved into Vancouver in order to protest their situation and seek some change in government policy. (Hoar, 1973: ix.) The work camps had been the sites of active propagandizing and organizing by the Communist Party of Canada, and by the time of the Vancouver assembly, the workers not only were in a mood for action, but had leaders ready and able to promote it. (Gray, 1967: 145.) Government authorities in Ottawa simply labelled the ensuing protest march as Communist-inspired. But it was much more broadly based than that, and it was a genuine act of disillusioned people who wished to work. With assistance from supporters such as the Liberal mayor of Vancouver, who sponsored a tag day netting $6,000, a march was organized, with Ottawa the objective. (Gray, 1967: 150.)

The marchers left Vancouver on June 3 and June 4, 1935, about 1,000 strong. (Gray, 1967: 151.) It now seems that, early on, the federal government had determined to stop the march, and Regina was the logical place for this, because of the concentration of Royal Canadian Mounted Police in that city. On June 14, 2,000 marchers arrived in Regina by freight train. (Gray, 1967: 152.) There they were ordered to halt by the government, and talks were arranged.

The talks proved to be utterly fruitless. As Gray reports, "It degenerated into a shouting match between the Prime Minister and Arthur Evans, the strike leader. Mr. Bennett called Evans a thief, and Evans called the Prime Minister a liar." (Gray, 1967; 155.) On July 1, a mass rally attended by an estimated 3,500 to 4,500 marchers and on-lookers was held in Market Square in Regina. (Gray, 1963: 158.) The city police and the RCMP were ordered in, and, at their appearance in force, the crowd panicked. Fighting developed, barricades were erected, and spectators, strikers, and police were injured. It lasted three hours and concluded with a policeman dead, many more injured, about seventeen civilians with bullet wounds, and 118 people arrested. (Gray, 1967: 159; Sherlock, 1985.)

The leaders were in jail and the trek was effectively broken. By July 5, the strikers had dispersed. (Hoar, 1973; xv–xviii.) At about the same time, other protesters in Winnipeg dispersed, just avoiding a similar police-striker confrontation. (Gray, 1967: 157–159.) Two weeks later some trekkers were attempting to carry on, and about 250 made it on foot to Kenora after their buses were stopped at the Manitoba-Ontario border by the Ontario Provincial Police. After three days, these trekkers gave up and returned to Winnipeg. (Gray, 1967; 160.)

As an ironic footnote to history, in June, 1985, several former trekkers at last made their way to Ottawa. Travelling this time by regular airline rather than by freight train or on foot, they arrived to protest the continued high rate of unemployment in Canada.

The specific clash in Regina would probably today be called a "police riot," for it resulted from police action taken on government orders. As in the Winnipeg General Strike, the entire trek was characterized by a class polarization of sentiment. James Gray, who covered the events as a reporter for the *Winnipeg Free Press*, states that the trekkers did have sympathetic treatment from the press, and were generally met with favour by the public, until the shouting match between Bennett and Evans. (Gray, 1967; 151–152; 155.) But even so, it seems fairer to say that both sides were locked into extreme views of each other; the government was callous and oppressive and the workers were communist. (Hoar, 1973: ix.)

The Dominion Day battle in Regina was merely the conspicuous event in a prolonged situation of class conflict. Protests against the relief programs had been occurring elsewhere before 1935: at Vancouver in 1931 and Winnipeg in 1934. Once again, western Canada was the setting for the more radical political action.

Source: Reprinted with permission — The Toronto Star Syndicate.

World War II marked the end of the Depression and of mass radical labour politics. Certainly the bitter memories lived on, not least among unemployed Canadians who found a secure income only in the armed forces. We recall the remark of one Canadian veteran, who in the 1970s summed up his analysis of the situation in the sentiment that, "Hitler was the one who got me a job!" Afterwards came the post-war industrial boom in North America. Canada in particular enjoyed a brief major-power status and a flurry of Canadian-controlled industry. Wages were high and welfare policies were extended to all classes. Yet even the gradual introduction of welfare security programs of the sort now taken for granted were occasions of class conflict. The most dramatic example also occurred in western Canada.

iii. The Saskatchewan Doctors' Strike

Our third example of class conflict involved a privileged occupational group within the middle class acting as the strikers, seeking to deter the extension of medical services to all classes. In July 1962, medical doctors in Saskatchewan commenced what would become a 23-day withdrawal of services in protest against the Saskatchewan government's comprehensive health care insurance program. The CCF government, abiding by its campaign promises, was determined to implement medical insurance to protect people against the economic fluctuations of the Saskatchewan economy. In a sense, one fraction of the middle class (the physicians) was in conflict with another segment of the middle class (the small rural landowners). But it was also clash of ideologies central to a class society, for the CCF government was seen to represent socialism, while the physicians saw themselves as medical entrepreneurs. The government was therefore stubbornly, and expensively, opposed by the doctors, who were determined to preserve their *"laissez-faire* definition of medical practice," or services for purchase. (Badgley and Wolfe, 1967: 5.) It also became, in part, a rural-urban conflict between the farm population and the doctors and their urban supporters. Fifty-four percent of Saskatchewan physicians practised in Regina and Saskatoon, where only 22 percent of the population lived. (Badgley and Wolfe, 1973: 28.)

The medical insurance legislation and the CCF government became the target of a very expensive campaign, with a Keep Our Doctors Committee in the vanguard. The KOD consisted of non-CCF politicians, druggists, dentists, businessmen, and some clergy, with ties to the provincial Liberal party. (Badgley and Wolfe, 1973: 52.) The KOD publicity equated medical insurance with "Marxism and Communism." (Badgley and Wolfe, 1973: 31.) To mount the campaign, aside from citizen donations, there was a $100 levy from all doctors in the province, plus $35,000 from the Canadian Medical Association. (Badgley and Wolfe, 1973: 74.)

Whatever the objective class support for the CCF, as now evaluated by historians and social scientists, it was clearly the case that, in 1966, little more than twenty years ago, the CCF was viewed as anathema by ruling and upper-middle-class interests. Saskatchewan may have been an unlikely social test-tube, but there is little doubt that there was a perception of clear, class-related, ideological cleavage.

In opposition to the KOD were the government, the trade unions, the farmers' union, and the co-op organizations. In 1961, a survey of small communities showed that 63 percent of the population favoured state-supported health care, but less than half (46 percent) of the upper class were in favour, as opposed to 70 percent of the lower class. (Badgley and Wolfe, 1973: 74.) Thus did the conflict polarize by class. In addition, publicity in the media was almost totally opposed to the government program. Except for the Canadian Broadcasting Corporation, the media supported the KOD. (Badgley and Wolfe, 1973: 74.)

Ultimately, of course, the doctors capitulated, in no small part because the government, rather than compromising, resorted to importing doctors from the United Kingdom.

Since 1962, Medicare programs have become available throughout

Canada. Medical resentment does continue to flare up, as in Ontario, where, with much publicity, physicians threaten to withdraw from the government service, and individuals occasionally do. Or, when governments threaten to end medical extra-billing, physicians threaten job actions. But although publicly-supported medical aid is well established, as is most legislation leading to an elaboration of the welfare state, ultimately, the benefits of medical insurance, though clearly aiding all classes, have most benefitted the middle class. Still, for a brief period, around this one issue, the reality of class conflict again crystallized and became overt in one region of Canadian society.

Conflict and Ethnicity

Intensive labour confrontations have often involved immigrant workers, reflecting the ethnic/class characteristics of Canada. Canadian capitalists and politicians worked with clear and explicit distinctions. At one time, Blacks and Orientals were "unassimilable" and were "to be used and, if possible, discarded;" Eastern and Southern Europeans were "candidates for Canadianization;" Brits and Yanks were the high-status candidates for Canadianization. (Avery, 1979: 7–8.) Mining, lumbering, farming, and railroad construction were key employment sectors for foreign workers, where there was explicit "priority to the imperatives of industrial capitalism and agricultural wage labour," drawn from the "transatlantic capitalist labour market." (Avery, 1979: 9.) These immigrant labourers were viewed as industrial fodder, and there is little doubt that, after the period of frontier settlement, immigration to Canada was manipulated in the interest of employers. Upper-class social sentiment revealed a sense of the European and Asian immigrants as somehow inferior and socially deviant. Speaking in 1944, for example, the Reverend Canon W.W. Judd of the Church of England in Canada addressed the boys at Upper Canada College. He urged them to remember with compassion the "refugees, Jews, Japanese Canadians, and juvenile delinquents." (Cameron, 1982: 14.)

The immigrants were prominent everywhere in Canada in struggling against industrial exploitation. In the West there developed a decisive commonality of interest between immigrant-fed industrial labour and agricultural labour and small land-holders; all perceived themselves to be subject to the exploitation of "Eastern" big money. Elsewhere, as in Quebec, the immigrant populations were in a minority, and yet crucial to the labour movement in single-industry towns such as Rouyn-Noranda. The 1934 "foreigners' strike" in Rouyn-Noranda, where perhaps at most 10 percent of the Noranda Mines workers were English or French, marked the power of the "Fros." (Dumas, 1975: 28–42.) The "Fros" were labelled as Communist agitators by management, government, and some Canadian unions. The Canadian Federation of Labour wrote in one of its publications that: "Reds invade the North" despite the company's "just and equitable treatment of the miners." (Dumas, 1975: 37.) The strike having been called for union recognition and better wages, it concluded with fifteen strike leaders tried, sentenced to penitentiary, and scheduled for deportation. Deportation had long been a powerful weapon of the state, as in the Winnipeg General Strike of 1919; in Rouyn-Noranda, ultimately two leaders were deported. (Dumas, 1975: 40.) The "foreigners' strike" boosted Quebec unionism, and briefly politicized it; in 1944 the northern mining communities of Quebec sent a CCF member to the Quebec Legislative Assembly — the only CCF member ever elected in Quebec. (Dumas, 1975: 129.)

Part of the historical labour struggle was between sectors of the labour force. Foreigners were often radical, while at other times they were brought in by labour brokers, companies, and the state as strike-breakers. In addition, labour was divided by an eastern crafts-union orientation in contrast to western industrial unionism. Additionally, of enduring import, American and Canadian unions were in competition. In 1919, for example, the Western Labour Conference and the formation of the OBU (One Big Union) was an attempt to resist American unionism. (Penner, 1977: 189.) As a counter, the federal government worked with the "Gomperist" Trades and Labour Congress (TLC) and resisted the One Big Union. (Penner, 1977: 189.)

The Examples of Class Conflict in Context

The examples of class conflict we have related may be taken in two ways. One might simply view them as interesting aberrations in the evolution of Canadian society, and therefore not of continuing relevance. Or, as we suggest, one may view them as symptomatic of and the product of fundamental stratification in Canada. Although conflict among classes usually remains subdued and invisible, incidents such as we have described were occasions in which the opposition of classes in Canada broke through. And they illustrate the manner in which social class in Canada is intimately interrelated with regional and ethnic differences, underlining the dominant status of the Anglo central-Canadian within Canadian society. The three examples stressed are probably the best known and documented in Canadian history, but they are not the only instances of conflict among classes. Others have been as violent, such as the famous Estevan, Saskatchewan, strike. Miners struck in Estevan in September, 1931, when their union was not recognized; ultimately, the RCMP again acted as strike-breakers and the strike was broken, with two dead.

At the other side of the continent, on the Atlantic, coal miners in Cape Breton, Nova Scotia, were in persistent struggle, often violently, with companies that provided poor wages and unsafe working conditions and opposed unionism. The companies also owned the workers' homes and the stores where they bought their staples. From the turn of the century to the mid-twenties, the mine workers were among Canada's most militant workers. (Mellor, 1983.)

In Cape Breton, Nova Scotia, many miners still honour Davis Day, June 11, in memory of Bill Davis, a miner killed by a company policeman during a strike in 1925. In March 1925, 12,000 coal miners had struck to oppose a 35 percent wage reduction of their daily average wage of $4.50. In the town of New Waterford, between 500–1,000 strikers marched to the company-owned power plant — water and power had been cut off to the town. Armed and mounted company police rode into the crowd. Strikers and policemen were injured — and Bill Davis was shot through the heart. A policeman was charged, but ultimately acquitted. (Davis, 1980: 45.)

In Ontario, the Oshawa strike of 1937 stands out as a significant, though non-violent, conflict. One expert estimates that, next to the Winnipeg General Strike, the Oshawa conflict was a "landmark." (Abella, 1974.) Auto workers struck General Motors, in response to a speed-up in the assembly line. The outcome was the firm introduction of the CIO in Canada. Another noteworthy Ontario strike was the 1941 strike of gold miners at Kirkland Lake. The miners struck in order to secure the right to organize and to bargain collectively. Ultimately, the strike was broken by the Ontario Provincial Police, in 1942. (MacDowell, 1983.)

In Quebec, the most important strike took place in the company towns of Asbestos and Thetford Mines in 1949. On February 13 of that year, 5,000 miners begun their struggle against the mining companies and the Quebec government. The struggle lasted four months, until the end of June, with police interventions, beatings, and mass arrests. (Trudeau, 1974; Isbister, 1974.)

Other contemporary events in Quebec are also illustrative. Racial/class violence was a feature of the destruction of a computer centre at Sir George Williams University in Montreal in 1969. And, among other violent strikes, the Murray Hill taxi strike in Montreal resulted in a death. The labour violence in 1974 at the James Bay Hydroelectric Development in northern Quebec is another instance, one that seemed to involve not only labour and management, but also a conflict between a Quebec union and an international union — not insignificant, given the previously-remarked less radical role of American-based unions in Canada. Lastly, we cannot fail to note that Quebec separatism of the 1970s was a class movement as well as an ethnic movement, one in which the new middle class of post-war Quebec had in some considerable degree committed itself to radical action, with the end both independence and socialism.

If such conflict is not abnormal but a continuing feature of Canadian society, deriving from the class distinctions that exist in Canada, then the prospects of change in aid of a non-violent and genuinely egalitarian or minimally stratified society must concern us.

Class Conflict and Welfare Politics

Organized Labour and Change

i. *Middle Class Unionism*

Labour unions have come to be broadly accepted, with the right to strike extended to public as well as private employees; increasing numbers of middle-class workers, as in universities and in government bureaucracies, are unionized. One poll demonstrated that 58 percent of Canadians view unions as necessary to protect workers' rights. The occupational group most pro-union were professionals, with an approval rate of 75 percent. (*Weekend Magazine*, September 2, 1978: 3.) It is significant that efforts to increase unionization, and, as noted above, the greatest pro-union sentiment, are found among the more privileged Canadian employees — the middle-class — and not among the working class.

The influence of the "internationals," as will be discussed, remains a significant feature of modern Canadian unionism. Also noteworthy in the present context of unionism is the unions' apparent lack of interest in organizing the marginal and unskilled work force. Recent organizing gains have been made among middle-class occupational groups, professionals such as teachers, university professors, and public servants. This has also meant an increase in the number of women joining unions, especially in the service, commercial, and professional sectors.

Female membership in unions is now increasing more rapidly than male membership, although women's total numbers lag behind. By 1980, women made up 38 percent of the labour force, but only 27 percent of Canadian union membership, and they held only 17 percent of leadership or executive positions. (White, 1980: 22–23.) Women work predominantly in service occupations or the finance sector, where unionization has traditionally been resisted. In banks, for example, women make up 73 percent of the work force. (White, 1980: 31.)

As female unionists grow in numbers, they do affect the character of unions. Working women produce a new group of workers to be "radicalized" — probably not so formidable a task in itself. But the increasing number of married women in the labour force over 35 years of age means second incomes in many families, especially middle-class families. (Westley and Westley, 1971: 11.) The disposable income for the family unit increases as women go to work, often markedly, perhaps depressing economic dissatisfaction and any consequent politics of dissent, whether from working-class women working from necessity or middle-class women working for intellectual stimulus and for luxuries.

The tactics of organized labour have become respectable, almost fashionable, with increased middle-class membership. Strikes are no longer the exclusive prerogative of industrial workers, but are used with vigorous rhetoric by highly-salaried professionals. It is doubtful, however, whether this fashionable "radical chic" unionism translates into genuine radicalism or interest in social change. Middle-class unionists, like those belonging to the Canadian Union of Public Employees (CUPE) have shifted the weight of the union movement from the internationals to the nationals. Attempts have been made to generate a real middle-class militancy, as in 1981, when three CUPE officers, including the national president, Grace Hartman, were sentenced to jail terms for failing to obey a Supreme Court injunction ordering striking non-medical hospital workers back to work. (The Canadian Press, June 15, 1981.) But insofar as members are functionaries of the state, there is unlikely to be any inclination for thoroughgoing change.

The actual number of strikes in Canada is high, many of them still stemming from the problem of union recognition. For example, in 1979, in Ontario alone, there were at least 37 strikes over first contracts after certification (*Ottawa Journal*, October 31, 1979), the initial bargaining where unions and management test one another and a union may break. Similarly, violence is not an obsolete feature of labour conflict, with the intervention of private and public police agencies to curtail strikes, and workers themselves resorting to violence as strike bitterness mounts. An example was the strike of Amoco Fabrics workers in Hawkesbury, Ontario; through its four weeks, violence was frequently threatened and finally occurred, with public damage to civic buildings and the arrest of 45 strikers. (*The Citizen*, August 14, 1980.) At times too, there is a hint of the potential for a general strike. In 1978, in Manitoba, 7,500 workers in the construction industry, supermarkets, breweries, and meat packers were off the job at one point. (*The Globe and Mail*, July 10, 1978.) Right across western Canada, workers in these industries were also contesting contracts and walking out. (The Canadian Press, August 19, 1978.)

Nor is dedicated employer resistance lacking today. In the early days of industrial organizing, it was common to find employers hiring thugs to act as "private police" to intimidate and beat workers. In 1918, for example, a brief general strike in Vancouver was broken by a force of 300 men recruited and paid by local business. But even in recent years there have been elaborate efforts to deter union organizing, as when, in 1974, K-Mart executives spent $167,000 to hire a firm of private investigators to infiltrate and sabotage organizing efforts by the International Brotherhood of Teamsters. Three company officials were charged under the Ontario Labour Relations Act, and given conditional discharges and one year of probation, but not jail sentences. Significantly, the Crown Prosecutor, the voice of the state, supported a conditional discharge and community service rather than other punishment, describing the offenders as "misguided executives." (The Canadian Press, June 4, 1981.) The firm was fined a mere $25,000. (The Canadian Press, June 13, 1981.)

Although such conflict exists, it must also be noted that generally speaking, unionized labour action is a poor indicator of working-class power.

A lower proportion of Canadians is unionized than is the case in other industrial societies — only about one worker in three. Fragmented among national and international unions, craft and industrial unions, old working class and middle class, males and females, separated by religion, ethnicity, and region, Canada's labour movement presents an uncertain mixture of interests. Reflecting our federated society, labour is a patchwork of employee organizations without a concerted ideology or objective.

ii. *Nationals and Internationals*

Within Canadian unionism, the division between national versus international unionism is related to that between working-class versus middle-class unions. Contention among rival unions has served to segment the Canadian labour movement. Not only are the many unions not well integrated within the umbrella structure of the Canadian Labour Congress, they are riven by competition of interest, and, in some measure, ideology, between the international unions and various national unions. A prominent example is to be found in the Quebec construction industry, where the Quebec Federation of Labour has combatted the internationals and supported a dues boycott. (The Canadian Press, September 27, 1980.) Similarly, in 1980, the CLC contested with twelve international building trades unions for membership, resorting to overt conflict in the form of membership raids. (*The Sunday Star*, April 12, 1981.)

The domination of the Canadian labour movement by international, that is, American-based, unions, is of long standing, as are its consequences. The American union tradition has explicitly rejected politicization and embraced the notion of unions as agencies for the improved marketing of labour. Such a view clearly suits the nature of the Canadian affiliates. It is less consistently a feature of the Canadian independents, especially those in regions of the country with a long history of union-generated social conflict, as in British Columbia. (Abella, 1975; Lipton, 1973.)

American-based unions became active in Canada, not as unwelcome aliens, but because they were perceived by Canadian workers to be effective. In particular, the politically-active unionism of western Canada was not admired by central Canadian workers who wanted tangible economic gains and security. Thus the Congress of Industrial Organization (CIO) was invited into Canada by Oshawa auto workers and Sarnia foundry workers. (Abella, 1973: 217.) By the beginning of World War II, the internationals were numerically dominant, although the organizing initiative and leadership as well as the funding were, in the main, strictly Canadian. (Abella, 1973: 217.) Thus, although "Gomperism" may be aptly criticized for castrating Canadian labour politics, commentators have correctly pointed out that there were indigenous Canadian reasons for conservative labour attitudes and practices. Canadian unionists themselves largely welcomed the American Federation of Labour and the prospect of more efficient

American labour organization. Moreover, "in an era of racism, individualism, and uncertainty," Canadians from all quarters, including workers themselves, opposed radical union politics. (Abella, 1978: 5.) In this context, "migration took the place of militancy" (Abella, 1978: 5), as workers moved in large numbers to the United States; similarly replacing militancy, efforts were devoted to importing American union stability and efficiency.

Over the last decade, there has been a clear though gradual trend toward re-establishing majority status for Canadian unions, judging by the size of their membership. In 1978, most union members in Canada belonged to American affiliates. Data for 1978 indicate that 52.5 percent of total union membership was in internationals, as contrasted to 67.1 percent in 1965. The rate increase in international memberships was only 1 percent, in contrast to 4.3 percent for national unions. By 1980, American-based union membership was approximately 46 percent of the total. (The Canadian Press, July 17, 1980.)

For the most part, the nationals' increase is attributable to the considerable growth of white-collar unions, especially in the state sectors, where the rate of growth in 1978 was 7.8 percent. State workers affiliated with the Canadian Union of Public Employees (CUPE) are now a conspicuous national presence, with organized affiliates representing occupational groups as varied as clerks, police officers, and "professionals." Noteworthy, too, is the breakaway in 1985 of the Canadian arm of the United Auto Workers, separating more than 100,000 Canadian industrial workers from the American-dominated international union.

iii. Union Economism

The continental economy, with United States' corporate domination of Canada's economy and the parallel influence of American-based unions, has been a potent deterrent to Canadian unions' having an indigenous political character. Labour is absorbed into the American pluralist democratic ideology, where employee groups are supposed to be apolitical and patriotic. American labour leaders urged conscription in World War I, obstructed the Winnipeg General Strike, opposed militant miners in Cape Breton Island, led American-style "commie" hunts (Salutin, 1977: 8), opposed unemployment insurance throughout the Depression (Levinson, 1974: 74–78), raided Canadian unions for members and revenues, and generally imposed a bland economism on Canadian labour.

It appears that the recent and belated "Canadianization" of unionism may reinforce rather than alter the economism of organized labour in Canada. Strikes occur, but almost invariably, and quite understandably, the dominant issue is salary, and not social change or even political partisanship. Because union expansion has concentrated upon middle-class occupations, especially in the massive, public-sector Canadian Union of Public Employees (CUPE), union activists do have an enormous stake in social stability, whatever their grievances.

Union interest in organizing the middle class has generated some conflict, palely reminiscent of the recognition strikes of the early 20th century. Often with the explicit intervention of the state, there is still employer resistance to union organization. Hence the still largely unsuccessful attempt to organize the approximately 100,000 tellers and clerks in Canada's thousands of chartered banks, and to unionize the Royal Canadian Mounted Police. In the former instance there are publicly recognized indications of "unfair labour practices and intimidation of unionized workers" in Canadian banks, as illustrated in a Canadian Labour Relations Board ruling in 1979 that concerned three branches of the Bank of Commerce. (*The Gazette*, December 2, 1980.)

There are about 4,000 branches of the chartered banks in Canada. In 1981 only 118 branches were certified, and, since 1977, at least 40 previous certifications have been revoked. In the period from April 1, 1980, to January 31, 1981 there were only 15 applications for certification, and 16 applications for decertification. (*The Gazette*, April 4, 1981: 75.) The necessity of organizing branch by branch, despite a high transfer and turnover rate; an ideological disinclination to unionism among the predominantly female staff (about two-thirds of the approximately 150,000 employees); and the deliberate opposition of the banks and the state — all have effectively thwarted large-scale bank unionism.

Yet management/state opposition simply obscures the advantages that middle-class unionism provides the class system. The extension of the routine of collective bargaining, and its respectability and legitimacy, act to reinforce the character of Canadian class society. In this general context of benign union action, state workers may occasionally be aggressively militant in Canada, at times challenging the state to the extent of going out on illegal strikes. For example, in 1981, the CUPE-sponsored strike of hospital workers in Ontario was illegal, and, for a brief period, defied a court injunction. However, such militance or willingness to resort to job action is infrequent and sporadic, and therefore not in itself synonymous with radicalism or politicization in the sense of an intent to alter political circumstances and so achieve a potentially more thoroughgoing economic redistribution.

Militant tactics such as illegal strikes employed to achieve short-term, job-related benefits may be rather disruptive in contrast to more conventional collective bargaining, arbitration, and legal strikes, but only marginally so. The objectives remain limited, and the strikes often may be safely ignored, for no real loss or deprivation of service or production is incurred, as was the case in the 1981 strike of Canadian Broadcasting Corporation (CBC) workers. Even police strikes usually prove less disruptive than the public thinks, or than is hoped for by police unionists whose power is premised upon a perceived public need for police protection. In fact, in most police strikes, for example, in St. John, New Brunswick, and Halifax, Nova Scotia, in 1981, there was little disruption. Street rowdyism occurred, but there was generally no increase, and perhaps a diminution, in offences against persons and property, as residents employed other means of protection, including self-protection.

Even where there is militancy or radicalism and politicization, it should not be assumed to be oriented around far-reaching change. As the organization and mechanisms of industrial labour become pervasive, they are used to perpetuate not only relative labour market advantage, but also the ideologies of the status quo. Moreover, union tactics can readily be expropriated by advantaged groups, such as academics or physicians, or occupational groups like the police, responsible for maintaining social control and order.

iv. Controlled Conflict

Class conflict persists in the present state of labour relations, of course, and is manifest in strike action. Especially in the 1960s, the number of strikes, including many illegal and violent strikes, was conspicuous. And, in 1972, a brief but effective general strike took place in Quebec. (Jamieson, 1971; Rinehart, 1975.)

If the number of strikes, and their duration, are taken as indicators, Canada is now experiencing aggressive labour-union activity. Consistently, Canada loses more time on the job through strike action than all but two of the industrial nations of the world. In large part, increased labour demands are a response to inflation and relate to a pursuit of immediate or short-term economic advantage, rather than any drive for basic change in social organization. In such two-party economic bargaining, unions are relatively successful in terms of gaining wage concessions. But when they have shown interest in influencing government policies, they have not been effective. Presthus has reported that, although many elected representatives in Canada believe unions to be effective pressure groups, an analysis of actual government decisions shows that, in fact, it is professional and business interests that are dominantly effective in this respect. (Presthus, 1974: 207.) Union influence seems to carry weight only at the point of specific bargaining confrontation. Unlike previous instances of conflict in Canada, labour actions have become conventionalized or institutionalized in a time of relative public affluence and general acceptance and legitimation of collective bargaining. Class conflict has not disappeared but, rather than becoming extreme, it has become and likely will continue to be increasingly oriented to wages rather than to significant structural change.

As previously noted, organized economic bargaining has increasingly extended to white-collar workers and professionals. Teachers' unions, professors' unions on most Canadian campuses, and the large Public Service Alliance of Canada are examples of such unionization and, perhaps, despite their affluence, the mobilization of the hitherto placid middle class. What is absent in such action, however, is an ideological component or sentiment that differs from hitherto prevailing "centre" attitudes of middle-class Canadians. Insofar as people are becoming increasingly engaged in confrontation with employers, it is purely out of local, short-term interest, and not an interest in the fundamental improvement of a class economic situation or any ideological conviction of an egalitarian sort.

The extent to which such pedestrian activities become radicalized will depend, in part, on the response of the government and employers, and on whether or not a major economic crisis occurs. Given economic disruption, middle-class persons have educational and organizational skills that are translatable into effective opposition politics. But that opposition is as apt to be conservative, as in the Saskatchewan doctors' strike, as it is to be change-oriented. A crucial variable will be perceived, relative, deprivation: economic jeopardy could bring about the class polarization Marxists anticipated so long ago. Hypothetically, massive inflation could precipitate a middle-class "revolution" — again, not necessarily or probably a left-wing revolution — involving skilled workers and professionals. Ominously, the conditions of the pre-war German Weimar Republic resembled such a hypothetical situation. But the likelihood for Canada is improbable.

Strikes, especially violent strikes characterized by vandalism, picket-line fighting, and police intervention, are bitter labour actions. However, the bitterness and anger do not render them challenges to the basic legitimacy of the society, with its established system of stratification and corporate and political authorities ranged in opposition to a union. Strikes are almost invariably wage-related, and not political challenges. Occasionally, the root grievance may relate to working conditions, job security, technological change, or management supervisory practices, as in the Canada Post Corporation or the strikes of the International Typographical Union (ITU). But even in such actions, the strikes are job-specific, and do not constitute a fundamental rejection of or attempt to alter the existing political and corporate systems. Moreover, striking unions in Canada are characteristically isolated. Not only is there rarely union solidarity with other unions, but often a striking union is pitted against a non-striking union, as in the case of striking inside postal workers pitted against mail carriers. In 1978, the Canadian Union of Postal Workers was, in fact, repudiated by other representatives of organized labour.

Massive strike action like the Winnipeg General Strike of 1919 may not have been initiated as a clearly articulated political action. But it became such a challenge, characterized by labour solidarity and a refusal to conform to government directive. In contrast, the labour union movement today is simply not cohesive. Rather, it consists of numerous non-coordinated organizations, diffused loyalties, and a quest for respectability.

In this context of limited labour action, there are, nonetheless, numerous illegal strikes and strike violence. Where such incidents produce police intervention, there is some exacerbation of class opposition, but it is usually fleeting and isolated. The Fleck strike, for example, where the Ontario Provincial Police intervened, had such a consequence, but it was not enduring. Similarly, when the CUPW refused federal government back-to-work legislation in October of 1978, that was an explicit challenge to government authority. But the challenge was, in turn, repudiated by the rest of organized labour, and CUPW capitulated, with some public humiliation.

Rejection of government authority is a more fundamental union and class action than are mere strikes over wage and other job-related issues. Yet it must be observed that its occurrences are few and far between, and seem to stem from government as much as from union initiative. For example, there is reason to suggest that the CUPW confrontation with the Trudeau government was not entirely unwished for by the government, who were seeking to re-establish a lost public popularity by ''being tough'' with a relatively isolated, unpopular, and militant union. Thereby, in sum, government legitimacy was enhanced, not eroded, and the union's standing suffered.

To exert serious pressure on government, and to make any inroads on class differentiation, inter-union co-operation is crucial in actions discrediting the government status quo. Failing this, as Rinehart remarks, ''What collective bargaining does is institutionalize the conflict by subsuming it under a web of rules which is made explicit in a union contract.'' (Rinehart, 1975: 154.) Currently. we have a situation in which unions tend to be chiefly interested in wages and to display the passive respectability that repudiates more militant labour groups, as when, in 1978, the Canadian Labour Congress failed to support the striking inside postal workers. Conforming to the norms of bargaining effectively reinforces the system, and blunts the effects of class conflict.

Broadly speaking, the early phases of Canadian labour-capitalist relations, until approximately the end of the 1930s, were characterized by labour organization and strikes for recognition, with frequent intervention by the state. Since World War II, labour relations have been characterized by ritualization. Labour unions now largely confine their activities to questions of wages and working conditions, while the state has provided a statutory legitimacy that has institutionalized collective bargaining and neutered periodic withdrawals of labour. Progression to a strike situation proceeds through extended periods of negotiation, conciliation, mediation, and arbitration. This paced ritualization allows the employer and the state a measure of predictability and protection that effectively reduces the value and power of the strike. In fact, the strike may now be planned for, costed out, and even timed, to allow an employer the opportunity to reduce a surplus inventory and/or effect wage savings that translate into a profit for the corporate or public operation. Because it violates the rules of the game, and deters the predictability and planning alluded to above, the illegal or wildcat strike best expresses the power that is inherent in organized labour, challenging owners, management, the state, and often the union officers themselves.

v. Unions and the Labour Market

Ironically, insofar as labour unions and labour leaders themselves enforce compliance with the laws and conventions of Canada's collective bargaining system, they deter the power of labour, and sustain employers. Rather than challenge the industrial system, as in change-oriented political action or in national labour solidarity, Canada's unions win short-run economic benefits in exchange for collaborating in stabilizing the socio-economic system. The scenario of the political power of the strike, above all the "general strike," has scant bearing in modern Canada. The economism of Canadian unions is expressed as a tacit concession that welfare capitalism, controlled labour supply, underemployment, and unemployment are to be accepted, and no fundamental redistribution of resources is to be sought.

The dilemma of trade unionism is that worker solidarity, cooperation, and class consciousness are unlikely, if not impossible, without trade union organization. Yet, with trade unionism, a structure of controlled adversarial game playing is institutionalized, effectively controlling and curtailing labour power and reinforcing the authority of employers and the state. Unions win concessions, they frustrate and deter authority and unbridled management, but they also sustain the fundamental relations of labour, capital, and the state. Thus one finds many experienced unionists and observers of unionism remarking upon unions as "policemen for the bosses" (Pfeffer, 1979: 317–326; Garson, 1975) with labour locked into contracts, bounded by laws, and monitored by both management and labour leaders. One writer, an academic who spent seven months as a factory worker in order to experience a workplace quite unlike the academic environment, remarks upon unions contributing to "the pacification, demoralization, and disorganization of [their] members as workers with a class interest." (Pfeffer, 1979: 137.) This consequence was anticipated by Marx. In a letter to Engels, in 1875, Marx described a union as "the real class organization of the proletariat, in which it carries on its daily struggle with capitalism." (Marx and Engels, 1968: 338.) Yet, as he also noted, the "guerrilla war" waged by unions dealt rather more with the effects rather than the bases of capitalism (Marx and Engels, 1968: 229), and, in consequence, allowed labour's accommodation to a capitalist class society rather than that society's destruction or change.

A modern comment is offered by Stanley Aronowitz (1973), by no means an academic merely passing through the working-class world. He spent almost fifteen years as an industrial worker and a labour organizer, finally withdrawing, having concluded that American unionism was consolidating and reinforcing capitalism. More specifically, he argues that unions, and stratification or differentiation among grades of workers, sustain the myths of nationhood, mobility, and opportunity previously nurtured by school, church, and mass media. Moreover, the unions reinforce and concede the natural order of the labour market, with labour as just another commodity. (Aronowitz, 1973: 10.) In this way, labour unions become one of the institutional pillars of modern society and its class structure.

Ultimately, the role of organized labour in modern Canadian society is best summed up by an appreciation of its having conceded the essential acceptability of the labour market. As Marx, Weber, and so many others have agreed, capitalism is, above all, characterized by its ability to treat labour as a commodity for sale and a source of profit. Unions organize labourers, and thereby secure for workers some material benefits, security, and protection. But they also stabilize and channel the labour supply, and, in effect, auction off their commodity, labour power. Whatever conscious motives one may attribute to labour leaders, the consequence of their activity is a symbiotic relation between unions and employers, with both of them intent upon economic regulation and stability. (Stewart, 1977: 14.)

Labour organizations formed to meet working-class objectives and enhance labour power have nevertheless maintained class society and insulated the state from conflict. Insofar as unions organize, systematize, and control the labour supply for employers, they are, as Mills wrote of union leaders, (1948: 6) ''jobbers of labor power,'' with the task of selling workers ''to the highest bidder on the best terms available.'' Unions also channel and resolve disputes and problems by vetting grievances, effectively sharing in the management of an operation. Similar generalizations are to be found throughout the sociological literature, whatever the theoretical school, whether functionalists or Marxists, with impressive agreement despite ideological differences. Although trade unions are a means to more effective worker opposition to capitalism, they tend to be ''too much aloof from general social and political movements,'' just as Marx feared. They respond to ''effects'' rather than resorting to basic political action. (Marx and Engels, 1968: 229.)

Crucial to industrial capitalism and stratification, as Weber insisted, is an occupational market of gradated skills or scarcity and, consequently, of gradated market value. The evolution of a society such as ours is marked by such occupational and class differentiation, serving to divide labour and to normalize the labour market. Educational institutions and credentialism sustain belief in social mobility and thereby in the validity of the occupational hierarchy and market. Sustained by major institutions and by law, bureaucratized and legitimated, class tensions and conflicts are muted and moderated, just as the adversarial relations of union and employer are carefully contained and routinized. Consequently, the wildcat strike may be seen as not only a response to the employer, but also a lashing out against a union-management compact and its consequent routinization of conflict relations and containment of labour power.

vi. Strikes

While routinization is achieved, privileged class interests also enjoy the benefits of union scapegoating. Strikes are perceived by most Canadians as costly and damaging, and the majority of Canadians who might otherwise support unions willingly would accept limitation upon the right to strike. A Quebec poll, for example, found that approximately 75 percent of respondents believed that hospital workers should not have the right to strike. (*The Gazette*, March 30, 1981.) Especially, so-called ''essential services,'' such as health care or policing, are readily seen as not suitable to be allowed strike privileges. Strikes of hospital workers, firemen, police officers, and public sector workers generally (where the strike directly affects the public as much or more than employers), prevent rather than encourage class solidarity.

Yet strikes are actually the tolerable and controlled manifestations of routinized class conflict, a means of regulating and defusing class antagonisms. Although statistically Canada has one of the worst records of working time lost to strike action, in effect the consequences are far less dramatic than presumed. As previously remarked, such legal withdrawals of labour frequently play into the hands of the employer, at great cost to the striking worker. Often there is no real loss in production, in that, as predictable events, strikes may be preceded by production speed-up (Forrest, 1978: 8), or, during the course of a strike, by supervisory production. Meanwhile, an employer enjoys massive wage-savings often more than sufficient to pay for increased benefits in any new contract. The worker, on the other hand, forfeits income, often never compensated for by any nominal gain in wage rate.

Moreover, in a labour-market system of union- and employer-controlled adversarial relations and economism, and in a society characterized by other divisive allegiances such as ethnicity or region, strikes may work to the advantage of capitalists and the state by generating a widespread public hostility, as indicated in the poll data cited above. Canadians, most of whom, objectively, are themselves workers or wage-earners, tend to sympathize with management, in so far as modern strikes are frequently perceived to be to their own cost as much or more than to the employers'. In fact, the perception is partially valid, for the public is more often harmed by the strike action, while employers are protected. Increasingly, strikes alienate a public of fellow class members by withdrawing a service or products enjoyed by the mass public and otherwise unobtainable, whereas the affluent employer will have access to alternate supply. Strikes of private and especially of public workers tend not to damage an employer or members of a dominant class so much as other workers;

rather than challenging corporate or state authorities, modern strikes create support for state intervention and "labour-busting." Thereby strikes may offer the employer not only economic advantages, but also clear ideological advantages, deterring class solidarity and class consciousness. The striking workers will sometimes experience a measure of increased cohesion and of more pronounced hostility to an employer. But such increments are transitory, however great the emotion, for the fundamental relation of accepting economic dependency is not altered, and the employer is often economically regenerated and the union fiscally drained.

At times, too, rather than keep its solidarity, a union will split, as members divide over the suitability and duration of a strike. A recent (1981) strike of Voyageur-Colonial bus drivers in Ontario revealed such a membership split, as workers finally accepted a contract that failed to compensate for lost wages. Another example of union loss in strike action was the bitter eight-month strike in 1979 of Local 6500 of the United Steelworkers of America against INCO Limited of Sudbury—"a strike that cost Canada more lost work days than any strike in this country's history." It ended in anger and frustration, and, ultimately, acceptance of terms favourable to the company. (Price, 1979: 18.) The company profited economically, too, in this instance, by reducing a massive stockpile of nickel while not having to meet its payroll. (Price, 1979: 18.)

Strikes are a manifestation of class conflict, and represent labour's most powerful tactic. However, that power is squandered if withdrawals of service become routinized, ill-timed, and misdirected. Increasingly, they sustain industrial capitalism, in that they occur as segmented or local events, oriented around short-term benefits, and targetted ineffectively against employers and the state. Ironically, collective bargaining and legal strikes become a means of institutionalizing and diminishing class conflict, rather than focussing such conflict. Insofar as such institutionalized conflict is characteristic of Canada and other modern industrialist capitalist societies (Giddens, 1973: 287), class conflict is limited, and any potential for radical or revolutionary action is obviated.

Further, the conflict is often diluted and directed back to fellow class members. Not only are other unionists often the direct victims, as in public service strikes, but employers are more thoroughly protected from the consequences of a strike than are members of the public. In addition, there is conflict among unions, between better- and less well-educated workers, between rank-and-file members and union executives and hired experts (Westley and Westley, 1971: 37), between workers in one region and those of another, or between workers of one language group and those of another.

In sum, Canadian welfare capitalism and the inequalities vested in Canadian society persist because they meet no wide-ranging challenges or disruptions. Periodic disturbances are more apt to be directly experienced and suffered by wage-earning Canadians than by owners who are insulated by considerable wealth and resources. The disadvantaged are divided by contending allegiances, and by a "false consciousness" that is repeatedly reinforced in the daily experiences of first-hand contacts and media socialization. The working class is fractionalized and controlled to such a degree that drastic change is all but inconceivable, and effectively unrealizable. Piecemeal reformism or welfarism, a concession to the endurance of the industrial class system, is the empirical reality. Classes and expressions of class conflict exist, but the potential for producing action and change is slight, especially as Canadian unions avoid or prove incapable of sustained political partisanship or action.

For many years, some social theorists have been predicting the development of white-collar or middle-class consciousness, meaning a recognition of economic affinity to other workers and opposition to owners. (Mills, 1951; Lockwood, 1958.) But there is a sense in which the middle class has been aware of its interests, and they have been perceived neither to be altogether akin to the working class nor opposed to upper-class economic dominance. Periodic pique is generated by "corporate rip-offs" and large corporate profits, but so, too, is there animosity over labour unions, despite growing middle-class union participation.

For the securely employed blue- or white-collar worker, there is as yet no fundamental dissatisfaction with the existing system of economic distribution. For the marginally employed or the unemployed, shunned as much by organized labour as by corporate and government interests, protest organization and action is even more rare.

The Impoverished and the Welfare State

Unemployment is a basic indication of social inequity. The extent to which a society will tolerate the existence of a reserve labour army, dependent upon state payments for sustenance, is an indication of social morality. In Canada, unemployment is massive, the highest among comparable western industrial nations including the United States, the United Kingdom, and Australia. Moreover, unemployment is far higher than official employment rates indicate. Underemployment and marginal work, accounts, in some estimates, for 30 percent of the labour force. (Gonick, 1978: 22–23; Braverman, 1974: 439–40.) Unemployment rates are diminished by periodic work. In addition, among the "hidden unemployed" are those on welfare assistance and not seeking work, those who have not registered, often in despair, as well as a massive student population, many of whom are students involuntarily in school by law and not for education. Witness the substantial enrolment increases experienced by Canadian universities in the 1980s, no doubt in part a response to diminished employment opportunities. One economist accounts for this in estimating the real Canadian unemployment rate as at least 20 percent. (Gonick, 1978: 22.)

The unemployed and marginally employed are not a significant force for change, cut off as they are from organization and sustained in their subordination by welfare programs. The welfare state effectively pacifies deprived individuals, unless their ranks are drastically enlarged by persons previously enjoying superior economic advantage. Piven and Cloward (1971) have proposed that the history of welfare policy in the United States is one of response to successive economic crises. We might consider Canadian government welfare response to the Depression of the 1930s and currently to inflation and unemployment, as such. They are not policies that alter the distribution of resources or the structure of class, but stabilize them. As one not-so-radical group (the Senate Committee on Poverty) put it, the welfare system "has treated the symptoms of poverty and left the disease itself untouched." (Canada, 1971: xv.) But the programs were not designed to do otherwise. Moreover, stabilization is secured using revenues in large part obtained from wage and salary earners, rather than from business, in no way challenging the economic dominance of the ruling class. In a period of inflation and rising welfare costs, corporations in Canada, especially the banks, report record profits.

Welfare programs, or, in the current euphemism favoured by the Economic Council of Canada, "transfer payments to individuals," amount to taking from the not-so-poor and not-so-rich and giving to the utterly deprived. But only giving a little to the deprived; most of it comes back to the middle class. Remarkable biases exist in programs ostensibly designed to provide equitable systems of security. For example, a 1978 analysis of the Canada Pension Plan demonstrates the advantage to higher-income groups. In effect, allowing for savings from tax deductions, a person with an income of $6,000 would make a net Canada Pension Plan contribution of $90.00. Moreover, the $6,000 income earner is entitled ultimately to a mere 58 percent of the full pension entitlement. In contrast, the person earning $50,000 is entitled to 100 percent. Proportionately, the wealthier income earner pays much less for much more than the lower income earner. (See Table 5-1.)

The taxes that support "transfer payments" are paid by workers. In 1970, over 80 percent of total income taxes in Canada were collected from persons earning under $20,000 per year. More startling, 41.6 percent of total taxes were paid by persons earning between $5,000 and $10,000. (Tarasoff, 1973: 1.) Taxes fail to redistribute income significantly, because the income share after taxes of widely disparate income groups is virtually unaltered. A slight income gain of one percent may be measured for each of the two lowest income groups, and a mere two percent income drop for the highest income group. (See Table 5-2.)

The very privileged tend to pay proportionately much less than wage workers. The Progressive Conservative budget of 1985, for example, merely exaggerated the advantage of the prosperous, especially in its capital gains provisions. The income tax system is notoriously regressive,

Table 5-1: Net contributions to the Canada Pension Plan for 1978

Earned Income	Required CPP Contribution	Tax Saving from Deduction	Net CPP Contribution	Pension Entitlement
$ 6,000	$ 90.00	$ 0	$ 90.00	58%
8,000	126.00	0	126.00	77
10,000	162.00	41.99	120.01	96
12,000	169.20	46.29	122.91	100
15,000	169.20	51.17	118.03	100
20,000	169.20	60.91	108.29	100
25,000	169.20	68.22	100.98	100
50,000	169.20	87.71	81.49	100

Source: National Council of Welfare, (March 1978).

Table 5-2: 1975 Data Before and After Tax Share of Total Income

	Share before income tax	Share after	Differences
Bottom 20%	4.0%	4.6	+ .6
2nd	10.6%	11.5	+ .9
Middle	17.6%	18.2	+ .6
Fourth	25.1%	25.1	0
Top	42.6%	40.6	− 2.0

Source: National Council of Welfare.

making deductions to the advantage of persons with higher income. Rather than being a redistributive mechanism, the tax system consolidates privilege. (Gillespie, 1978.) When indirect taxes are also considered, such as those on clothing and all consumer items, we have all the more clearly regressive rather than progressive tax systems, insofar as the taxes paid by low-income earners constitute a far greater proportion of their income than do the taxes paid by higher-income earners, particularly those enjoying business profits rather than wages or salaries.

Most of these tax revenues, then, benefit the middle class, and are a further indication of the essential stability or maintenance of the system. In 1973–74, projected federal spending of tax revenues only apportioned 28 cents of the tax dollar for "health and welfare," and an additional 13 cents of the tax dollar for "economic development and support." (Tarasoff, 1973.) And much of this goes to middle- and upper-class persons, not only insofar as they receive profits from economic develop-

Table 5-3: Average Income from Public Pension Plans and Private
Sources, Poor and Non-poor Aged Couples and Unattached
Individuals, 1981

Income Source	Aged Couples*		Aged Unattached Individuals	
	Poor	Non-Poor	Poor	Non-Poor
C/QPP	$1,824	$ 2,263	$1,276	$1,973
Private pensions	1,075	4,885	1,679	4,787
Investments	748	7,161	1,176	7,107
Employment	913	10,984	1,206	7,731

* Couples in which both spouses were 65 or older in 1981.
Source: National Council of Welfare.

ment schemes, but also in that ''health and welfare'' spending includes medicare payments and hospital insurance payments to the provinces, family allowances, and veterans' allowances. A similar pattern of ''redistribution'' operates at the provincial level. The aged — especially women — suffer most from meagre levels of state-mediated support. (See Table 5-3.)

Generally, therefore, present government systems act to reinforce the class structure. Wage earners are taxed, whereas corporate profits remain relatively unscathed. Taxes, then, are returned as benefits to the relatively privileged. Extremes of wealth and poverty are not seriously affected, except for some necessary support of the impoverished, which, however humane, also serves to deepen the dependent state of its recipients and gloss over the persistence of disparities. There is no significant redistribution of wealth, but only a circular distribution.

Rather than offer genuine redistributive and security benefits for all Canadians, present state intervention only subsidizes employee-derived benefits for the middle class. Of particular concern in Canada, where we have an aging population, is that few pension plans are comparable to the indexed pensions available to state employees. Moreover, increasingly, accumulated pension funds have been used by corporations and the state as a source of capital, with the funds ''borrowed'' at nominal interest charges. (Myles, 1979: 11–23.) Wages ''banked'' by workers are, in effect, reappropriated by the state or industry for their own investment and regulatory purposes. As a result, the Canadian welfare state, like other capitalist states, has not ultimately been the impartial arbiter of class interests, as it expanded so vastly throughout this century. Whatever the measure of relative bureaucratic or state autonomy and the extension of citizen rights to fundamental economic subsistence (defined relative to national standards of wealth) the state has nonetheless acted to legitimate and stabilize class society. The ruthlessness and indignity of pre-welfare class societies have been muted, but the class structure has been reinforced.

Canada is obviously not unique in these applications and consequences of welfarism. Michael Harrington has convincingly argued that the welfare state apparatus of the United States is effectively a mechanism of social control, neither effecting genuine income redistribution nor offering genuine challenges to dominant capitalist class interests. (Harrington, 1976.) The state welfare apparatus is managed by middle-class bureaucrats and elected political masters with middle- or ruling-class origins in business or law, and whose interests are patently to stabilize and maintain the socioeconomic status quo. The modern welfare state is, thereby, a direct and non-disruptive extension of capitalist relations of dominance, managing to accommodate populist political sentiments with relative deprivation of the working class.

A relatively new economic device for the state is the promotion of lotteries. So lucrative as a source of revenue have public lotteries proven to be in Canada that the provinces and the federal government contested control of them—ultimately ceded to the provinces. Despite their wide acceptability as voluntary purchases, lotteries are a cruel form of taxation, disproportionately drawing monies from the disadvantaged with the lure of quick riches. In a sense, lotteries are welfare capitalism's Horatio Alger equivalent, insofar as they are a seductive promise of the possibility of better things. Yet the monies are applied by the state to finance its operations,

Table 5-4: Maximum benefits from Federal Programs for the Aged and Provincial Supplements, 1983

	Single Persons			Couples		
	Federal Programs*	Provincial Supplements	Total	Federal Programs*	Provincial Supplements	Total
Newfoundland	$6,147	—	$6,147	$10,883	—	$10,883
Prince Edward Island	6,147	—	6,147	10,883	—	10,883
Nova Scotia	6,147	$ 219	6,366	10,883	$ 438	11,321
New Brunswick	6,147	—	6,147	10,883	—	10,833
Quebec	6,147	—	6,147	10,883	—	10,833
Ontario	6,147	587	6,734	10,883	1,922	12,805
Manitoba	6,147	188	6,335	10,833	405	11,288
Saskatchewan	6,147	300	6,477	10,883	540	11,423
Alberta	6,147	1,140	7,287	10,883	2,280	13,163
British Columbia	6,147	467	6,614	10,883	1,196	12,079
Yukon	6,147	1,200	7,347	10,883	2,400	13,283
Northwest Territories	6,147	900	7,047	10,883	1,800	12,683

* Old Age Security and Guaranteed Income Supplement.
Source: National Council of Welfare.

often directly applied to recreational benefits for the middle and upper class rather than the working class. Ironically, the early success story in Canadian lotteries was Manitoba's — introduced by the New Democratic Party government of Edward Schreyer before lotteries were common elsewhere in Canada.

Traditionally, industrial capitalist societies have been characterized by an ostensible separation of economy and polity, incorporating the myth of the state as impartial mediator. (Giddens, 1973: 281.) However, the modern interventionist state, with origins in the Great Depression of the thirties, and earlier, in Canada, from the very inception of the Canadian nation, has also been characterized by state action to maintain the system. In addition to the legitimation of inequity achieved through welfarism, the state has been a major actor in the protection of entrepreneurs, and generally in the accumulation and application of capital to the advantage of the already advantaged social classes.

Social Change and Politics

A token lament is heard in the legislatures, the media, and the social science literature of the industrial democracies, to the effect that public participation in politics is slight. Voter turnout may be appraised as too low, party affiliation as too infrequent, and, generally, rates of participation in political campaigns and events too skimpy and apathetic. (Swartz, 1973.) Yet this level of political activity is precisely consistent with the persistence of "democratic" class societies, as Lipset (1965) approvingly acknowledged in his functionalist analysis of social stability. Lipset's reasoning is offensive, premised as it is upon notions of working-class authoritarianism, irrational extremism, and ideological gullibility. But the conclusion is apt: stable class societies depend upon economism and limited and ritualized political action. Lipset (1960) observed that stable politics obtained when the degree of participation was modest, and when it was confined to electoral politics. Extremist political movements of the right or of the left, oriented to drastic change, are apt to achieve political success when they coincide with an extraordinarily high rate of political participation, including voting. For Lipset, this also means that extremist groups won power when they elicited the participatory support of the sectors of society normally inactive, specifically the working class. Insofar as unions are apolitical, and discouraging of class-oriented politics, they therefore may be seen as securing stable electoral systems.

Class politics seemed most pronounced in Canada in the period surrounding World War I as unionism was struggling for recognition, culminating in the 1919 Winnipeg General Strike, and, in the 1930s, as economic crisis nurtured a plethora of political movements and parties, such as

Social Credit and the Co-operative Commonwealth Federation. Both of the latter depended upon rural and working-class support, and were initially rather supportive of one another, despite differing ideological labels and content, the former presumably of the "right" and the latter of the "left." (Shackleton, 1975.) During the 1930s, class political division was also evident in several fascist movements, and in anti-semitism. Generally there was middle-class support of fascism, and working class opposition to it, primarily by organized labour. (Betcherman, 1975.) Small businessmen especially were fascist supporters, seeing themselves in "economic rivalry with Jewish competitors, large department stores, and retail chains." (Betcherman, 1975: 6; 40.) There were not, of course, clear and unequivocal class divisions; as always, the lines between the right and left were unclear and fluid. Adrien Arcand, the Quebec fascist leader and propagandist, for example, graduated from a classical college, and came from a family whose mother was employed as a teacher, and whose father was a labour organizer. (Betcherman, 1965: 5.) Ethnic preferences also intruded. French-Canadian support for fascist groups was fostered by sentiments in the Roman Catholic church that were reflected in the concordat between Pope Pius XI and Hitler in 1933. (Betcherman, 1965: 5.) In the West, fascist groups tended to receive a greater support in German and Ukrainian communities, and in Toronto were associated with "Anglo-Saxon nativism" and a population of British origins who were antagonistic to the Jewish community. (Betcherman, 1965: 47; 61–65.)

In contrast to the fragmented and unpredictable politics of the 1930s, normal democratic politics are premised upon generalist centre parties that combine a variety of public interests. Above all, the Liberal Party in Canada has achieved such centre blandness, offering if not delivering something for everyone. Stable politics depend upon the dominant participation of the politically orthodox middle class, and their support of the centre parties. In Canada, for example, placid politics or normal politics are those in which the centre Liberal Party is hegemonic, as it has been through most of Canadian history, having elicited the support of the middle class — the social class to which the majority of voters belong. In 1985, the Progressive Conservatives under Brian Mulroney successfully, if perhaps only temporarily, displaced centre Liberal appeal, and, as the Liberal Party had done, achieved their electoral strength by appealing to the middle class. Middle-class political hegemony is not only tolerated but generally supported by organized labour. The Liberal Party and not the New Democrats have received the majority of working-class votes (Alford, 1963) an historic consistency that has encouraged the futile shift of the New Democrats to an indistinguishable and undistinguished centre position.

There have been several attempts in Canada to translate labour interests into a political party, most explicitly in support for the CCF/NDP. Yet one finds cleavage, tension, and conflict within the party (Westley and Westley, 1971: 38), as well as a general inability to demonstrate its utility to the working class, and so to win anything but a small minority of the working-class vote. In the main, the NDP party is perceived as the plaything of the "eggheads," of the middle-class intelligentsia who thus far have failed to live up to the traditionally-anticipated potential of providing effective and convincing leadership for the working class. Although, on the one hand, one can point to a Canadian "intelligentsia" having been crucial to the CCF/NDP and to Canadian "socialism" as founding influences (Avakumovic, 1978), the feeling is prevalent that the party does not really reach the working class. In Ontario, for example, Michael Cassidy's Ontario NDP leadership victory over Ian Deans was a conspicuous instance of the so-called intellectuals' domination of the party, and translated into ineffectual electoral appeal.

The national NDP's commitment to cautious evolutionary politics, intended gradually to displace one of the older parties, has had the consequence of an increasingly bland and undistinguished "socialist" alternative — far from forming an official opposition, let alone a government in Ottawa. The glory of its early policy initiatives in the West has dissipated, and the party seems to have chosen the role of permanent critic or devil's advocate, responding in an *ad hoc* manner to circumstances, rather than generating and systematically promoting its own policy initiatives. In consequence, the party seems long since to have reached its saturation point where public support is concerned, with approximately 17 percent of the popular vote in the last fifteen years. The centre character of the NDP has featured middle-class political candidates and leaders, especially teachers and university instructors (Forcese and de Vries, 1977), and reactive political positions devoted to social criticism rather than policy positions. The de-radicalization of the NDP has won it some formal labour support, in endorsement and financial support from the Canadian Labour Congress (CLC). However, CLC contributions, amounting to $1.2 million in 1979 when the Liberals were defeated by Joe Clark's Progressive Conservatives, did not translate into votes and NDP seats; in fact, the NDP lost a seat in Ontario in 1979. (*The Gazette*, May 24, 1979.) Similarly, the NDP survived, but did not break out, in the Mulroney landslide victory that came after.

The significance of stable politics has to do fundamentally with the maintenance of a system of economic distribution. Insofar as legitimate politics are defined as consisting essentially of electoral politics, and especially the act of voting, the potential of politics for opposition and change is inhibited. All Western democracies depend upon routinized and narrowly defined politics (Giddens, 1973), wherein extended periods of public inattention give way to periodic, ritualized, media events known as elections. Governments find routinized lobbies acceptable between elections, and a measure of conventional criticism. But group actions that challenge the operation of the state are threatening and intolerable for the dominant class interests in Canada.

Notably, politicized labour union action is intolerable. In North America, labour unions have allowed themselves to be defined as utterly apolitical. The economism of unions in Canada, as in the United States, has been institutionalized so thoroughly as to render political action by unions a form of deviance. Such, for example, is manifest in the attitude of the Canadian Labour Congress with respect to the militant activities of the Canadian Union of Postal Workers. Labour unions exist, in the view of union leaders as well as that of business and government, in order to enhance the market value of their commodity, labour. Moreover, that limited objective is further restricted to the routinized behaviours associated with the collective bargaining process. The stressful features of the process, such as strikes, are directed explicitly to short-term economic benefit, or some comparable improvement in working conditions, and tend to affect the immediate employer and public consumers rather than the real employers, such as the head office of a multinational corporation or the government. Additionally, such actions are themselves routinized and orderly.

Short-run objectives are, of course, not without significance to the lives of employees. But they are inherently limited objectives that offer no prospect of a fundamental or far-reaching change in the system of economic distribution. Nor does such institutionalized unionism tolerate job actions that constitute a challenge to the character and composition of the state. In 1976, with the imposition of wage and price controls, organized labour leaders began briefly to talk of political strikes. Joe Morris of the CLC speculated publicly that traditional opposition to political strikes might have to be abandoned. (*The Globe and Mail*, February 14, 1976.) Yet this union sabre-rattling was a passing thing and never developed into a course to be seriously pursued. Traditionally in Canada, except in the West before the 1930s, strikes as political weapons have been considered abhorrent. Unions as political actors are abhorrent.

In Canadian unions, anyone calling for politicization is labelled an ''ultra left'' radical or communist. For example, when the Canadian Labour Congress was condemned for its failure to support striking postal workers, and a motion of censure was put by CUPE members at a CLC convention, the president of the CLC, Dennis McDermott, called for a purge of the ''ultra left'' in the labour movement. When such statements exemplify union executives and policies, organized labour is limited to seeking economic benefits within the parameters of the dominant class system, and deterred from seeking more thoroughgoing redistribution. The working class is co-opted, and fails to ever seriously threaten the basic inequities of class society. Manipulation by corporate interests and the state is not only tolerated, but ends in collaboration. Organized labour, therefore, is not a threat to the welfare capitalist society of North America, as at times it is represented to be. Rather, it is a legitimate participant in the process of maintaining the basic nature or profile of class society. This ''adversarial'' fashion of North American industrial relations is as much a process of "co-determination" in the sense of co-maintenance as are European systems of so-called "industrial democracy" or corporatism.

Even in more class-conscious societies than Canada, one finds that the activities of organized labour are preoccupied with immediate advantage. The frequency of strikes, or the willingness to resort to strike or other job action, does not usually translate into political action. In the United Kingdom, for example, the militant character of labour has not been expressed as an "effective political radicalism; and it has rarely been revolutionary." (Westergaard and Reisler, 1975: 7.) Although, in contrast to Canada, the British working class is politicized, by affiliation with the Labour Party, this is itself a routinization, an activity within the rules of the game, and the rules are those of the dominant interests in society. The situation of British unions, unable to alter the character of British class society, merely points up more sharply the far more thoroughly apolitical unionism of the United States and Canada, tied to the continental economic grid. Especially as unions also become a fashionable organizational device of the Canadian middle class, the labour movement in this country ceases to press for profound change.

Barring a major economic catastrophe, or some external intervention, there is little prospect of drastic action being taken within the Canadian class structure. The ruling class is not apt to undertake the erosion of its advantages, the middle- and working-classes are entwined in a feedback system of affluent, short-term economic competition, and the destitute are restrained in a web of welfare dependency. A proletarian consciousness consisting of an organized and effective opposition to the ruling stratum is improbable under existing conditions of competitive economic gamesmanship. In his optimism, Mills offered the remark that, "Because men are not 'class conscious' at all times and in all places does not mean that 'there are no classes' or that 'in America everybody is middle class.'" (Mills, 1951: 294.) But neither is it true that because people are class conscious sometimes, and because classes are real, that class contestation of a magnitude sufficient to realize structural change is likely.

Wage and salary workers hold the potential for political action, but it is not a potential apt to crystallize without a major catalyst. Economic breakdown on the scale of the 1930s, which economists confidently assure us is impossible, would be such a crisis. Conceivably, nationalist movements in Canada could also serve politicizing class actions. However, there is certainly no assurance that it would be action to the "left," and in aid of a more egalitarian society.

Johnson has argued that Canada has experienced a decline in the size and influence of the petite bourgeoisie — that is, small businessmen and farmers. In the past, he argues, such people have been in opposition to the working class, a statement not altogether correct in light of periodic working-class-farm alliance in Saskatchewan. But in the deterioration of their positions he suggests that perhaps there has been a polarization of class interests.

(Johnson, 1972.) Similarly, Clement has argued that there has been a crystallization of class interests insofar as the capitalist élite in Canada has become more exclusive and difficult of entry. (Clement, 1975.) The validity of the arguments rests on a number of assumptions, not the least of which relates to the character of labour and white-collar action. Labour organized in international unions has always been very moderate in ideology and action, and salaried workers have always been conservative. (Mills, 1951.) The middle class has replaced the small entrepreneur or petite bourgeoisie in our stratification system, growing from 15.2 percent of the labour force in 1901 to 38.8 percent in 1961. (Meltz, 1969.) This group mediates now between the owners and the working class. Should it become radicalized in its union relations with its employers, then the polarization of which Johnson speaks may be realized. But it seems a tenuous hope, especially in light of the increasing entry of women into the labour force, constituting a new group to be ''educated'' to class consciousness while contributing to two-income family affluence.

In all probability, class-related hostility will continue to be most viably expressed as a reaction to regional differences. The regions in Canada have distinct interests and identities. Particularly as peripheral regions move effectively to develop in competition with central Canada, class conflict will manifest itself in regional conflict. But such regional/class conflict is itself subsumed within legitimated federal constitutional politics. The so-called rise of the middle class in Quebec, (Guindon, 1969), a feature of industrial development and urbanization in the province, led to a vigorous separatist movement launched by the middle class, with the support of organized labour, who viewed their interests in opposition to Anglophone Canada. But, in the 1980s, separatism has waned. Similarly, the surge of western Canadian separatism in the western provinces, exploiting the capital generated by sales of oil and natural gas, evolved as nothing more than a move to industrialize and compete with eastern Canada in secondary production.

Political exchanges between federal and provincial governments will produce some regional redistribution. But the radical tradition of the West and its well-established NDP socialist power base and, similarly, the language-based interests of Quebec at best produce intermittent regional separatist efforts that to some extent achieve redistribution of economic resources in amelioration of class distinctions. Fundamentally, however, Ontario and the Maritimes remain relatively unaltered in social structure and benefits. As the theory of relative deprivation would suggest, those regions that are experiencing developmental changes and social instability are those wherein deprivation will be perceived as salient and prompt social action. To put it crudely, central Ontario is on top, the Atlantic on the bottom, and the West and Quebec are the middle class who are apt to incite the Canadian middle-class revolution and perhaps along the way seriously alter the basic structure of inequality in Canada. But to count on the influence of such separatist movements, and to further expect that they would necessarily make for autonomous or semi-autonomous political entities that are more egalitarian than the present Canadian federal system, is to engage in naïve speculation. At best we could predict some redistribution of wealth in the nation's regions, but among the privileged classes.

Generally, it is probable that the basic class structure of Canadian society will change little in the future. The ruling class is well established, and the centre parties, the Liberals and the alternative Progressive Conservatives, and the remaining "alternative," the NDP, seem committed to variations of the theme of "welfarism" rather than fundamental structural change. Policies that would alter the inheritance of unequal resources and opportunities do not seem imminent; rather, present and anticipated policies emphasize variations on existing patterns of ownership, taxation, and administration of welfare programs, thereby tolerating and reinforcing the class system.

The rituals of conventional politics are limited to such a conception. Effective challenge to conventional politics may to some extent come from regional movements, as has been the case historically. And it will come in some part from the activities of trade unions. However, failing a class polarization, which we have already suggested is improbable, effective change in the stratification system is not imminent.

Only some issue or event that will override present, conventional, welfare-related, political opportunities is apt to challenge the existing system of stratification. Hence our reference to regional separatism, and perhaps also nationalist opposition to foreign economic control, that might serve as foci of radical action, even though these issues are themselves readily distorted or conventionalized. But in the meantime, the privileged enjoy their advantage, and the underprivileged suffer the "structural violence" inherent in Canada's system of institutionalized inequalities.

Conclusion

Processes of social control and socialization render social systems and their patterns of privilege remarkably resistant to fundamental change. There is no human precedent that would lead one to expect a ruling class to divest itself of power and privilege. We have seen that the Canadian ruling class is well established and effectively in control of conventional politics in Canada. Their position is only likely to be altered by the action of less privileged strata in Canadian society. But that action is unlikely. In reading a prize-winning book that develops a devastating critique of welfare policies in the United States, one wonders, at first, how its authors could conclude by recommending the provision of further welfare. (Piven and Cloward, 1971: 347.) Their reason now seems obvious: in the face of the improbability of basic economic reform and change in the class structure, welfare, despite an admission of the evil of class society, is at least humane. But it is a very poor approximation of a redistribution of wealth and opportunity sufficient to realize the ideal of minimal stratification.

Some people would place their expectations of change in the prospect of extreme and perhaps violent class conflicts; from such crises, rather than from the ritual of everyday politics, would change emerge. Canadian society has experienced numerous instances of overt class conflict, often including acts of violence. These do indicate the reality of class relations and of class consciousness. In that sense, such conflict is a normal feature of class stratification and not a mere aberration.

But it is also the case that class confrontations have become ritualized or institutionalized. Violent opposition will periodically occur as it always has in Canada, but labour relations have become conventional, and restricted to short-term economic bargaining, after the American fashion of establishment labour action. Wealth is not really redistributed in Canadian society so as to challenge the viability of classes. Nor are there serious demands for such redistribution. Rather, the circulation of economic resources remains within the parameters of the class structure, and reinforces it.

There are stubborn theoretical projections of prospects for increased class consciousness and action. These characteristically have resorted to proletarization of the middle class and the polarization of the class structure. (Mills, 1951: 301–350; Lockwood, 1958; Johnson, 1972; Clement, 1975.) There is some plausibility to such arguments, but also a lot of wishful thinking. It is possible to overemphasize the extent of middle-class unionization and its resort to bargaining tactics, but, more fundamentally, also to misjudge the goals of such activity. We judge them to be of the order of conventional, non-disruptive, politics, and of bargaining for short-term economic gain, as is typical of labour-owner relations generally in Canada.

It seems, therefore, that prospects for considerable and rapid change in Canada's class structure are remote. Unless one is prepared to trust in a radical variant of "aristocratic responsibility," the ruling class is not likely to institute far-reaching social change, but only an elaboration of welfare as crisis-response. Given the history of Canadian protest politics, we could expect demands for change increasingly to be associated with regional identities, in particular Quebec and the Canadian West, the latter perhaps bifurcated between the Prairies and the west coast. As these regions experience greater economic gains, their perceptions of relative deprivation vis-à-vis Ontario industrial interests are likely to promote more vigorous demands, which could bring about a redistribution of advantage affecting the various classes to some degree. This would only really be significant, however, if the regional contestation were itself radicalized because of federal opposition and through regional ideologies; the prospects of

Quebec separatism seemed in the 1970s most likely to be of this sort, but in the 1980s to be on the wane.

Any such radicalization cannot be predicted to be necessarily in the direction of egalitarian principles, as minimizing stratification would be, but, rather, is apt to amount to mere regional redeployment of advantage, to the benefit of privileged regional populations. Generally, regional action is even more likely to remain within the context of conventional provincial-federal negotiations, the alteration in the distribution of advantage amounting only to an altered geographical distribution of benefits, and not an altered class distribution.

A massive social crisis in Canada could conceivably precipitate a violent revolutionary mobilization of the subordinate social classes. But such a prospect, whether far-fetched or not, does not carry with it the probability of an improved society, free of social classes and their oppositions. Historically, revolution has redistributed wealth to the advantage of some of the formerly disadvantaged and to the disadvantage of some of the formerly advantaged. It has not redistributed wealth to the point of equality of condition. If there were a sound mode of human calculus—and there is not —we would probably find that the human costs of revolutionary violence are not demonstrably less than the evils of a persisting, liberal, class society, especially with the prospect of achieving amended class societies rather than minimally-stratified societies in the post-revolutionary situation.

Consequently, the correct political position would seem to be that which promotes a class conflict and challenge that stops short of revolutionary carnage. Social change in the direction of a more egalitarian Canada is possible through constant and unremitting contestation of established Canadian privilege and its legitimacy. Such aggravated class conflict is premised upon a mobilization of the working and the middle classes, with perhaps the latter bearing the greater potential for escalation of conflict. Perhaps such controlled class mobilization is not practical, although the empirical and historical record is surely unclear. What is clear is that the alternatives are unpalatable. In the absence of such class action, the extremes of violent revolution or the more probable evolutionary welfare elaboration will simply reinforce and crystallize the existing structure of differential privilege. ''Post-industrial'' Canada would be characterized by ever-reduced mobility opportunities and a stable structure of inequity.

Bibliography

Abella, Irving, *Nationalism, Communism, and Canadian Labour*. Toronto: University of Toronto Press, 1973.

Abella, Irving, "Oshawa, 1937" in I. Abella (ed.), *On Strike: Six Key Labour Struggles in Canada 1919–1949*. Toronto: James Lorimer, 1974.

Adams, Ian, "Living with Automation in Winnipeg" in G. Humius *et al.* (eds.), *Workers' Control*. New York: Vintage Books, 1973.

Adorno, T.W.; Frenkel-Brunswik, Else; Levinson, D.J.; and Sanford, R.N. *The Authoritarian Personality*. New York: Harper, 1950.

Alberta. "A Study of Native Youth in Edmonton." Department of Culture, Youth, and Recreation, Edmonton, 1971.

Alford, R. *Party and Society*. Chicago: Aldine, 1963.

Alford, R. "Class Voting in the Anglo-American Political Systems" in S.M. Lipset and S. Rokkan (eds.), *Party Systems and Voter Alignments*. New York: The Free Press, 1967.

Alford, R. "The Social Bases of Political Cleavage in 1962" in J. Meisel (ed.), *Papers on the 1962 Election*. Toronto: University of Toronto Press, 1964.

Allen, Marg. "Hatred Building at Carleton School." *Ottawa Journal* (March 18, 1980).

Allingham, John. "Religious Affiliation and School Class in Ontario." Hamilton: M.A. thesis, Department of Sociology, McMaster University, May 1962.

Anderson, Charles. *The Political Economy of Social Class*. Englewood Cliffs, N.J.: Prentice-Hall, 1974.

Anderson, Grace. "Voting Behaviour and the Ethnic-Religious Variable: A Study of a Federal Election in Hamilton, Ontario." *Canadian Journal of Economics and Political Science* xxxii (1966).

Armstrong, Pat, and Armstrong, M. *A Working Majority: What Women Must Do for Pay*. Ottawa: Canadian Advisory Council on the Status of Women, 1983.

Aronowitz, Stanley. *False Promises*. New York: McGraw-Hill, 1973.

Avakumovic, Ivan. *Socialism in Canada*. Toronto: McClelland and Stewart, 1978.

Avery, Donald. *Dangerous Foreigners*. Toronto: McClelland and Stewart, 1979.

Badgley, Robin F., and Wolfe, Samuel. *Doctor's Strike: Medical Care and Conflict in Saskatchewan*. Toronto: Macmillan of Canada, 1967.

Balawyder, A. *The Winnipeg General Strike*. Toronto: Copp Clark, 1967.

Baldus, B., and Tribe, V. "The Development of Perceptions and Evaluations of Social Inequality Among Public School Children." *CRSA* 15 (1978).

Bancroft, George (ed.). *Outreach for Understanding*. Toronto: Ministry of Culture and Recreation, Government of Ontario, 1976.

Barber, Bernard. *Social Stratification*. New York: Harcourt, Brace and World, 1957.

Beattie, C., and Spencer B. "Career Attainment in Canadian Bureaucracies: Unscrambling the Effects of Age, Seniority, Education, and Ethnolinguistic Factors." *AJS* 77 (1971).

Beattie, Christopher. *Minority Men in a Majority Setting*. Toronto: McClelland and Stewart (The Carleton Library), 1975.

Beck, R.G., and Horne, J.M. "Economic Class and Risk Avoidance: Experience under Public Medical Care Insurance." *Journal of Risk and Insurance*, Vol. 43.

Bell, C. and Newby, H. *Community Studies*. London: George Allen and Unwin, 1971.

Bennett, John. *Hutterite Brethren: The Agricultural Economy and Social Organization of a Communal People*. Stanford: Stanford University Press, 1967.

Bennett, J., and Krueger, C. "Agrarian Pragmatism and Radical Politics" in S.M. Lipset, *Agrarian Socialism* (new ed., Part 2). Berkeley: University of California Press, 1968.

Bercuson, David. *Confrontation at Winnipeg*. Montreal: McGill-Queens University Press, 1974.

185

Best, Michael. "Our Indians: Victims of a Failed Policy." *The Toronto Star*, September 25, 1982.

Betcherman, Lita-Rose. *The Swastika and the Maple Leaf.* Toronto: Fitzhenry and Whiteside, 1975.

Blishen, B.R. "The Construction and Use of an Occupational Class Scale." *Canadian Journal of Economics and Political Science* 24 (1958).

Blishen, B.R. "A Socio-Economic Index for Occupations in Canada." *CRSA* 4 (November 1967).

Blishen, B.R. "Social Class and Opportunity in Canada." *CRSA* 17, (1970).

Blishen, B.R., and McRoberts, H. "A Revised Socioeconomic Index for Occupations in Canada." *CRSA* 13 (February 1976).

Boroway, Alan. "Indian Poverty in Canada" in J. Harp and J. Hofley, (eds.) *Poverty in Canada.* Toronto: Prentice-Hall Canada, 1971.

Bottomore, T.B. *Classes in Modern Society.* London: George Allen and Unwin, 1965.

Boyd, M., Goyder, J., Jones, F., McRoberts, M., Pineo, P., Porter, J. *Ascription and Achievement.* Ottawa: Carleton University Press, 1985.

Braverman, Harry. *Labour and Monopoly Capital.* New York: Monthly Review Press, 1974.

Breton, Raymond. "Academic Stratification in Secondary Schools and the Educational Plans of Students." *CRSA* 7 (August 1970).

Breton, Raymond. *Social and Academic Factors in the Career Decisions of Canadian Youth.* Ottawa: Manpower and Immigration, 1972.

Breton, R., Reitz, J., Valentine, V. *Cultural Boundaries and the Cohesion of Canada.* Montreal: The Institute for Research on Public Policy, 1980.

Brown, L., and Brown, C. *An Unauthorized History of the RCMP.* Toronto: James Lewis and Samuel, 1973.

Brinkerhoff, M.B. "Women Who Want to Work in a Man's World." *CJS* 2 (Summer 1977).

Burbidge, Scott. "Structural Factors and Occupational Mobility: A Study of Parental and Peer Group Influences on the Career Patterns of Lower Class Males." Halifax: M.A. Thesis, Department of Sociology, Dalhousie University, April 1965.

Campbell, Kenneth. "Regional Disparity and Interregional Exchange Imbalance" in D. Glenday et al. (eds.), *Modernization and the Canadian State.* Toronto: Macmillan of Canada, 1978.

Cameron, Elspeth. "Newman's Progress." *Saturday Night* (September 1982).

Canada. *Illness and Health Care in Canada: Canadian Sickness Survey, 1950–51.* Ottawa: Queen's Printer, 1960.

Canada. *Selected Statistics on Children.* Ottawa: Queen's Printer, 1965.

Canada. *Report of the Royal Commission on Bilingualism and Biculturalism (Book III, The Work World).* Ottawa: Queen's Printer, 1969.

Canada. *Earnings of Dentists in Canada, 1959–1968.* Ottawa: Queen's Printer, 1970.

Canada. *Poverty in Canada: Report of the Special Senate Committee on Poverty.* Ottawa: Information Canada, 1971.

Canada. *Household Facilities by Income and Other Characteristics for 1968.* Ottawa: Information Canada, 1972.

Canada. *Canada Year Book 1972.* Ottawa: Information Canada, 1972A.

Canada. *Perspective Canada: A Compendium of Social Statistics.* Ottawa: Information Canada, 1974.

Canada. *Some Characteristics of Post-Secondary Students in Canada.* Ottawa: Secretary of State, 1976.

Canada. *The Distribution of Income in Canada.* Ottawa: Department of National Health and Welfare, March 1977.

Canada. *Perspectives Canada.* Ottawa: Information Canada, 1977; 1980.

Canada. *The Changing Dependence of Women.* Ottawa: Ministry of National Health and Welfare, April 1978.

Canada. *Annual Report to Parliament on Immigration Levels 1982.* Ottawa: Employment and Immigration Canada, November 1981.

Canada. *Trends in Canadian Education, 1961–62 to 1983–84.* Ottawa: Statistics Canada, September 1982.

Canada. *Charting Canadian Incomes, 1951–1981.* Ottawa: Statistics Canada, March 1984.

Canada. *Highlights: 1981 Census of Canada.* Ottawa: Statistics Canada, April 1984.

Canada. *Changes in Income in Canada: 1970–1980.* Ottawa: Statistics Canada, May 1984.

Canada. *Women in the Work World.* Ottawa: Statistics Canada, September 1984.

Canadian Advisory Council on the Status of Women (CACSW). *What Will Tomorrow Bring? A Study of the Aspirations of Adolescent Women.* Ottawa: CACSW, March 1985.

Canadian Council on Social Development. *Canadian Fact Book on Poverty,* Ottawa, 1975.

Chapin, F.S. "A Quantitative Scale for Rating of the Home and Social Environment of Middle Class Families in an Urban Environment." *Journal of Educational Psychology* 19 (1928).

Clark, Peter. "Leadership Succession among the Hutterites." *CRSA* 14, (August 1977).

Clark, S.D. "Foreword" in D.C. Masters, *The Winnipeg General Strike.* Toronto: University of Toronto Press, 1950.

Clark, S.D. *The Suburban Society.* Toronto: University of Toronto Press, 1966.

Clark, S.D. "The Position of the French-Speaking Population in Northern Industrial Communities" in R. Ossenberg (ed.), *Canadian Society: Pluralism, Change, and Conflict.* Toronto: Prentice-Hall Canada, 1971.

Clement, Wallace. "Parasites, Satellites, and Stratification." Ottawa: Department of Sociology and Anthropology, Carleton University, February 1973.

Clement, Wallace. "The Social Origins of the Industrial Elite, 1885–1910," Ottawa: Carleton University, 1973 A.

Clement, Wallace, and Olsen, D. "Official Ideology and Ethnic Power: Canadian Elites, 1953–1973." Montreal: Meetings of the ASA, August 1974.

Clement, Wallace. *The Canadian Corporate Elite: Economic Power in Canada.* Toronto: McClelland and Stewart (The Carleton Library), 1975.

Conway, J.F. "Populism in the United States, Russia, and Canada: Explaining the Roots of Canada's Third Parties." *Canadian Journal of Political Science* XI: (March 1978).

Creighton, Donald. *Canada's First Century.* Toronto: Macmillan of Canada, 1972.

Crysdale, Stewart. "Occupational and Social Mobility in Riverdale, A Blue Collar Community." Toronto: Ph.D. thesis, Department of Sociology, University of Toronto, March 1968.

Crysdale, Stewart, and Beattie, C. *Sociology Canada: An Introductory Text,* Butterworth, 1973.

Curtis, James, and Scott, William (eds.). *Social Stratification in Canada.* Toronto: Prentice-Hall Canada, 1973.

Dahrendorf, Ralf. *Class and Class Conflict in Industrial Society.* Stanford: Stanford University Press, 1959.

D'Antini, B. "The Quiet Desperation of the Immigrant," in Bancroft, George (ed.), *Outreach for Understanding.* Toronto: Ministry of Culture and Recreation, 1978.

Data Laboratories Research Consultants. "Collective Bargaining." *The Weekend Magazine* 28 (September 2, 1978).

Darroch, A., and Marston, W. "The Social Class Basis of Ethnic Residential Segregation: The Canadian Case." *AJS* 77 (1971).

Davidson, H., and Lang, G. "Children's Perceptions of their Teachers' Feelings Towards Them Related to Self-Perception, School Achievement, and Behaviour." *Journal of Experimental Education* 29 (1960).

Davis, Arthur K. "Canadian Society and History as Hinterland Versus Metropolis" in R. Ossenberg (ed.), *Canadian Society: Pluralism, Change, and Conflict.* Toronto: Prentice-Hall Canada, 1971.

Davis, Kingsley, and Moore, Wilbert E. "Some Principles of Stratification." *ASR* 10 (April 1945).

Dawson, R., and Prewitt, K. *Political Socialization.* Boston: Little, Brown, 1969.

Djilas, Milovan. *The New Class*. New York: Frederick A. Praeger, 1957.

Drucker, Philip. *Cultures of the North Pacific Coast*. San Francisco: Chandler Publishing Co., 1965.

Dumas, Evelyn. *The Bitter Thirties in Quebec*. Montreal: Black Rose Books, 1975.

Engelmann, F.C., and Schwartz, M.A. *Canadian Political Parties* (rev. ed.). Toronto: Prentice-Hall Canada, 1975.

Enterline, P.E. "The Distribution of Medical Services Before and After 'Free' Medical Care — the Quebec Experience." *New England Journal of Medicine* 289 (1973).

Ewing, Anthony. "Social Class and Voting in Vancouver Civic Elections." Ottawa: M.A. thesis, Department of Sociology and Anthropology, Carleton University, 1972.

Ferri, John. "Streaming Down a Dead-end River?" *The Toronto Star*, July 1, 1985.

Forcese, D. "Leadership in a Depressed Primary Industry." Winnipeg: M.A. thesis, Department of Sociology, The University of Manitoba, 1964.

Forcese, D., and Siemens, L.B. *School-Related Factors and the Aspiration Levels of Manitoba Senior High School Students*. Winnipeg: Faculty of Agriculture and Home Economics, University of Manitoba, 1965.

Forcese, D., Richer, S, de Vries, J. and McRoberts, H. "The Methodology of Crisis Survey." St. John's, Nfld.: Meetings of the Canadian Sociology and Anthropology Association, June 1971.

Forcese, D., and de Vries, J. "Occupation and Electoral Success in Canada: The 1974 Federal Election." *CRSA* 14 (August 1977).

Forcese, D. "Elites and Power in Canada," in J. Redekop (ed.), *Approaches to Canadian Politics*. Toronto: Prentice-Hall Canada, 1978.

Forcese, D., Begin, P., and Gould, D. "Policing in a Multicultural Society: Ottawa Police Relations with Immigrant and Public Housing Residents." Ottawa: Department of Sociology and Anthropology, Carleton University, 1978.

Forrest, Anne. *Unions in the Collective Bargaining Process*. Toronto: OISE 1978.

Francis, Diane. "Where Will it all End"? *The Toronto Star*, November 11, 1984.

Fraser, Howard. "Socio-economic Status, Morbidity, and the Utilization of Health Resources of Calgary." Calgary: M.A. thesis, Department of Sociology, University of Calgary, 1968.

Garcia, John. "I.Q.: The Conspiracy." *Psychology Today* 6 (September 1972).

Garson, Barbara. *All the Livelong Day*. New York: Doubleday, 1975.

Giddens, Anthony. *The Class Structure of Advanced Societies*. London: Hutchinson University Library, 1973.

Gilbert, Sid. "Educational and Occupational Aspirations of Ontario High School Students: A Multivariate Analysis." Ottawa: Ph.D. thesis, Department of Sociology and Anthropology, Carleton University, 1973.

Gilbert, Sid, and McRoberts, Hugh. "Differentiation and Stratification: The Issue of Inequality" in D. Forcese and S. Richer (contrib. eds.), *Issues in Canadian Society: An Introduction to Sociology*. Toronto: Prentice-Hall Canada, 1975.

Gilbert, Sid, and McRoberts, Hugh. "Academic Stratification and Education Plans" *CRSA* 14: (February 1977).

Gillespie, W. Irwin. *In Search of Robin Hood*. Montreal: C.D. Howe Research Institute, 1978.

Glass, D.V. *Social Mobility in Britain*. London: Routledge and Kegan Paul, 1945.

Gockel, G. "Income and Religious Affiliation: A Regression Analysis." *AJS* 74 (1969).

Gonick, Cy. *Out of Work*. Toronto: James Lorimer, 1978.

Goodall, Raymond. "Religious Style and Social Class." Vancouver: M.A. thesis, Department of Sociology, University of British Columbia, 1970.

Goulder, Alvin. *The Coming Crisis of Western Sociology*. New York: Avon Books, 1971.

Goyder, John, and Curtis, James. "Occupational Mobility in Canada over Four Generations." *CRSA* 14 (August 1977).

Gray, James. *The Winter Years*. Toronto: Macmillan of Canada, 1966.

Guindon, Hubert. "Social Unrest, Social Class, and Quebec's Bureaucratic Revolution." *Queen's Quarterly* LXXI (1964).

Gunderson, Morley. "Work Patterns" in Gail Cook (ed.), *Opportunity for Choice*. Ottawa: Information Canada, 1976.

Guppy, L.N., and Siltanen, J.L. "A Comparison of Allocation for Male and Female Occupational Prestige." *CRSA* 14 (August 1977).

Guttman, Louis. "A Revision of Chapin's Social Status Scale." *ASR* 7 (1942).

Hall, Oswald. "The Canadian Division of Labour Revisited," in J. Curtis and W. Scott (eds.), *Social Stratification in Canada*. Toronto: Prentice-Hall Canada, 1973.

Hall, Oswald, and Richard Carlton. "Basic Skills at School and Work." Toronto: Ontario Economic Council, 1977.

Hamilton, R., and Pinard, M. "Poverty in Canada: Illusion and Reality." *CRSA* 14 (May 1977).

Harp, John, and Hofley, John, eds. *Poverty in Canada*. Toronto: Prentice-Hall Canada, 1971.

Harrington, Michael. *The Twilight of Capitalism*. New York: Simon & Schuster, 1976.

Heap, James (ed.). *Everybody's Canada: The Vertical Mosaic Reviewed and Re-examined*. Toronto: Burns and MacEachern, 1974.

Hoar, Victor. "Introduction" in R. Liversedge, *Recollections of the On to Ottawa Trek*. Toronto: McClelland and Stewart, 1973.

Hoare, Michael. "Social Origins of Nurses and Career Stratification: A Study of Student Nurses in Three Metropolitan Halifax Schools of Nursing." Halifax: M.A. thesis, Department of Sociology, Dalhousie University, 1969.

Horn, Jack. "Bored to Sickness." *Psychology Today* (November 16, 1975).

Horowitz, Gad. *Canadian Labour in Politics*. Toronto: University of Toronto Press, 1968.

Hughes, Everett. *French Canada in Transition*. Chicago: University of Chicago Press, 1943.

Hunter, Alfred A. *Class Tells: On Social Inequality in Canada*. Toronto: Butterworths, 1981.

Hunter, Floyd. *Community Power Structure*. Chapel Hill: University of North Carolina Press, 1952.

Isbister, Fraser. "Asbestos 1949" in I. Abella (ed.), *On Strike: Six Key Labour Struggles in Canada 1919–1949*. Toronto: James Lorimer, 1974.

Institute for Social Research. "Are We a Classless Society?" *ISR Newsletter*, Autumn 1982.

Jackson, J.E.W., and Poushinsky, N. *Migration to Northern Mining Communities: Structural and Social-Psychological Dimensions*. Winnipeg: Centre for Settlement Studies, University of Manitoba, 1971.

Jansen, Clifford. "The Italian Community in Toronto" in Jean Elliott (ed.), *Minority Canadians: Immigrant Groups*. Toronto: Prentice-Hall Canada, 1971.

Johnson, Laura. *The Seam Allowance*. Toronto: The Women's Press, 1982.

Johnson, Leo A. "The Development of Class in Canada in the Twentieth Century" in Gary Teeple (ed.), *Capitalism and the National Question in Canada*. Toronto: University of Toronto Press, 1972.

Johnson, Leo A. "Illusions or Realities: Hamilton's and Pinard's Approach to Poverty." *CRSA* 14 (August 1977).

Johnson, Leo A. *Poverty in Wealth*. Toronto: New Hogtown Press, 1977.

Jones, Frank. "The Social Origins of High School Teachers in a Canadian City." *CJEPS* XXIX (November 1963).

Karabel, J. "Community Colleges and Social Stratification." *Harvard Educational Review* 42 (1972).

Kashmeri, Zuhair. "Apartheid Mild in Comparison with Caste System." *The Globe and Mail* (June 10, 1985).

Kerchoff, Alan. *Socialization and Social Class*. Englewood Cliffs, New Jersey: Prentice-Hall, 1972.

Kerr, Donald. "Metropolitan Dominance in Canada" in John Warkentin (ed.), *Canada, A Geographical Interpretation*. Toronto: Methuen, 1970.

Kirkopoulos, G. "Education", in G. Bancroft, *Outreach for Understanding*. Toronto, 1976.

Kluckhohn, F., and Strodtbeck, F. *Variations in Value Orientation*. Evanston, Illinois: Row, Peterson, 1961.

Lane, David. *The End of Inequality? Stratification under State Socialism*. Middlesex: Penguin Books, 1971.

Langton, Kenneth. *Political Socialization*. New York: Oxford University Press, 1969.

Laskin, Richard. *Organizations in a Saskatchewan Town*. Saskatoon: Centre for Community Studies, 1961.

Lenski, Gerhard E. *Power and Privilege*. New York: McGraw-Hill, 1966.

Levison, Andrew. *The Working Class Majority*. New York: Coward, McCann and Geohagen, 1974.

Leyton, Elliott. *Dying Hard*. Toronto: McClelland and Stewart, 1975.

Lipset, Seymour M. *Agrarian Socialism*. Berkeley: University of California Press, 1950.

Lipset, Seymour M. *The First New Nation*. New York: Basic Books, 1963.

Lipset, Seymour M. *Political Man*. Garden City, N.Y.: Doubleday, 1965.

Lipset, Seymour M. *Agrarian Socialism* (rev. ed.). Garden City, N.Y.: Doubleday, 1968.

Liversedge, Ronald. *Recollections of the On to Ottawa Trek*. V. Hoar, (ed.). Toronto: McClelland and Stewart (The Carleton Library), 1973.

Lockwood, David. *The Blackcoated Worker*. London: Unwin University Books, 1958.

Lorimer, J., and Phillips, M. *Working People: Life in a Downtown City Neighbourhood*. Toronto: James Lewis and Samuel, 1971.

Lower, J. Arthur. *Western Canada: An Outline History*. Vancouver: Douglas and McIntyre, 1983.

Lucas, Rex. *Minetown, Milltown, Railtown: Life in Canadian Communities of Single Industry*. Toronto: University of Toronto Press, 1971.

Lynd, R.S., and Lynd, H.M. *Middletown: A Study in Modern American Culture*. New York: Harcourt, Brace and World, 1929.

Lynd, R.S., and Lynd, H.M. *Middletown in Transition*. New York: Harcourt, Brace and World, 1937.

MacDowell, Laurel S. *Remember Kirkland Lake: The Gold Miners' Strike of 1941–42*. Toronto: University of Toronto Press, 1983.

Macpherson, C.B. *Democracy in Alberta*. Toronto: University of Toronto Press, 1953.

Manga, P. *The Income Distribution Effect of Medical Insurance in Ontario*. Toronto: Ontario Economic Council, 1978.

Manzer, R. *Canada: A Socio-Political Report*. Toronto: McGraw-Hill Ryerson, 1974.

Marchak, Pat. *Ideological Perspectives on Canada*. Toronto, McGraw-Hill Ryerson, 1975.

Marx, Karl, and Engels, Friedrich. *The Communist Manifesto*. R. Pascal (ed.). New York: International Publishers, 1947.

Marx, Karl, and Engels, Friedrich. *The German Ideology*, Parts I and III. R. Pascal, ed. New York: International Publishers, 1947.

Marx, Karl, and Engels, Friedrich. *Selected Works*. New York: International Publishers, 1968.

Masters, D.C. *The Winnipeg General Strike*. Toronto: University of Toronto Press, 1950.

Matthiasson, J. "Resident Mobility in Resource Frontier Communities" in John Matthiasson (ed.), *Two Studies on Fort McMurray*. Winnipeg: Centre for Settlement Studies, University of Manitoba, 1971.

Mayer, K., and Buckley, W. *Class and Society*, 3rd ed. New York: Random House, 1969.

McCrorie, James N. "Change and Paradox in Agrarian Social Movements: The Case of Saskatchewan" in R. Ossenberg (ed.), *Canadian Society: Pluralism, Change, and Conflict*. Toronto: Prentice-Hall Canada, 1971.

McKenzie, R., and Silver, A. "The Delicate Experiment: Industrialism, Conservatism and Working-Class Tories in England" in S.M. Lipset and S. Rokkan (eds.), *Party Systems and Voter Alignments*. New York: The Free Press, 1967.

McNaught, Kenneth. "Violence in Canadian History" in John Moir (ed.), *Character and Circumstance*. Toronto: Macmillan of Canada, 1970.

McRoberts, Hugh A. "Follow-up of Grade 12 Students from the Blishen/Porter Study of Educational Aspirations." Ottawa: Department of Sociology and Anthropology, Carleton University, 1973.

Mehmet, O. *Who Benefits from the Ontario University System?* Toronto: Ontario Economic Council, 1978.

Mellor, John. *The Company Store: James Bryson McLachlan and the Cape Breton Coal Miners, 1900-1925.* Toronto, Doubleday, 1983.

Meltz, Noah. *Manpower in Canada, 1931-1962.* Ottawa: Queen's Printer, 1959.

Merton, Robert K. *Social Theory and Social Structure.* New York: The Free Press, 1957.

Michels, Robert. *Political Parties: A Sociological Study on the Oligarchical Tendencies of Modern Democracy* (E. Paul and C. Paul, trans.). New York: Collier Books, 1962.

Milbrath, Lester. *Political Participation.* Chicago: Rand McNally, 1965.

Miliband, Ralph. *The State in Capitalist Society.* New York: Basic Books, 1969.

Mills, C. Wright. *The New Men of Power.* New York: Harcourt, Brace and World, 1948.

Mills, C. Wright. *White Collar.* New York: Oxford University Press, 1951.

Mills, C. Wright. *The Power Elite.* New York: Oxford University Press, 1956.

Mohs, Mayo. "I.Q." *Discover*, September 1982.

Montero, Gloria. *We Stood Together.* Toronto: James Lorimer, 1979.

Morton, W.L. *The Progressive Party in Canada.* Toronto: University of Toronto Press, 1950.

Mosca, Gaetano. *The Ruling Class* (ed. and rev. by A. Livingston; trans. by H. Kahn). New York: McGraw-Hill, 1939.

Murphy, R. "Societal Values and the Reaction of Teachers to Students' Backgrounds." *CRSA* 14 (February 1977).

Myers, Gustavus. *A History of Canadian Wealth.* Toronto: James Lewis and Samuel, 1972.

Myles, John. *Old Age in the Welfare State.* Boston, Toronto: Little, Brown & Co., 1984.

Myles, John. "Pensions, Power, and Profits: The Political Economy of Old Age Security in Canada." Saskatoon: Annual Meetings of the CISAA, 1979.

Nagnur, Ohruva. "Longevity and Historical Life Tables (Abridged) Canada and Provinces, 1921-1981." Ottawa: Statistics Canada, 1982.

National Council of Welfare. *One Child, One Chance.* Ottawa: 1973.

———. *Prices and the Poor.* Ottawa: 1974.

———. *Poor Kids.* Ottawa: 1975.

———. *The Hidden Welfare System.* Ottawa: 1976.

———. *Jobs and Poverty.* Ottawa: June 1977.

———. *Bearing the Burden, Sharing the Profits.* Ottawa: March 1978.

———. *The Working Poor.* Ottawa: May 1981.

———. *Medicare: The Public Good and Private Practice.* Ottawa: May 1982.

———. *Sixty-five and Older.* Ottawa: February 1984.

———. *1984 Poverty Lines.* Ottawa: March 1984.

National Opinion Research Center. "Jobs and Occupation: A Popular Evaluation." *Public Opinion News* 9 (1974).

Neatby, H. Blair. *The Politics of Chaos: Canada in the Thirties.* Toronto: Macmillan of Canada, 1972.

Newman, Peter C. *The Canadian Establishment* (Vol. I) rev. Toronto: McClelland and Stewart 1979.

Ogmundson, Rick. "Mass-Elite Linkages and Class Issues in Canada." *CRSA* 13 (February 1976).

Olsen, Dennis. "The State Elites" in Leo Panitch (ed.), *The Canadian State: Political Economy and Political Power.* Toronto: University of Toronto Press, 1977.

Or, Michael. "A Comparison of High School Graduates and Dropouts in Halifax." Halifax: M.A. thesis, Department of Sociology, Dalhousie University, 1970.

Osberg, Lars. *Economic Inequality in Canada.* Toronto: Butterworths, 1981.

Ossenberg, Richard. "Social Pluralism in Quebec: Continuity, Change, and Conflict" in R. Ossenberg (ed.), *Canadian Society: Pluralism, Change, and Conflict.* Toronto: Prentice-Hall Canada.

Panitch, Leo. "The Role and Nature of the Canadian State", in Leo Panitch (ed.), *The Canadian State: Political Economy and Political Power.* Toronto: University of Toronto Press, 1977.

Penner, Norman (ed.) *Winnipeg 1919.* Toronto: James Lewis and Samuel, 1973.

Perez, Fatima. "Adjustment Problems of the Portuguese Mother" in G. Bancroft, *Outreach for Understanding.* Toronto: 1976.

Peters, Victor. *All Things Common.* Winnipeg: The University of Manitoba Press, 1965.

Pfeffer, Richard. *Working for Capitalism.* New York: Columbia University Press, 1979.

Pike, Robert. *Who Doesn't Get to University and Why.* Ottawa: Association of Universities and Colleges of Canada, 1970.

Pike, R., and Zureik, E. (eds.) *Socialization and Values in Canadian Society* (Vol. 2). Toronto: McClelland and Stewart (The Carleton Library), 1975.

Pinard, Maurice. "Working Class Politics: An Interpretation of the Quebec Case." *CRSA* 7 (1970).

Pinard, Maurice. *The Rise of a Third Party.* Englewood Cliffs, New Jersey: Prentice-Hall, 1971.

Pineo, P., and Porter, J. "Occupational Prestige in Canada." *CRSA* 4 (1967).

Pineo, P., Porter, J. and McRoberts, H. "The 1971 Census and the Socioeconomic Classification of Occupations." *CRSA* 13 (February 1977).

Piven, A., and Cloward R. *Regulating the Poor.* New York: Pantheon Books, 1971.

Plaskin, Robert. "A Stake in the Future." *The Globe and Mail,* Toronto, October 9, 1978.

Podoluk, Jenny. *Incomes of Canadians.* Ottawa: Dominion Bureau of Statistics, 1968.

Porter, John. "The Concentration of Economic Power and the Economic Elite in Canada." *CJEPS* XXII (May 1956).

Porter, John. *The Vertical Mosaic.* Toronto: University of Toronto Press, 1965.

Porter, John. *Canadian Social Structure: A Statistical Profile.* Toronto: McClelland and Stewart (The Carleton Library), 1979.

Porter, John. "Politics and Minorities: Canada and The United States." Michigan: Intercollegiate Conference on Canadian-American Relations, Michigan State University, February 1968.

Porter, M., Porter, J. and Blishen, B. *Does Money Matter?* (rev. ed.), Toronto: Macmillan of Canada (The Carleton Library), 1979.

Presthus, Robert. *Elite Accommodation in Canadian Politics.* Toronto: Macmillan of Canada, 1973.

Presthus, Robert, *Elites in the Policy Process.* London: Cambridge University Press, 1974.

Price, Bonnie. "The INCO Syndrome." *The Gazette,* May 12, 1979.

Rainwater, Lee (ed.) *Inequality and Justice.* Chicago: Aldine, 1974.

Reitz, Jeffrey. "Immigrants, Their Descendants, and the Cohesion of Canada" in R. Breton *et al.* Montreal: Institute for Research on Public Policy, 1980.

Rennie, Douglas. "The Ethnic Division of Labour in Montreal from 1931–1951." Montreal: M.A. thesis, Department of Sociology, McGill University, 1953.

Richardson, James. "Education and Social Mobility: Changing Conceptions of the Role of Educational Systems." *CJS* 2: (Fall 1977).

Richer, Stephen. "Middle-Class Bias of Schools—Fact or Fancy?" *Sociology of Education* 47: (Fall 1974).

Richmond, A. "Social Mobility of Immigrants in Canada" in B. Blishen *et al.* (eds.). *Canadian Society* (3rd ed.). Toronto: Macmillan of Canada, 1968.

Riffel, J.A. *Quality of Life in Resource Towns.* Ottawa: Information Canada, 1975.

Rinehart, James. *The Tyranny of Work.* Toronto: Longman Canada, 1975.

Rioux, Marcel. *Quebec in Question.* Toronto: James Lewis and Samuel, 1971.

Robb, A.L., and Spencer, B. "Education: Enrolment and Attainment" in Gail Cook (ed.) *Opportunity for Choice.* Ottawa: Information Canada, 1976.

Robertson, Heather. *Grass Roots.* Toronto: James Lorimer, 1973.

Robin, Martin. *Radical Politics and Canadian Labour 1880–1930*. Kingston: Industrial Relations Centre, Queen's University, 1968.

Rocher, Guy. "Formal Education: The Issue of Opportunity" in S. Richer, D. Forcese, *Issues in Canadian Society: An Introduction to Sociology*. Toronto: Prentice-Hall Canada, 1975.

Rosenberg, M. "On the Location of Physicians in Metropolitan Toronto 1951–1971." *Horizon* 27, 1979.

Rosenberg, M. "Accessibility to Health Care." *Progress in Human Geography* 7, 1983.

Rubin, L.B. *Worlds of Pain*. New York: Basic Books, 1976.

Russell, George. "Bound Together in the Fear of a Harsh God." *Weekend Magazine*, April 6, 1974.

Ryan, John. *The Agricultural Economy of Manitoba Hutterite Colonies*. Toronto: McClelland and Stewart (The Carleton Library), 1977.

Schwartz, Mildred. "Canadian Voting Behaviour," in Richard Rose (ed.). *Electoral Behavior: A Comparative Handbook*. New York: Free Press, 1974.

Seeley, John; Sims, R.; and Loosely, A. *Crestwood Heights*. New York: Wiley, 1957.

Shackleton, Doris. *Tommy Douglas*. Toronto: McClelland and Stewart, 1975.

Sherlock, Karen. "Protest Ends in Defeat, Tragedy." *The Citizen*, July 3, 1985.

Siemens, Leonard B., and Jackson, J.E. *Educational Plans and Their Fulfillment: A Study of Selected High School Students in Manitoba*. Winnipeg: Faculty of Agriculture and Home Economics, University of Manitoba, 1965.

Siemens, L.B. *Single Enterprise Community Studies in Northern Canada*. Winnipeg: Centre for Settlement Studies, University of Manitoba, 1973.

Sinclair, Peter. "Class Structure and Populist Protest: The Case of Western Canada." *CJS* 1: (1975) 1–17.

Smith, Joel. "Melting-Pot-Mosaic: Consideration for a Prognosis." Michigan: Intercollegiate Conference on Canadian-American Relations, Michigan State University, February 1968.

Stevenson, Paul. "Class and Left-Wing Radicalism." *CRSA* 14 (August 1977).

Stewart, Walter. *Strike!* Toronto: McClelland and Stewart, 1977.

Stone, Leroy O. *Migration in Canada: Some Regional Aspects*. Ottawa: Dominion Bureau of Statistics, 1969.

Stub, Holger (ed.) *Status Groups in Modern Society: Alternatives to Class Analysis*. New York: Dryden Press, 1972.

Svalastoga, Kaare. *Social Differentiation*. New York: David McKay, 1965.

Swartz, Donald. "The Politics of Reform," in Leo Panitch (ed.), *The Canadian State*. Toronto: University of Toronto Press, 1977.

Tarasoff, Nadya. "Some Notes on 'Government Transfer Payments To Individuals'." Ottawa: Social Planning Council of Ottawa, November 28, 1973.

Tataryn, Lloyd. "The Tortured Future of Elliot Lake." *Saturday Night* (June 1976).

Taylor, K.W., and Wiseman, N. "Class and Ethnic Voting in Winnipeg: The Case of 1931." *CRSA* 14: (May 1977).

Teeple, Gary. "Land, Labour, and Capital in Pre-Confederation Canada" in Gary Teeple (ed.), *Capitalism and the National Question in Canada*. Toronto: University of Toronto Press, 1972.

Teevan, James J., Jr. and Jackson, J.E. Winston. "Religion and Social Class in Toronto." Montreal: Meetings of the Canadian Sociology and Anthropology Associations, June 1972.

Tenszen, Michael. "Battling a Dropout Crisis." *The Globe and Mail*, April 27, 1985.

Thoenes, Piet. *The Elite in the Welfare State*. London: Faber and Faber, 1966.

Trudeau, Pierre Elliott. *The Asbestos Strike*. Toronto: James Lewis and Samuel, 1974.

Ward, Norman. *The Canadian House of Commons: Representation*. Toronto: University of Toronto Press, 1950.

Warner, W. Lloyd, and Lunt, P.S. *The Status System of a Modern Community*. New Haven: Yale University Press, 1947.

Warner, W. Lloyd (with M. Meeker and K. Eells). *Social Class in America: The Evaluation of Status.* New York: Science Research Associates, 1949.

Weber, Max. *From Max Weber* (trans. by H. Gerth and C.W. Mills). New York: Oxford University Press, 1958.

Westergaard, John and Henrietta Resler. *Class in a Capitalist Society.* London: Heinemann, 1975.

Westley, William and Margaret Westley. *The Emerging Worker.* Montreal: McGill-Queen's University Press, 1971.

Weyer, E.M. *The Eskimos: Their Environment and Folkways.* New Haven: Yale University Press, 1932.

White, Julie. *Women and Unions.* Ottawa: Canadian Advisory Council on the Status of Women, 1980.

Wichern, P.H. *Two Studies in Political Development on Canada's Resource Frontier.* Winnipeg: Centre for Settlement Studies, University of Manitoba, 1972.

Wiseman, N., and Taylor K.W. ''Ethnic versus Class Voting: The Case of Winnipeg, 1945.'' *Canadian Journal of Political Science* 7: (1974).

Index

Abella, I., 150, 157, 160
Aberhart, William, 129, 139
achievement, 22; by class, 101; educational, 94-98; female, 82-86; occupational, 101; university, population of, 78-80
Adams, I., 120
Adorno, T.W., 125
affluence, 35
Africa, 49
age, and health care, 106; and income, 68; and inequality, 69; old age security benefits, 174; and role, 6, 9
agrarian protest, 137-140
agriculturalists, corporate, 8
Alberta, province of, expenditure on dentists' services, 108; family income, 43; French immersion enrolment, 82; interprovincial migration, 44; old age security, 174; patients per doctor, 109; school attendance rates, 77; women in labour force, 54-56, 59
Alert Bay, British Columbia, 111
Alford, R., 128, 132-133, 135
"aliens," deportation of, 145
All Canadian Congress of Labour (1927), 150, 151
Allen, M., 96
Allingham, J., 127
amenities, by region, 113
"American dream," 1
American Federation of Labor (AFL), 150
American frontier, ("Wild West"), 72
American unions, 160, 161
Americans, 26, 51, 63
Amish, 8
Anabaptists, 8
Anderson, Charles, 2, 20, 63, 128
Anglican Church, 127, 129
Anglo-Canadians, 31, 34-35; in high-status occupations, 63; in politics, 63
Arcand, Adrien, 176
"aristocratic compact," 45
"aristocratic responsibility," 72, 99
Aronowitz, S., 120, 167
Asbestos, Quebec, strike, 157
ascription, 5, 11, 21
aspirations, educational, 91-103; as function of social class level, 91; of native peoples, 91; and school preparation, 94; and socialization, 97, 98; and streaming, 100; working-class, and teacher encouragement, 93
Atlantic provinces, 29, 33, 42, 70, 113

attitudes, class, to education, 91-103; to punishment, 122, 124; of teachers, 93, 95
Australia, and class identification with political parties, 134; and voting by class, 133
"authoritarianism," 125
Avakumovic, I., 177
Avery D., 155

Badgley, R., 154
Balawyder, A., 148-149
Bank of Montreal, 41-43, 69, 70
banks, 60; control of, 45
Barber, Bernard, 13
bargaining, economic, 161-165
Beattie, Christopher, 64, 129
Beck, R.G., 106
Becket, Archbishop Thomas, 12
Begin, P., 123
behaviour, 4, 29, 121-123; class attitudes influencing, 125; class, in relation to religion, 126-129; deviant, 121-123; motivating of, 2; political, 131-141; violent, 123
Bennett, John, 8, 28, 29, 30, 140
Bennett, R.B., 152
Bercuson, D., 149-150
Berton, Pierre, 26
Betcherman, L.-R., 176
Biggar, Saskatchewan, 31
biological inheritance, 22-23
black Canadians, 53
"black lung," 119
Blau, Peter, 18
Blishen, Bernard, 17, 51, 91, 99-100; Blishen rankings, 18
"Bloody Saturday," 148
"Bolshevism," 148
Bottomore, Tom, 2
bourgeoisie, 2; petite, 19, 179-180
Boyd, M., 46, 101
Brandon, Manitoba, 117
Braverman, H., 96, 170
Breton, R., 91, 94
Brinkerhoff, M., 91
British, 46, 59
British Columbia, province of, expenditure on dentists' services, 108; family income, 43; French immersion enrolment, 82; interprovincial migration, 44; old age security, 174; patients per doctor, 109; school attendance rates, 77; women in labour force, 54-56, 59

195